Who Rules the World?

Noam Chomsky is the author of numerous bestselling political works, including *Hegemony or Survival* and *Failed States*. A professor emeritus of linguistics and philosophy at MIT, he is widely credited with having revolutionized modern linguistics. He lives in Cambridge, Massachusetts.

ALSO BY NOAM CHOMSKY

Who Rules the World?

NOAM CHOMSKY

HAMISH HAMILTON
an imprint of
PENGUIN BOOKS

HAMISH HAMILTON

UK | USA | Canada | Ireland | Australia
India | New Zealand | South Africa

Hamish Hamilton is part of the Penguin Random House group of companies
whose addresses can be found at global.penguinrandomhouse.com.

First published in the United States of America by Metropolitan Books,
Henry Holt and Company, New York 2016
First published in the United Kingdom by Hamish Hamilton 2016
001

Portions of this book previously appeared, in different form, in the following
publications: *Al-Akhbar*, *Boston Review*, chomsky.info, CNN.com, *Mondoweiss*,
The New York Times syndicate, *The Oslo Accords: A Critical Assessment*
(Petter Bauck and Mohammed Omer, eds.), *TomDispatch* and *Z* magazine

The moral right of the copyright holder has been asserted

Set in 11.45/16.03 pt by Minion Pro
Printed in Great Britain by Clays Ltd, St Ives plc

A CIP catalogue record for this book is available from the British Library

HARDBACK ISBN: 978–0–241–18943–6
TRADE PAPERBACK ISBN: 978–0–241–18944–3

www.greenpenguin.co.uk

CONTENTS

INTRODUCTION

The question raised by the title of this book cannot have a simple and definite answer. The world is too varied, too complex, for that to be possible. But it is not hard to recognize the sharp differences in ability to shape world affairs, and to identify the more prominent and influential actors.

Among states, since the end of World War II the United States has been by far the first among unequals, and remains so. It still largely sets the terms for global discourse, ranging from such concerns as Israel-Palestine, Iran, Latin America, the "war on terror," international economic organization, rights and justice, and others like them to the ultimate issues of survival of civilization (nuclear war and environmental destruction). Its power, however, has been diminishing since it reached a historically unprecedented peak in 1945. And with the inevitable decline, Washington's power is to some extent shared within the "de facto world government" of the "masters of the universe," to borrow the terms of the business press—referring to the leading state capitalist powers (the G7 countries) along with the institutions they control in the "new imperial age," such as the International Monetary Fund and the global trade organizations.[1]

The "masters of the universe" are of course very far from representative of the populations of the dominant powers. Even in the more democratic states, the populations have only limited impact on policy decisions. In the United States, prominent researchers have produced compelling evidence that "economic elites and organized groups representing business interests have substantial independent impacts on U.S. government policy, while average citizens and mass-based interest groups have little or no independent influence." The results of their studies, the authors conclude, "provide substantial support for theories of Economic Elite Domination and for theories of Biased Pluralism, but not for theories of Majoritarian Electoral Democracy or Majoritarian Pluralism." Other studies have demonstrated that the large majority of the population, at the lower end of the income/wealth scale, are effectively excluded from the political system, their opinions and attitudes ignored by their formal representatives, while a tiny sector at the top has overwhelming influence; and that over a long period, campaign funding is a remarkably good predictor of policy choices.[2]

One consequence is so-called apathy: not bothering to vote. It has a significant class correlation. Likely reasons were discussed thirty-five years ago by one of the leading scholars of electoral politics, Walter Dean Burnham. He related abstention to a "crucial comparative peculiarity of the American political system: the total absence of a socialist or laborite mass party as an organized competitor in the electoral market," which, he argued, accounts for much of the "class-skewed abstention rates" as well as the downplaying of policy options that may be supported by the general population but are opposed to elite interests. The observations reach to the present. In a close analysis of the 2014 election, Burnham and Thomas Ferguson show that rates of voting "recall the earliest days of the nineteenth century," when voting rights were virtually restricted to propertied free males. They conclude that "both direct poll evidence and common sense confirm that huge numbers of Americans are now wary of both major political parties and increasingly upset about prospects in the long term. Many are convinced that a few big interests control policy. They crave effective action to reverse long term economic decline and runaway economic inequality, but nothing on the scale required will be offered to them by either of America's money-driven major parties. This is likely only to accelerate the disintegration of the political system evident in the 2014 congressional elections."[3]

In Europe, the decline of democracy is no less striking, as decision making on crucial issues is shifted to the Brussels bureaucracy and the financial powers that it largely represents. Their contempt for democracy was revealed in the savage reaction in July 2015 to the very idea that the people of Greece might have a voice in determining the fate of their society, shattered by the brutal austerity policies of the troika— the European Commission, the European Central Bank, and the International Monetary Fund (specifically the IMF's political actors, not its economists, who have been critical of the destructive policies). These austerity policies were imposed with the stated goal of reducing Greece's debt. Yet they have in fact increased the debt relative to GDP, while Greek social fabric has been torn to shreds, and Greece has served as a funnel to transmit bailouts to French and German banks that made risky loans.

There are few surprises here. Class war, typically one-sided, has a long and bitter history. At the dawn of the modern state capitalist era, Adam Smith condemned the "masters of mankind" of his day, the "merchants and manufacturers" of England, who were "by far the principal architects" of policy, and who made sure their own interests were "most peculiarly attended to" no matter how "grievous" the effect on others (primarily the victims of their "savage injustice" abroad, but much of the population of England as well). The neoliberal era of the past generation has added its own touches to this classic picture, with the masters drawn from the top ranks of increasingly monopolized economies, the gargantuan and often predatory financial institutions, the multinationals protected by state power, and the political figures who largely represent their interests.

Meanwhile, scarcely a day passes without new reports of ominous scientific discoveries about the pace of environmental destruction. It is not too comforting to read that "in the middle latitudes of the Northern hemisphere, average temperatures are increasing at a rate that is equivalent to moving south about 10 meters (30 feet) each day," a rate "about 100 times faster than most climate change that we can observe in the geological record"—and perhaps 1,000 times faster, according to other technical studies.[4]

No less grim is the growing threat of nuclear war. The well-informed former Defense Secretary William Perry, no Cassandra, regards "the probability of a nuclear calamity [as] higher today" than during the Cold War, when escape from unimaginable disaster was a near miracle. Meanwhile the great powers doggedly pursue their programs of "national insecurity," in the apt phrase of longtime CIA analyst Melvin Goodman. Perry is also one of those specialists who called on President Obama to "kill the new cruise missile," a nuclear weapon with improved targeting and lower yield that might encourage "limited nuclear war," quickly escalating by familiar dynamics to utter disaster. Worse yet, the new missile has both nuclear and nonnuclear variants, so that "a foe under attack might assume the worst and overreact, initiating nuclear war." But there is little reason to expect that the advice will be heeded, as the Pentagon's planned trillion-dollar enhancement of nuclear weapons systems proceeds apace, while lesser powers take their own steps towards Armageddon.[5]

The foregoing remarks seem to me to sketch a fair approximation to the cast of primary characters. The chapters that follow seek to explore the question of who rules the world, how they proceed in their efforts, and where these lead—and how the "underlying populations," to borrow Thorstein Veblen's useful phrase, may hope to overcome the power of business and nationalist doctrine and become, in his words, "alive and fit to live."

There is not much time.

1

The Responsibility of Intellectuals, Redux

Before thinking about the responsibility of intellectuals, it is worth clarifying to whom we are referring.

The concept of "intellectuals" in the modern sense gained prominence with the 1898 "Manifesto of the Intellectuals" produced by the Dreyfusards, who, inspired by Émile Zola's open letter of protest to France's president, condemned both the framing of French artillery officer Alfred Dreyfus for treason and the subsequent military cover-up. The Dreyfusards' stance conveys the image of intellectuals as defenders of justice, confronting power with courage and integrity. But they were hardly seen that way at the time. A minority of the educated classes, the Dreyfusards were bitterly condemned in the mainstream of intellectual life, in particular by prominent figures among the "immortals of the strongly anti-Dreyfusard Académie Française," as sociologist Steven Lukes writes. To the novelist, politician, and anti-Dreyfusard leader Maurice Barrès, Dreyfusards were "anarchists of the lecture-platform." To another of these immortals, Ferdinand Brunetière, the very word "intellectual" signified "one of the most ridiculous eccentricities of our time—I mean the pretension of raising writers, scientists, professors and philologists to the rank of supermen" who dare to "treat our generals as idiots, our social institutions as absurd and our traditions as unhealthy."[1]

Who then were the intellectuals? The minority inspired by Zola (who was sentenced to jail for libel and fled the country), or the immortals of the academy? The question resonates through the ages, in one form or another.

INTELLECTUALS: TWO CATEGORIES

One answer came during World War I, when prominent intellectuals on all sides lined up enthusiastically in support of their own states. In their "Manifesto of the Ninety-Three," leading figures in one of the world's most enlightened states called on the West to "have faith in us! Believe, that we shall carry on this war to the end as a civilized nation, to whom the legacy of a Goethe, a Beethoven, and a Kant, is just as sacred as its own hearths and homes."[2] Their counterparts on the other side of the intellectual trenches matched them in enthusiasm for the noble cause, but went beyond in self-adulation. In the *New Republic* they proclaimed that the "effective and decisive work on behalf of the war has been accomplished by . . . a class which must be comprehensively but loosely described as the 'intellectuals.'" These progressives believed they were ensuring that the United States entered the war "under the influence of a moral verdict reached, after the utmost deliberation by the more thoughtful members of the community." They were, in fact, the victims of concoctions of the British Ministry of Information, which secretly sought "to direct the thought of most of the world," but particularly to direct the thought of American progressive intellectuals who might help to whip a pacifist country into war fever.[3]

John Dewey was impressed by the great "psychological and educational lesson" of the war, which proved that human beings—more precisely, the "intelligent men of the community"—can "take hold of human affairs and manage them . . . deliberately and intelligently" to achieve the ends sought.[4] (It took Dewey only a few years to shift from responsible intellectual of World War I to "anarchist of the lecture-platform," denouncing the "un-free press" and questioning "how far genuine intellectual freedom and social responsibility are possible on any large scale under the existing economic regime."[5])

Not everyone toed the line so obediently, of course. Notable figures such as Bertrand Russell, Eugene Debs, Rosa Luxemburg, and Karl Liebknecht were, like Zola, sentenced to prison. Debs was punished with particular severity—a ten-year prison term for raising questions about President Wilson's "war for democracy and human rights." Wilson refused him amnesty after the war ended, though President Harding finally relented. Some dissidents, such as Thorstein Veblen, were chastised but treated less harshly; Veblen was fired from his position in the Food Administration after preparing a report showing that the shortage of farm labor could be overcome by ending Wilson's brutal persecution of unions, specifically the Industrial Workers of the World. Randolph Bourne was dropped by the progressive journals after criticizing the "league of benevolently imperialistic nations" and their exalted endeavors.[6]

The pattern of praise and punishment is a familiar one throughout history: those who line up in the service of the state are typically praised by the general intellectual community, and those who refuse to line up in service of the state are punished.

In later years, the two categories of intellectuals were distinguished more explicitly by prominent scholars. The ridiculous eccentrics are termed "value-oriented intellectuals," who pose "a challenge to democratic government which is, potentially at least, as serious as those posed in the past by aristocratic cliques, fascist movements, and communist parties." Among other misdeeds, these dangerous creatures "devote themselves to the derogation of leadership, the challenging of authority," and even confront the institutions responsible for "the indoctrination of the young." Some sink so far as to doubt the nobility of war aims, like Bourne. This castigation of the miscreants who defy authority and the established order was delivered by the scholars of the liberal internationalist Trilateral Commission—the Carter administration was largely drawn from their ranks—in their 1975 study *The Crisis of*

Democracy. Like the *New Republic* progressives during the First World War, they extend the concept of "intellectual" beyond Brunetière to include the "technocratic and policy-oriented intellectuals," responsible and serious thinkers who devote themselves to the constructive work of shaping policy within established institutions, and to ensuring that indoctrination of the young proceeds on course.[7]

What particularly alarmed the Trilateral scholars was the "excess of democracy" during the time of troubles, the 1960s, when normally passive and apathetic parts of the population entered the political arena to advance their concerns: minorities, women, the young, the old, working people . . . in short, the population, sometimes called "the special interests." They are to be distinguished from those whom Adam Smith called the "masters of mankind," who are the "principal architects" of government policy and who pursue their "vile maxim": "All for ourselves and nothing for other people."[8] The role of the masters in the political arena is not deplored, or discussed, in the Trilateral volume, presumably because the masters represent "the national interest," like those who applauded themselves for leading the country to war "after the utmost deliberation by the more thoughtful members of the community" had reached its "moral verdict."

To overcome the excessive burden imposed on the state by the special interests, the Trilateralists called for more "moderation in democracy," a return to passivity on the part of the less deserving, perhaps even a return to the happy days when "Truman had been able to govern the country with the cooperation of a relatively small number of Wall Street lawyers and bankers," and democracy therefore flourished.

The Trilateralists could well have claimed that they were adhering to the original intent of the Constitution, "intrinsically an aristocratic document designed to check the democratic tendencies of the period," by delivering power to a "better sort" of people and barring "those who were not rich, well born, or prominent from exercising political power," in the words of the historian Gordon Wood.[9] In Madison's defense, however, we should recognize that his mentality was precapitalist. In determining that power should be in the hands of "the wealth of the nation," "the more capable set of men," he envisioned those men on the model of the "enlightened statesman" and "benevolent philosopher" of the imagined Roman world. They would be "pure and noble," "men of intelligence, patriotism, property, and independent circumstances" "whose wisdom may best discern the true interest of their country, and whose patriotism and love of justice will be least likely to sacrifice it to temporary or partial considerations." So endowed, these men would "refine and enlarge the public views," guarding the public interest against the "mischiefs" of democratic majorities.[10] In a similar vein, the progressive Wilsonian intellectuals might have taken comfort in the discoveries of the behavioral sciences, explained in 1939 by the psychologist and education theorist Edward Thorndike:[11]

> It is the great good fortune of mankind that there is a substantial correlation between intelligence and morality including good will toward one's fellows. . . . Consequently our superiors in ability are on the average our benefactors, and it is often safer to trust our interests to them than to ourselves.

A comforting doctrine, though some might feel that Adam Smith had the sharper eye.

REVERSING THE VALUES

The distinction between the two categories of intellectuals provides the framework for determining the "responsibility of intellectuals." The phrase is ambiguous: Does it refer to their moral responsibility as decent human beings, in a position to use their privilege and status to advance the causes of freedom, justice, mercy, peace, and other such sentimental concerns? Or does it refer to the role they are expected to play as "technocratic and policy-oriented intellectuals," not derogating but serving leadership and established institutions? Since power generally tends to prevail, it is those in the latter category who are considered the "responsible intellectuals," while the former are dismissed or denigrated— at home, that is.

With regard to enemies, the distinction between the two categories of intellectuals is retained, but with values reversed. In the old Soviet Union, the value-oriented intellectuals were perceived by Americans as honored dissidents, while we had only contempt for the apparatchiks and commissars, the technocratic and policy-oriented intellectuals. Similarly, in Iran we honor the courageous dissidents and condemn those who defend the clerical establishment. And so on elsewhere generally.

In this way, the honorable term "dissident" is used selectively. It does not, of course, apply, with its favorable connotations, to value-oriented intellectuals at home or to those who combat U.S.-supported tyranny abroad. Take the interesting case of Nelson Mandela, who was only removed from the official State Department terrorist list in 2008, allowing him to travel to the United States without special authorization. Twenty years earlier, he was the criminal leader of one of the world's "more notorious terrorist groups," according to a Pentagon report.[12] That is why President Reagan had to support the apartheid regime, increasing trade with South Africa in violation of congressional sanctions and supporting South Africa's depredations in neighboring countries, which led, according to a UN study, to 1.5 million deaths.[13] That was only one episode in the war on terrorism that Reagan declared to combat "the plague of the modern age," or, as Secretary of State George Shultz had it, "a return to barbarism in the modern age."[14] We may add hundreds of thousands of corpses in Central America and tens of thousands more in the Middle East, among other achievements. Small wonder that the Great Communicator is worshipped by Hoover Institution scholars as a colossus whose "spirit seems to stride the country, watching us like a warm and friendly ghost."[15]

The Latin American case is revealing. Those who called for freedom and justice in Latin America are not admitted to the pantheon of honored dissidents. For example, a week after the fall of the Berlin Wall, six leading Latin American intellectuals, all Jesuit priests, had their heads blown off on the direct orders of the Salvadoran high command. The perpetrators were from an elite battalion armed and trained by Washington that had already left a gruesome trail of blood and terror.

The murdered priests are not commemorated as honored dissidents, nor are others like them throughout the hemisphere. Honored dissidents are those who called for freedom in enemy domains in Eastern Europe and the Soviet Union—and those thinkers certainly suffered, but not remotely like their counterparts in Latin America. This assertion is not seriously in question; as John Coatsworth writes in the *Cambridge History of the Cold War*, from 1960 to "the Soviet collapse in 1990, the numbers of political prisoners, torture victims, and executions of non-violent political dissenters in Latin America vastly exceeded those in the Soviet Union and its East European satellites." Among the executed were many religious martyrs, and there were mass slaughters as well, consistently supported or initiated by Washington.[16]

Why then the distinction? It might be argued that what happened in Eastern Europe matters far more than the fate of the global South at our hands. It would be interesting to see that argument spelled out, and also to see the argument explaining why we should disregard elementary moral principles in thinking about U.S. involvement in foreign affairs, among them that we should focus our efforts on where we can do the most good—typically, where we share responsibility for what is being done. We have no difficulty demanding that our enemies follow such principles.

Few of us care, or should, what Andrei Sakharov or Shirin Ebadi says about U.S. or Israeli crimes; we admire them for what they say and do about those of their own states, and this conclusion holds far more strongly for those who live in more free and democratic societies, and therefore have far greater opportunities to act effectively. It is of some interest that, in the most respected circles, the practice is virtually the opposite of what elementary moral values dictate.

The U.S. wars in Latin America from 1960 to 1990, quite apart from their horrors, have long-term historical significance. To consider just one important aspect, they were in no small measure wars against the Catholic Church, undertaken to crush a terrible heresy proclaimed at Vatican II in 1962. At that time, Pope John XXIII "ushered in a new era in the history of the Catholic Church," in the words of the distinguished theologian Hans Küng, restoring the teachings of the gospels that had been put to rest in the fourth century when the emperor Constantine established Christianity as the religion of the Roman Empire, thereby instituting "a revolution" that converted "the persecuted church" to a "persecuting church." The heresy of Vatican II was taken up by Latin American bishops, who adopted the "preferential option for the poor."[17] Priests, nuns, and laypersons then brought the radical pacifist message of the gospels to the poor, helping them organize to ameliorate their bitter fate in the domains of U.S. power.

That same year, 1962, President John F. Kennedy made several critical decisions. One was to shift the mission of the militaries of Latin America from "hemispheric defense" (an anachronism from World War II) to "internal security"—in effect, war against the domestic population, if they raised their heads.[18] Charles Maechling Jr., who led U.S. counter-insurgency and internal defense planning from 1961 to 1966, describes the unsurprising consequences of the 1962 decision as a shift from tol-eration of "the rapacity and cruelty of the Latin American military" to "direct complicity" in their crimes, to U.S. support for "the methods of Heinrich Himmler's extermination squads."[19] One major initiative was a military coup in Brazil, backed by Washington and implemented shortly after Kennedy's assassination, that instituted a murderous and brutal national security state there. The plague of repression then spread through the hemisphere, encompassing the 1973 coup that installed the Pinochet dictatorship in Chile and later the most vicious of all, the Argentine dictatorship—Ronald Reagan's favorite Latin American regime. Central America's turn—not for the first time—came in the 1980s under the leadership of the "warm and friendly ghost" of the Hoover Institution scholars, who is now revered for his achievements.

The murder of the Jesuit intellectuals as the Berlin Wall fell was a final blow in defeating the heresy of liberation theology, the culmination of a decade of horror in El Salvador that opened with the assassination, by much the same hands, of Archbishop Óscar Romero, the "voice for the voiceless." The victors in the war against the Church declared their responsibility with pride. The School of the Americas (since renamed), famous for its training of Latin American killers, announced as one of its "talking points" that the liberation theology initiated at Vatican II was "defeated with the assistance of the US army."[20]

Actually, the November 1989 assassinations were *almost* a final blow; more effort was yet needed. A year later Haiti had its first free election, and to the surprise and shock of Washington—which had anticipated an easy victory for its own candidate, handpicked from the privileged elite—the organized public in the slums and hills elected Jean-Bertrand Aristide, a popular priest committed to liberation theology. The United States at once moved to undermine the elected government and, after the military coup that overthrew it a few months later, lent substantial support to the vicious military junta and its elite supporters who took power. Trade with Haiti was increased, in violation of international sanctions, and increased further under President Clinton, who also authorized the Texaco oil company to supply the murderous rulers, in defiance of his own directives.[21] I will skip the disgraceful aftermath, amply reviewed elsewhere, except to point out that in 2004, the two traditional torturers of Haiti, France and the United States, joined by Canada, forcefully intervened once more, kidnapped President Aristide (who had been elected again), and shipped him off to central Africa. Aristide and his party were then effectively barred from the farcical 2010–11 elections, the most recent episode in a horrendous history that goes back hundreds of years and is barely known among those responsible for the crimes, who prefer tales of dedicated efforts to save the suffering people from their grim fate.

Another fateful Kennedy decision in 1962 was to send a Special Forces mission, led by General William Yarborough, to Colombia. Yarborough advised the Colombian security forces to undertake "paramilitary, sabotage and/or terrorist activities against known communist proponents," activities that "should be backed by the United States."[22] The meaning of the phrase "communist proponents" was spelled out by the respected president of the Colombian Permanent Committee for Human Rights, former minister of foreign affairs Alfredo Vázquez Carrizosa, who wrote that the Kennedy administration "took great pains to transform our regular armies into counterinsurgency brigades, accepting the new strategy of the death squads," ushering in

> what is known in Latin America as the National Security Doctrine. . . . [not] defense against an external enemy, but a way to make the military establishment the masters of the game . . . [with] the right to combat the internal enemy, as set forth in the Brazilian doctrine, the Argentine doctrine, the Uruguayan doctrine, and the Colombian doctrine: it is the right to fight and to exterminate social workers, trade unionists, men and women who are not supportive of the establishment, and who are assumed to be communist extremists. And this could mean anyone, including human rights activists such as myself.[23]

Vázquez Carrizosa was living under heavy guard in his Bogotá residence when I visited him there in 2002 as part of a mission of Amnesty International, which was opening its yearlong campaign to protect human rights defenders in Colombia in response to the country's horrifying record of attacks against human rights and labor activists and mostly the usual victims of state terror: the poor and defenseless.[24] Terror and torture in Colombia were supplemented by chemical warfare ("fumigation") in the countryside under the pretext of the war on drugs, leading to misery and a huge flight of the survivors to urban slums. Colombia's attorney general's office now estimates that more than 140,000 people have been killed by paramilitaries, often acting in close collaboration with the U.S.-funded military.[25]

Signs of the slaughter are everywhere. In 2010, on a nearly impassible dirt road to a remote village in southern Colombia, my companions and I passed a small clearing with many simple crosses marking the graves of victims of a paramilitary attack on a local bus. Reports of the killings are graphic enough; spending a little time with the survivors, who are among the kindest and most compassionate people I have ever had the privilege of meeting, makes the picture more vivid, and only more painful.

This is merely the briefest sketch of terrible crimes for which Americans bear substantial culpability, and that we could at the very least have easily ameliorated. But it is more gratifying to bask in praise for courageously protesting the abuses of official enemies: a fine activity, but not the priority of a value-oriented intellectual who takes the responsibilities of that stance seriously.

The victims within our domains of power, unlike those in enemy states, are not merely ignored and quickly forgotten but are also cynically insulted. One striking illustration of this fact came a few weeks after the murder of the Latin American intellectuals in El Salvador, when Václav Havel visited Washington and addressed a joint session of Congress. Before his enraptured audience, Havel lauded the "defenders of freedom" in Washington who "understood the responsibility that flowed from" being "the most powerful nation on earth"—crucially, their responsibility for the brutal assassination of his Salvadoran counterparts shortly before. The liberal intellectual class was enthralled by his presentation. Havel reminded us that "we live in a romantic age," Anthony Lewis gushed in the *New York Times*.[26] Other prominent liberal commentators reveled in Havel's "idealism, his irony, his humanity," as he "preached a difficult doctrine of individual responsibility" while Congress "obviously ached with respect" for his genius and integrity and asked why America lacks intellectuals who "elevate morality over self-interest" in this way.[27] We need not tarry on what the reaction would have been had Father Ignacio Ellacuría, the most prominent of the murdered Jesuit intellectuals, spoken such words at the Duma after elite forces armed and trained by the Soviet Union assassinated Havel and half a dozen of his associates—a performance that would, of course, have been inconceivable.

Since we can scarcely see what is happening before our eyes, it is not surprising that events at a slight distance are utterly invisible. An

instructive example: President Obama's dispatch of seventy-nine com-
mandos into Pakistan in May 2011 to carry out what was evidently a
planned assassination of the prime suspect in the terrorist atrocities of
9/11, Osama bin Laden.[28] Though the target of the operation, unarmed
and with no protection, could easily have been apprehended, he was
simply murdered and his body dumped at sea without an autopsy—an
action that was "just and necessary," we read in the liberal press.[29] There
would be no trial, as there was in the case of Nazi war criminals—a fact
not overlooked by legal authorities abroad, who approved of the operation but objected to the procedure. As Harvard professor Elaine Scarry
reminds us, the prohibition on assassination in international law traces
back to a forceful denunciation of the practice by Abraham Lincoln, who
condemned the call for assassination as "international outlawry" in 1863,
an "outrage" which "civilized nations" view with "horror" and that mer-
its the "sternest retaliation."[30] We have come a long way since then.

There is much more to say about the bin Laden operation, including
Washington's willingness to face a serious risk of major war and even
the leakage of nuclear materials to jihadis, as I have discussed elsewhere.
But let us keep to the choice of its nomenclature: Operation Geronimo.
The name caused outrage in Mexico and was protested by indigenous
groups in the United States, but there seems to have been no other notice
of the fact that Obama was identifying bin Laden with the Apache
Indian chief who led his people's courageous resistance to invaders.
The casual choice of the name is reminiscent of the ease with which we
name our murder weapons after victims of our crimes: Apache, Black-
hawk, Cheyenne. How would we have reacted if the Luftwaffe had
called its fighter planes "Jew" and "Gypsy"?

Denial of these "heinous sins" is sometimes explicit. To mention a few
recent cases, two years ago in one of the leading left-liberal intellectual
journals, the New York Review of Books, Russell Baker outlined what he
had learned from the work of the "heroic historian" Edmund Morgan:
namely, that when Columbus and the early explorers arrived they "found
a continental vastness sparsely populated by farming and hunting

people . . . In the limitless and unspoiled world stretching from tropical jungle to the frozen north, there may have been scarcely more than a million inhabitants."[31] That calculation is off by many tens of millions, and the "vastness" included advanced civilizations throughout the continent. No reactions appeared, though four months later the editors issued a correction, noting that in North America there may have been as many as 18 million people—yet still unmentioned were tens of millions more "from tropical jungle to the frozen north." This was all well-known decades ago—including the advanced civilizations and the crimes that were to come—but not important enough even for a casual phrase. In the *London Review of Books* a year later, the noted historian Mark Mazower mentioned American "mistreatment of the Native Americans," again eliciting no comment.[32] Would we accept the word "mistreatment" for comparable crimes committed by our enemies?

THE SIGNIFICANCE OF 9/11

If the responsibility of intellectuals refers to their moral responsibility as decent human beings in a position to use their privilege and status to advance the causes of freedom, justice, mercy, and peace—and to speak out not simply about the abuses of our enemies but, far more significantly, about the crimes in which we are implicated and which we can ameliorate or terminate if we choose—how should we think of 9/11?

The notion that 9/11 "changed the world" is widely held, and understandably so. The events of that day certainly had major consequences, domestic and international. One was to lead President Bush to redeclare Reagan's war on terrorism—the first one has been effectively "disappeared," to borrow the phrase of our favorite Latin American killers and torturers, presumably because its results did not fit well with our preferred self-image. Another consequence was the invasion of Afghanistan and then Iraq, and more recently military interventions in several other countries in the region, as well as regular threats of an attack on

Iran ("all options are open," in the standard phrase). The costs, in every dimension, have been enormous. That suggests a rather obvious question, asked here not for the first time: Was there an alternative?

A number of analysts have observed that bin Laden won major successes in his war against the United States. "He repeatedly asserted that the only way to drive the US from the Muslim world and defeat its satraps was by drawing Americans into a series of small but expensive wars that would ultimately bankrupt them," the journalist Eric Margolis writes. "The United States, first under George W. Bush and then Barack Obama, rushed right into bin Laden's trap. . . . Grotesquely overblown military outlays and debt addiction . . . may be the most pernicious legacy of the man who thought he could defeat the United States."[33] A report from the Costs of War Project at Brown University's Watson Institute for International and Public Affairs estimates that the final bill will be $3.2–4 trillion.[34] Quite an impressive achievement by bin Laden.

That Washington was intent on rushing into bin Laden's trap was evident at once. Michael Scheuer, the senior CIA analyst responsible for tracking bin Laden from 1996 to 1999, wrote, "Bin Laden has been precise in telling America the reasons he is waging war on us." The al-Qaeda leader, Scheuer continued, was "out to drastically alter US and Western policies toward the Islamic world."

And, as Scheuer explains, bin Laden largely succeeded. "US forces and policies are completing the radicalization of the Islamic world, something Osama bin Laden has been trying to do with substantial but incomplete success since the early 1990s. As a result, I think it is fair to conclude that the United States of America remains bin Laden's only indispensable ally."[35] Arguably, it remains so even after his death.

There is good reason to believe that the jihadi movement could have been split and undermined after the 9/11 attack, which was criticized harshly within the movement. Furthermore, that "crime against humanity," as it was rightly called, could have been approached as a crime, with an international operation to apprehend the likely suspects. That was recognized in the immediate aftermath of the attack, but no such idea was even considered by decision makers in Washington. It seems no thought was given to the Taliban's tentative offer—how serious an offer we cannot know—to present the al-Qaeda leaders for a judicial proceeding.

At the time, I quoted Robert Fisk's conclusion that the horrendous crime of 9/11 was committed with "wickedness and awesome cruelty"— an accurate judgment. The crimes could have been even worse: Suppose that Flight 93, downed by courageous passengers in Pennsylvania, had hit the White House, killing the president. Suppose that the perpetrators of the crime planned to, and did, impose a military dictatorship that killed thousands and tortured tens of thousands. Suppose the new dictatorship established, with the support of the criminals, an international terror center that helped install similar torture-and-terror states elsewhere, and, as the icing on the cake, brought in a team of economists—call them "the Kandahar Boys"—who quickly drove the economy into one of the worst depressions in its history. That, plainly, would have been a lot worse than 9/11.

As we all should know, this is not a thought experiment. It happened. I am, of course, referring to what in Latin America is often called "the first 9/11": September 11, 1973, when the United States succeeded in its intensive efforts to overthrow the democratic government of Salvador Allende in Chile via the military coup that placed General Augusto Pinochet's ghastly regime in office. The dictatorship then installed the Chicago Boys—economists trained at the University of Chicago—to reshape Chile's economy. Consider the economic destruction and the torture and kidnappings, and multiply the numbers killed by twenty-five to yield per-capita equivalents, and you will see just how much more devastating the first 9/11 was.

The goal of the overthrow, in the words of the Nixon administration, was to kill the "virus" that might encourage all those "foreigners [who] are out to screw us"—screw us by trying to take over their own resources and, more generally, to pursue a policy of independent development along lines disliked by Washington. In the background was the conclusion of Nixon's National Security Council that if the United States could not control Latin America, it could not expect "to achieve a successful order elsewhere in the world." Washington's "credibility" would be undermined, as Henry Kissinger put it.

The first 9/11, unlike the second, did not change the world. It was "nothing of very great consequence," Kissinger assured his boss a few days later. And judging by how it figures in conventional history, his words can hardly be faulted, though the survivors may see the matter differently.

These events of little consequence were not limited to the military coup that destroyed Chilean democracy and set in motion the horror story that followed. As already discussed, the first 9/11 was just one act in the drama that began in 1962 when Kennedy shifted the mission of the Latin American militaries to "internal security." The shattering aftermath is also of little consequence, the familiar pattern when history is guarded by responsible intellectuals.

INTELLECTUALS AND THEIR CHOICES

Returning to the two categories of intellectuals, it seems to be close to a historical universal that conformist intellectuals, the ones who support official aims and ignore or rationalize official crimes, are honored and privileged in their own societies, while the value-oriented are punished in one way or another. The pattern goes back to the earliest records. It was the man accused of corrupting the youth of Athens who drank the hemlock, much as Dreyfusards were accused of "corrupting souls, and, in due course, society as a whole" and the value-oriented intellectuals of the 1960s were charged with interference with "indoctrination of the young."[36] In the Hebrew scriptures there are figures who by contemporary standards are dissident intellectuals, called "prophets" in the English translation. They bitterly angered the establishment with their critical geopolitical analysis, their condemnation of the crimes of the powerful, their calls for justice and concern for the poor and suffering. King Ahab, the most evil of the kings, denounced the prophet Elijah as a hater of Israel, the first "self-hating Jew" or "anti-American" in the modern counterparts. The prophets were treated harshly, unlike the flatterers at the court, who would later be condemned as false prophets. The pattern is understandable. It would be surprising if it were otherwise.

As for the responsibility of intellectuals, there does not seem to me to be much to say beyond some simple truths: intellectuals are typically privileged; privilege yields opportunity, and opportunity confers responsibilities. An individual then has choices.

2

Terrorists Wanted the World Over

On February 13, 2008, Imad Mughniyeh, a senior commander of Hizbollah, was assassinated in Damascus. "The world is a better place without this man in it," State Department spokesperson Sean McCormack said. "One way or the other he was brought to justice."[1] Director of National Intelligence Mike McConnell added that Mughniyeh had been "responsible for more deaths of Americans and Israelis than any other terrorist with the exception of Osama bin Laden."[2]

Joy was unconstrained in Israel, too, as "one of the US and Israel's most wanted men" was brought to justice, the London *Financial Times* reported.[3] Under the headline "A Militant Wanted the World Over," an accompanying story reported that Mughniyeh was "superseded on the most-wanted list by Osama bin Laden" after 9/11 and so ranked only second among "the most wanted militants in the world."[4]

The terminology is accurate enough, according to the rules of Anglo-American discourse, which defines "the world" as the political class in Washington and London (and whoever happens to agree with them on specific matters). It is common, for example, to read that "the world" fully supported George Bush when he ordered the bombing of Afghanistan. That may be true of "the world," but hardly of the world, as revealed in an international Gallup poll after the bombing was announced. Global support was slight. In Latin America, which has some experience with U.S. behavior, support ranged from 2 percent in Mexico to 16 percent in Panama, and that support was conditional upon the culprits being identified (they still weren't eight months later, the FBI reported) and civilian targets being spared (they were attacked at once).[5] There was an overwhelming preference in the world for diplomatic/judicial measures, rejected out of hand by "the world."

FOLLOWING THE TERROR TRAIL

If "the world" were extended to the world, we might find some other candidates for the honor of most hated arch-criminal. It is instructive to ask why this might be true.

The *Financial Times* reported that most of the charges against Mughniyeh are unsubstantiated, but "one of the very few times when his involvement can be ascertained with certainty [is in] the hijacking of a TWA plane in 1985 in which a US Navy diver was killed."[6] This was one of two terrorist atrocities that led newspaper editors, in a poll, to select terrorism in the Middle East as the top story of 1985; the other was the hijacking of the passenger liner *Achille Lauro*, in which a crippled American, Leon Klinghoffer, was brutally murdered.[7] That reflects the judgment of "the world." It may be that the world saw matters somewhat differently.

The *Achille Lauro* hijacking was a retaliation for the bombing of Tunis ordered a week earlier by Israeli Prime Minister Shimon Peres. Among other atrocities, his air force killed seventy-five Tunisians and Palestinians with smart bombs that tore them to shreds, as vividly reported from the scene by the prominent Israeli journalist Amnon Kapeliouk.[8] Washington cooperated by failing to warn its ally Tunisia that the bombers were on the way, though the Sixth Fleet and U.S. intelligence could not have been unaware of the impending attack. Secretary of State George Shultz informed Israeli Foreign Minister Yitzhak Shamir that Washington "had considerable sympathy for the Israeli action," which, to general approbation, he termed "a legitimate response" to "terrorist attacks."[9] A few days later, the UN Security Council unanimously denounced the bombing as an "act of armed aggression" (with the United States abstaining).[10] "Aggression" is, of course, a far more serious crime than international terrorism. But giving the United States and Israel the benefit of the doubt, let us keep to the lesser charge against their leadership.

A few days after, Peres went to Washington to consult with the leading international terrorist of the day, Ronald Reagan, who denounced "the evil scourge of terrorism," again to general acclaim from "the world."[11]

The "terrorist attacks" that Shultz and Peres offered as the pretext for the bombing of Tunis were the killings of three Israelis in Larnaca, Cyprus. The killers, as Israel conceded, had nothing to do with Tunis, though they might have had Syrian connections.[12] Tunis was a preferable target, however; it was defenseless, unlike Damascus. And there was an extra benefit: more exiled Palestinians could be killed there.

The Larnaca killings, in turn, were regarded as retaliation by the perpetrators. They were a response to regular Israeli hijackings in international waters in which many victims were killed—and many more kidnapped, commonly to be held for long periods without charge in Israeli prisons. The most notorious of these prisons has been the secret prison/torture chamber Facility 1391. A good deal can be learned about it from the Israeli and foreign press.[13] Such regular Israeli crimes are, of course, known to editors of the national press in the United States, and occasionally receive some casual mention.

Klinghoffer's murder was properly viewed with horror and is very famous. It was the topic of an acclaimed opera and a made-for-TV movie, as well as much shocked commentary deploring the savagery of Palestinians, who have variously been deemed "two-headed beasts" (Prime Minister Menachem Begin), "drugged roaches scurrying around in a bottle" (Israeli Defense Forces Chief of Staff Raful Eitan), "like grasshoppers compared to us" whose heads should be "smashed against the boulders and walls" (Prime Minister Yitzhak Shamir)—or, more commonly, just "Araboushim," the slang counterpart of "kike" or "nigger."[14]

Thus, after a particularly depraved display of settler-military terror and purposeful humiliation in the West Bank town of Halhul in December 1982, which disgusted even Israeli hawks, the well-known military/political analyst Yoram Peri wrote in dismay that one "task of the army today [is] to demolish the rights of innocent people just because they are Araboushim living in territories that God promised to us," a task that became far more urgent, and was carried out with far more brutality, when the Araboushim began to "raise their heads" a few years later.[15]

We can easily assess the sincerity of the sentiments expressed about the Klinghoffer murder. It is only necessary to investigate the reaction to comparable U.S.-backed Israeli crimes. Take, for example, the murder in April 2002 of two crippled Palestinians, Kemal Zughayer and Jamal Rashid, by Israeli forces rampaging through the refugee camp of Jenin in the West Bank. Zughayer's crushed body and the remains of his wheelchair were found by British reporters, along with the remains of the white flag he was holding when he was shot dead while seeking to flee the Israeli tanks which then drove over him, ripping his face in two and severing his arms and legs.[16] Jamal Rashid was crushed in *his* wheelchair when one of Israel's huge U.S.-supplied Caterpillar bulldozers demolished his home in Jenin with his family inside.[17] The differential reaction, or rather nonreaction, has become so routine and so easy to explain that no further commentary is necessary.

CAR BOMBING AND "TERRORIST VILLAGERS"

Plainly, the 1985 Tunis bombing was a vastly more severe terrorist crime than either the *Achille Lauro* hijacking or the crime for which Mughniyeh's "involvement can be ascertained with certainty" in the same year.[18] But even the Tunis bombing had competitors for the prize of worst terrorist atrocity in the Mideast in the peak year of 1985.

One challenger was a car bombing in Beirut right outside a mosque, timed to go off as worshippers were leaving Friday prayers. It killed 80 people and wounded 256.[19] Most of the dead were girls and women who had been leaving the mosque, though the ferocity of the blast "burned babies in their beds," "killed a bride buying her trousseau," and "blew away three children as they walked home from the mosque." It also "devastated the main street of the densely populated" West Beirut suburb, reported Nora Boustany three years later in the *Washington Post*.[20]

The intended target had been the Shiite cleric Sheikh Mohammad Hussein Fadlallah, who escaped. The bombing was carried out by Reagan's CIA and his Saudi allies, with Britain's help, and was specifically authorized by CIA director William Casey, according to *Washington Post* reporter Bob Woodward's account in his book *Veil: The Secret Wars of the CIA, 1981–1987*. Little is known beyond the bare facts, thanks to rigorous adherence to the doctrine that we do not investigate our own crimes (unless they become too prominent to suppress, and the inquiry can be limited to some low-level "bad apples" who were, naturally, "out of control").

A third competitor for the 1985 Mideast terrorism prize was Prime Minister Peres's "Iron Fist" operations in southern Lebanese territories then occupied by Israel in violation of Security Council orders. The targets were what the Israeli high command called "terrorist villagers."[21] Peres's crimes in this case sank to new depths of "calculated brutality and arbitrary murder," in the words of a Western diplomat familiar with the area, an assessment amply supported by direct coverage.[22] They are, however, of no interest to "the world" and therefore remain uninvestigated, in accordance with the usual conventions. We might well ask again whether these crimes fall under international terrorism or the far more severe crime of aggression, but let us once more give the benefit of the doubt to Israel and its backers in Washington and keep to the lesser charge.

These are a few of the incidents that might cross the minds of people elsewhere in the world when considering "one of the very few times" Imad Mughniyeh was clearly implicated in a terrorist crime.

The United States also accuses Mughniyeh of responsibility for devastating double suicide truck-bomb attacks on the barracks occupied by U.S. Marines and French paratroopers in Lebanon in 1983, killing 241 Marines and 58 paratroopers, as well as a prior attack on the U.S. embassy in Beirut, killing 63, a particularly serious blow because of a meeting there of CIA officials at the time.[23] The *Financial Times* has, however, attributed the attack on the Marine barracks to Islamic Jihad, not Hizbollah.[24] Fawaz Gerges, one of the leading scholars on the jihadi movements and on Lebanon, has written that responsibility was taken by an "unknown group called Islamic Jihad."[25] A voice speaking in classical Arabic called for all Americans to leave Lebanon or face death. It has been claimed that Mughniyeh was the head of Islamic Jihad at the time, but to my knowledge, evidence is sparse.

The opinion of the world has not been sampled on the subject, but it is possible that there might be some hesitancy about calling an attack on a military base in a foreign country a "terrorist attack," particularly when U.S. and French forces were carrying out heavy naval bombardments and air strikes in Lebanon, and shortly after the United States provided decisive support for the 1982 Israeli invasion of Lebanon, which killed some twenty thousand people and devastated the southern part of the country while leaving much of Beirut in ruins. It was finally called off by President Reagan when international protest became too intense to ignore after the Sabra and Shatila massacres.[26]

In the United States, the Israeli invasion of Lebanon is regularly described as a reaction to Palestine Liberation Organization (PLO) terrorist attacks on northern Israel from their Lebanese bases, making our crucial contribution to these major war crimes understandable. In the real world, the Lebanese border area had been quiet for a year, apart from repeated Israeli attacks, many of them murderous, in an effort to elicit some PLO response that could be used as a pretext for the already planned invasion. Its actual purpose was not concealed at the time by Israeli commentators and leaders: to safeguard the Israeli takeover of the occupied West Bank. It is of some interest that the sole serious error in Jimmy Carter's book *Palestine: Peace Not Apartheid* is his repetition of this propaganda concoction about PLO attacks from Lebanon being the motive for the Israeli invasion.[27] The book was bitterly attacked, and desperate efforts were made to find some phrase that could be misinterpreted, but this glaring error—the only one—was ignored. Reasonably, since it satisfies the criterion of adhering to useful doctrinal fabrications.

KILLING WITHOUT INTENT

Another allegation is that Mughniyeh "masterminded" the bombing of Israel's embassy in Buenos Aires on March 17, 1992, which killed twenty-nine people, in response, as the *Financial Times* put it, to Israel's "assassination of former Hizbollah leader Abbas al-Musawi in an air attack in southern Lebanon."[28] About the assassination, there is no need for evidence: Israel proudly took credit for it. The world might have some interest in the rest of the story. Al-Musawi was murdered with a U.S.-supplied helicopter, well north of Israel's illegal "security zone" in southern Lebanon. He was on his way to Sidon from the village of Jibchit, where he had spoken at the memorial for another imam murdered by Israeli forces; the helicopter attack also killed his wife and five-year-old child. Israel then employed U.S.-supplied helicopters to attack a car bringing survivors of the first attack to a hospital.[29]

After the murder of the family, Hizbollah "changed the rules of the game," Yitzhak Rabin informed the Israeli Knesset.[30] Previously, no rockets had been launched at Israel. Until then, the rules of the game had been that Israel could launch murderous attacks anywhere in Lebanon at will, and Hizbollah would respond only within Israeli-occupied Lebanese territory.

After the murder of its leader (and his family), Hizbollah began to respond to Israeli crimes in Lebanon by rocketing northern Israel. The latter is, of course, intolerable terror, so Rabin launched an invasion that drove some five hundred thousand people out of their homes and killed well over a hundred. The merciless Israeli attacks reached as far as northern Lebanon.[31]

In the south, 80 percent of the city of Tyre fled, and Nabatiye was left a "ghost town."[32] The village of Jibchit was about 70 percent destroyed, according to an Israeli army spokesperson, who explained that the intent was "to destroy the village completely because of its importance to the Shiite population of southern Lebanon." The general goal was "to wipe the villages from the face of the earth and sow destruction around them," as a senior officer of the Israeli Northern Command described the operation.[33]

Jibchit may have been a particular target because it was the home of Sheikh Abdul Karim Obeid, kidnapped and brought to Israel several years earlier. Obeid's home "received a direct hit from a missile," British journalist Robert Fisk reported, "although the Israelis were presumably gunning for his wife and three children." Those who had not escaped hid in terror, wrote Mark Nicholson in the *Financial Times*, "because any visible movement inside or outside their houses is likely to attract the attention of Israeli artillery spotters, who were pounding their shells repeatedly and devastatingly into selected targets." Artillery shells were hitting some villages at a rate of more than ten rounds a minute at times.[34]

All of these actions received the firm support of President Bill Clinton, who understood the need to instruct the Araboushim sternly on the "rules of the game." And Rabin emerged as another grand hero and a man of peace, so different from the two-legged beasts, grasshoppers, and drugged roaches.

The world might find such facts of interest in connection with the alleged responsibility of Mughniyeh for the retaliatory terrorist act in Buenos Aires.

Other charges include that Mughniyeh helped prepare Hizbollah defenses against the 2006 Israeli invasion of Lebanon, evidently an intolerable terrorist crime by the standards of "the world." The more vulgar apologists for U.S. and Israeli crimes solemnly explain that, while Arabs purposely kill civilians, the U.S. and Israel, being democratic societies, do not intend to do so. Their killings are just accidental ones, hence not at the level of moral depravity of their adversaries. That was, for example, the stand of Israel's High Court of Justice when it recently authorized severe collective punishment of the people of Gaza by depriving them of electricity (hence also water, sewage disposal, and other such basics of civilized life).[35]

The same line of defense is common with regard to some of Washington's past peccadilloes, like the missile attack that in 1998 destroyed the al-Shifa pharmaceutical plant in Sudan.[36] The attack apparently led to the deaths of tens of thousands of people, but without intent to kill them, hence it was not a crime on the order of intentional killing.

In other words, we can distinguish three categories of crimes: murder with intent, accidental killing, and murder with foreknowledge but without specific intent. Israeli and U.S. atrocities typically fall into the third category. Thus, when Israel destroys Gaza's power supply or sets up barriers to travel in the West Bank, it does not specifically intend to murder the particular people who will die from polluted water or in ambulances that cannot reach hospitals. And when Bill Clinton ordered the bombing of the al-Shifa plant, it was obvious that it would lead to a humanitarian catastrophe. Human Rights Watch immediately informed him of this, providing details; nevertheless, he and his advisers did not intend to kill specific people among those who would inevitably die when half the pharmaceutical supplies were destroyed in a poor African country that could not replenish them.

Rather, they and their apologists regarded Africans much as we do the ants we crush while walking down a street. We are aware (if we bother to think about it) that it is likely to happen, but we do not intend to kill them because they are not worthy of such consideration. Needless to say, comparable attacks by Araboushim in areas inhabited by human beings are regarded rather differently.

If, for a moment, we can adopt the perspective of the world, we might ask which criminals are "wanted the world over."

3

The Torture Memos and Historical Amnesia

The torture memos released by the White House in 2008–9 elicited shock, indignation, and surprise. The shock and indignation are understandable—particularly the testimony in the Senate Armed Services Committee report on Dick Cheney and Donald Rumsfeld's desperation to find links between Iraq and al-Qaeda, links that were later concocted as justification for the invasion. Former army psychiatrist Major Charles Burney testified that "a large part of the time we were focused on trying to establish a link between Al Qaeda and Iraq. The more frustrated people got in not being able to establish this link . . . there was more and more pressure to resort to measures that might produce more immediate results"; that is, torture. McClatchy reported that a former senior intelligence official familiar with the interrogation issue added that "the Bush administration applied relentless pressure on interrogators to use harsh methods on detainees in part to find evidence of cooperation between al Qaida and the late Iraqi dictator Saddam Hussein's regime. . . . [Cheney and Rumsfeld] demanded that the interrogators find evidence of al Qaida–Iraq collaboration. . . . 'There was constant pressure on the intelligence agencies and the interrogators to do whatever it took to get that information out of the detainees, especially the few high-value ones we had, and when people kept coming up empty, they were told by Cheney's and Rumsfeld's people to push harder.'"[1]

These were the most significant revelations from the Senate inquiry, and they were barely reported.

While such testimony about the viciousness and deceit of the administration should indeed be shocking, the surprise at the general picture revealed is nonetheless surprising. For one thing, even without inquiry it was reasonable to suppose that Guantánamo was a torture chamber. Why else send prisoners where they would be beyond the reach of the law—a place, incidentally, that Washington is using in violation of a treaty forced on Cuba at the point of a gun? Security reasons were, of course, alleged, but they remain hard to take seriously. The same expectations held for the Bush administration's "black sites," or secret prisons, and for extraordinary rendition, and they were fulfilled.

More importantly, torture has been routinely practiced from the early days of the conquest of the national territory, and continued to be used as the imperial ventures of the "infant empire"—as George Washington called the new republic—extended to the Philippines, Haiti, and elsewhere. Keep in mind as well that torture was the least of the many crimes of aggression, terror, subversion, and economic strangulation that have darkened U.S. history, much as in the case of other great powers.

Accordingly, what's surprising is to see the reactions to the release of those Justice Department memos, even by some of the most eloquent and forthright critics of Bush malfeasance: Paul Krugman, for example, writing that we used to be "a nation of moral ideals" and that never before Bush "have our leaders so utterly betrayed everything our nation stands for."[2] To say the least, that common view reflects a rather slanted version of American history.

Occasionally, the conflict between "what we stand for" and "what we do" has been forthrightly addressed. One distinguished scholar who undertook the task was Hans Morgenthau, a founder of realist international relations theory. In a classic study published in 1964 in the glow of Kennedy's Camelot, Morgenthau developed the standard view that the United States has a "transcendent purpose": establishing peace and freedom at home and indeed everywhere, since "the arena within which the United States must defend and promote its purpose has become worldwide." But as a scrupulous scholar, he also recognized that the historical record was radically inconsistent with that "transcendent purpose."[3]

We should not be misled by that discrepancy, advised Morgenthau; we should not "confound the abuse of reality with reality itself." Reality is the unachieved "national purpose" revealed by "the evidence of history as our minds reflect it." What actually happened was merely the "abuse of reality." To confound the abuse of reality with reality is akin to "the error of atheism, which denies the validity of religion on similar grounds"—an apt comparison.[4]

The release of the torture memos led others to recognize the problem. In the *New York Times*, columnist Roger Cohen reviewed a new book, *The Myth of American Exceptionalism*, by British journalist Godfrey Hodgson, who concluded that the United States is "just one great, but imperfect, country among others." Cohen agreed that the evidence supports Hodgson's judgment, but nonetheless regarded as fundamentally mistaken Hodgson's failure to understand that "America was born as an idea, and so it has to carry that idea forward." The American idea is revealed in the country's birth as a "city on a hill," an "inspirational notion" that resides "deep in the American psyche," and by "the distinctive spirit of American individualism and enterprise" demonstrated in the Western expansion. Hodgson's error, it seems, is that he was keeping to "the distortions of the American idea in recent decades," "the abuse of reality."[5]

Let us then turn to "reality itself": the "idea" of America from its earliest days.

"COME OVER AND HELP US"

The inspirational phrase "city on a hill" was coined by John Winthrop in 1630, borrowing from the Gospels, as he outlined the glorious future of a new nation "ordained by God." One year earlier, his Massachusetts

Bay Colony had created its Great Seal, which depicted an Indian with a scroll coming out of his mouth. On that scroll are the words "Come over and help us." The British colonists were thus benevolent humanists, responding to the pleas of the miserable natives to be rescued from their bitter pagan fate.

The Great Seal is, in fact, a graphic representation of "the idea of America" from its birth. It should be exhumed from the depths of the American psyche and displayed on the walls of every classroom. It should certainly appear in the background of all of the Kim Il Sung–style worship of that savage murderer and torturer Ronald Reagan, who blissfully described himself as the leader of a "shining city on the hill" while orchestrating some of the more ghastly crimes of his years in office, notoriously in Central America but elsewhere as well.

The Great Seal was an early proclamation of "humanitarian intervention," to use the currently fashionable phrase. As has commonly been the case since, "humanitarian intervention" led to catastrophe for the alleged beneficiaries. The first U.S. secretary of war, General Henry Knox, described "the utter extirpation of all the Indians in most populous parts of the Union" by means "more destructive to the Indian natives than the conduct of the conquerors of Mexico and Peru."[6]

Long after his own significant contributions to the process were past, John Quincy Adams deplored the fate of "that hapless race of native Americans, which we are exterminating with such merciless and perfidious cruelty among the heinous sins of this nation, for which I believe God will one day bring [it] to judgement."[7] The "merciless and perfidious cruelty" continued until "the West was won." Instead of God's judgment, those heinous sins today bring only praise for the fulfillment of the "American idea."[8]

There was, to be sure, a more convenient and conventional version of the narrative, expressed, for example, by Supreme Court justice Joseph Story, who mused that "the wisdom of Providence" caused the natives to disappear like "the withered leaves of autumn" even though the colonists had "constantly respected" them.[9]

The conquest and settling of the West indeed showed "individualism

and enterprise"; settler-colonialist enterprises, the cruelest form of imperialism, commonly do. The results were hailed by the respected and influential senator Henry Cabot Lodge in 1898. Calling for intervention in
Cuba, Lodge lauded our record "of conquest, colonization, and territorial
expansion unequalled by any people in the 19th century," and urged that
it is "not to be curbed now," as the Cubans too were pleading with us, in
the Great Seal's words, to "come over and help us."[10]

Their plea was answered. The United States sent troops, thereby
preventing Cuba's liberation from Spain and turning it into a virtual
U.S. colony, as it remained until 1959.

The "American idea" was illustrated further by the remarkable campaign, initiated by the Eisenhower administration almost at once, to
restore Cuba to its proper place: economic warfare (with the clearly
articulated aim of punishing the Cuban population so that they would
overthrow the disobedient Castro government), invasion, the dedication of the Kennedy brothers to bringing "the terrors of the earth" to
Cuba (the phrase of historian Arthur M. Schlesinger Jr. in his biography of Robert Kennedy, who considered that task one of his highest
priorities), and other crimes in defiance of virtually unanimous world
opinion.[11]

American imperialism is often traced to the takeover of Cuba, Puerto
Rico, and Hawaii in 1898. But that is to succumb to what historian of
imperialism Bernard Porter calls "the saltwater fallacy," the idea that
conquest only becomes imperialism when it crosses salt water. Thus, if
the Mississippi River had resembled the Irish Sea, westward expansion
would have been imperialism. From George Washington to Henry Cabot
Lodge, those engaged in the enterprise had a clearer grasp of the truth.

After the success of humanitarian intervention in Cuba in 1898, the
next step in the mission assigned by Providence was to confer "the bless-
ings of liberty and civilization upon all the rescued peoples" of the
Philippines (in the words of the platform of Lodge's Republican party)—
at least those who survived the murderous onslaught and widespread
use of torture and other atrocities that accompanied it.[12] These fortu-
nate souls were left to the mercies of the U.S.-established Philippine

constabulary within a newly devised model of colonial domination, relying on security forces trained and equipped for sophisticated modes of surveillance, intimidation, and violence.[13] Similar models would be adopted in many other areas where the United States imposed brutal national guards and other client forces, with consequences that should be well-known.

THE TORTURE PARADIGM

Over the past sixty years, victims worldwide have endured the CIA's "torture paradigm," developed at a cost that reached $1 billion annually, according to historian Alfred McCoy in his book *A Question of Torture*. He shows how torture methods the CIA developed in the 1950s surfaced with little change in the infamous photos from Iraq's Abu Ghraib prison. There is no hyperbole in the title of Jennifer Harbury's penetrating study of the U.S. torture record: *Truth, Torture, and the American Way*.[14] It is highly misleading, to say the least, when investigators of the Bush gang's descent into the global sewers lament that "in waging the war against terrorism, America had lost its way."[15]

None of this is to say that Bush/Cheney/Rumsfeld et al. did not introduce important innovations. In ordinary American practice, torture was largely farmed out to subsidiaries, not carried out by Americans directly in their own government-established torture chambers. As Allan Nairn, who has done some of the most revealing and courageous investigations of torture, points out: "What the Obama [ban on torture] ostensibly knocks off is that small percentage of torture now done by Americans while retaining the overwhelming bulk of the system's torture, which is done by foreigners under US patronage. Obama could stop backing foreign forces that torture, but he has chosen not to do so."[16]

Obama did not shut down the practice of torture, Nairn observes, but "merely repositioned it," restoring it to the American norm, a matter of indifference to the victims. Since Vietnam, "the US has mainly seen its torture done for it by proxy—paying, arming, training and guiding foreigners doing it, but usually being careful to keep Americans at least one discreet step removed." Obama's ban "doesn't even prohibit direct torture by Americans outside environments of 'armed conflict,' which is where much torture happens anyway since many repressive regimes aren't in armed conflict . . . his is a return to the status quo ante, the torture regime of Ford through Clinton, which, year by year, often produced more US-backed strapped-down agony than was produced during the Bush/Cheney years."[17]

Sometimes the American engagement in torture was even more indirect. In a 1980 study, Latin Americanist Lars Schoultz found that U.S. aid "has tended to flow disproportionately to Latin American governments which torture their citizens . . . to the hemisphere's relatively egregious violators of fundamental human rights."[18] That trend included military aid, was independent of need, and ran through the Carter years. Broader studies by Edward Herman found the same correlation, and also suggested an explanation. Not surprisingly, U.S. aid tends to correlate with a favorable climate for business operations, commonly improved by the murder of labor and peasant organizers and human rights activists and other such actions, yielding a secondary correlation between aid and egregious violation of human rights.[19]

These studies took place before the Reagan years, when the topic became not worth studying because the correlations were so clear.

Small wonder that President Obama advises us to look forward, not backward—a convenient doctrine for those who hold the clubs. Those who are beaten by them tend to see the world differently, much to our annoyance.

ADOPTING BUSH'S POSITIONS

An argument can be made that implementation of the CIA's "torture paradigm" never violated the 1984 United Nations Convention against Torture, at least as Washington interpreted it. McCoy points out that the isticated CIA paradigm, developed at enormous cost in the 1960s and based on "the KGB's most devastating torture ," kept primarily to mental torture, not crude physical torture, which was considered less effective in turning people into pliant vegetables.

McCoy writes that the Reagan administration carefully revised the international torture convention "with four detailed diplomatic 'reservations' focused on just one word in the convention's 26-printed pages," the word "mental." He continues: "These intricately-constructed diplomatic reservations re-defined torture, as interpreted by the United States, to exclude sensory deprivation and self-inflicted pain—the very techniques the CIA had refined at such great cost."

When Clinton sent the UN convention to Congress for ratification in 1994, he included the Reagan reservations. The president and Congress therefore exempted the core of the CIA torture paradigm from the U.S. interpretation of the torture convention; and those reservations, McCoy observes, were "reproduced verbatim in domestic legislation enacted to give legal force to the UN Convention."[20] That is the "political land mine" that "detonated with such phenomenal force" in the Abu Ghraib scandal and in the shameful Military Commissions Act that was passed with bipartisan support in 2006.

Bush, of course, went beyond his predecessors in authorizing prima facie violations of international law, and several of his extremist innovations were struck down by the courts. While Obama, like Bush, eloquently affirms our unwavering commitment to international law, he seems intent on substantially reinstating the extremist Bush measures.

In the important case of *Boumediene v. Bush* in June 2008, the Supreme Court rejected as unconstitutional the Bush administration's claim that prisoners in Guantánamo are not entitled to the right of habeas corpus.[21] Glenn Greenwald reviewed the aftermath of the case in *Salon*. Seeking to "preserve the power to abduct people from around the world" and imprison them without due process, the Bush administration decided to ship them to the U.S. prison at Bagram Airfield in Afghanistan, treating "the *Boumediene* ruling, grounded in our most basic constitutional guarantees, as though it was some sort of a silly game—fly your abducted prisoners to Guantanamo and they have constitutional rights, but fly them instead to Bagram and you can disappear them forever with no judicial process." Obama adopted the Bush position, "filing a brief in federal court that, in two sentences, declared that it embraced the most extremist Bush theory on this issue," arguing that prisoners flown to Bagram from anywhere in the world (in the case in question, Yemenis and Tunisians captured in Thailand and the United Arab Emirates) "can be imprisoned indefinitely with no rights of any kind—as long as they are kept in Bagram rather than Guantanamo."[22]

Shortly after, a Bush-appointed federal judge "rejected the Bush/ Obama position and held that the rationale of *Boumediene* applies every bit as much to Bagram as it does to Guantanamo." The Obama administration announced that it would appeal the ruling, thus placing Obama's Department of Justice, Greenwald concludes, "squarely to the Right of an extremely conservative, pro-executive-power, Bush 43-appointed judge on issues of executive power and due-process-less detentions," in radical violation of the president's campaign promises and earlier stands.[23]

The case of *Rasul v. Rumsfeld* appears to be following a similar trajectory. The plaintiffs charged that Rumsfeld and other high officials were responsible for their torture in Guantánamo, where they were sent after being captured by Uzbeki warlord Abdul Rashid Dostum. The plaintiffs claimed that they had traveled to Afghanistan to offer humanitarian relief. Dostum, a notorious thug, was then a leader of the Northern Alliance, the Afghan faction supported by Russia, Iran, India, Turkey, the Central Asian states, and the United States as it attacked Afghanistan in October 2001.

Dostum turned them over to U.S. custody, allegedly for bounty money. The Bush administration sought to have the case dismissed. Obama's Department of Justice filed a brief supporting the Bush position that government officials should not be held liable for torture and other violations of due process at Guantánamo, on the grounds that the courts had not yet clearly established the rights that prisoners there enjoy.[24]

It was also reported that the Obama administration considered reviving military commissions, one of the more severe violations of the rule of law during the Bush years. There is a reason, according to William Glaberson of the *New York Times*: "Officials who work on the Guantanamo issue say administration lawyers have become concerned that they would face significant obstacles to trying some terrorism suspects in federal courts. Judges might make it difficult to prosecute detainees who were subjected to brutal treatment or for prosecutors to use hearsay evidence gathered by intelligence agencies."[25] A serious flaw in the criminal justice system, it appears.

CREATING TERRORISTS

There is much debate about whether torture has been effective in eliciting information—the assumption being, apparently, that if it is effective then it may be justified. By this argument, when Nicaragua captured U.S. pilot Eugene Hasenfus in 1986, after shooting down his plane as it delivered aid to U.S.-supported Contra forces, they should not have tried him, found him guilty, and then sent him back to the United States, as they did. Instead, they should have applied the CIA torture paradigm to try to extract information about other terrorist atrocities being planned and implemented in Washington—no small matter for a tiny, impoverished country under terrorist attack by the global superpower.

By the same standard, if the Nicaraguans had been able to capture the chief terrorism coordinator—John Negroponte, then the U.S. ambassador in Honduras (later appointed as the first director of national intelligence, essentially a counterterrorism czar, without eliciting a murmur)—they should have done the same. Cuba would have been justified in acting similarly, had the Castro government been able to lay hands on the Kennedy brothers. There is no need to bring up what their victims should have done to Henry Kissinger, Ronald Reagan, and other leading terrorist commanders, whose exploits leave al-Qaeda in the dust, and who doubtless had ample information that could have prevented further "ticking time bomb" attacks.

Such considerations never seem to arise in public discussion. Accordingly, we know at once how to evaluate the pleas about valuable information.

There is, to be sure, a response: our terrorism, even if surely terrorism, is benign, deriving as it does from the idea of the City on the Hill. Perhaps the most eloquent exposition of this thesis was presented by *New Republic* editor Michael Kinsley, a respected spokesman of "the left." Americas Watch (part of Human Rights Watch) had protested State Department confirmation of official orders to Washington's terrorist forces to attack "soft targets"—undefended civilian targets—and to avoid the Nicaraguan army, as they could do thanks to CIA control of Nicaraguan airspace and the sophisticated communications systems provided to the Contras. In response, Kinsley explained that U.S. terrorist attacks on civilian targets are justified if they satisfy pragmatic criteria: a "sensible policy [should] meet the test of cost-benefit analysis," an analysis of "the amount of blood and misery that will be poured in, and the likelihood that democracy will emerge at the other end"[26]— "democracy" as U.S. elites determine its shape.

Kinsley's thoughts elicited no public comment; to my knowledge, they were apparently deemed acceptable. It would seem to follow, then, that U.S. leaders and their agents are not culpable for conducting such sensible policies in good faith, even if their judgment might sometimes be flawed.

Perhaps culpability would be greater, by prevailing moral standards, if it were discovered that Bush administration torture had cost American lives. That is, in fact, the conclusion drawn by Major Matthew Alexander (a pseudonym), one of the most seasoned U.S. interrogators in Iraq, who elicited "the information that led to the US military being able to locate Abu Musab al-Zarqawi, the head of al-Qa'ida in Iraq," correspondent Patrick Cockburn reports.

Alexander expresses only contempt for the Bush administration's harsh interrogation methods: "The use of torture by the US," he believes, not only elicits no useful information but "has proved so counter-productive that it may have led to the death of as many US soldiers as civilians killed in 9/11." From hundreds of interrogations, Alexander discovered that foreign fighters came to Iraq in reaction to the abuses at Guantánamo and Abu Ghraib, and that they and their domestic allies turned to suicide bombing and other terrorist acts for the same reasons.[27]

There is also mounting evidence that the torture methods Dick Cheney and Donald Rumsfeld encouraged created terrorists. One carefully studied case is that of Abdallah al-Ajmi, who was locked up in Guantánamo on the charge of "engaging in two or three fire fights with the Northern Alliance." He ended up in Afghanistan after having failed to reach Chechnya to fight against the Russians. After four years of brutal treatment in Guantánamo, he was returned to Kuwait. He later found his way to Iraq and, in March 2008, drove a bomb-laden truck into an Iraqi military compound, killing himself and thirteen Iraqi soldiers—"the single most heinous act of violence committed by a former Guantanamo detainee," according to the *Washington Post*, and according to his lawyer, the direct result of his abusive imprisonment.[28]

All much as a reasonable person would expect.

UNEXCEPTIONAL AMERICANS

Another standard pretext for torture is the context: the "war on terror" that Bush declared after 9/11. A crime that rendered traditional international law "quaint" and "obsolete"—so George W. Bush was advised by his legal counsel, Alberto Gonzales, later appointed attorney general. The doctrine has been widely reiterated in one form or another in commentary and analysis.[29]

The 9/11 attack was doubtless unique in many respects. One is where the guns were pointing: typically it is in the opposite direction. In fact, it was the first attack of any consequence on the national territory of the United States since the British burned down Washington, DC, in 1814.

The reigning doctrine of the country is sometimes called "American exceptionalism." It is nothing of the sort; it is probably close to universal among imperial powers. France hailed its "civilizing mission" in its colonies while the French minister of war called for "exterminating the indigenous population" of Algeria. Britain's nobility was a "novelty in the world," John Stuart Mill declared, while urging that this angelic power delay no longer in completing its liberation of India. Mill's classic essay on humanitarian intervention was written shortly after the public revelation of Britain's horrifying atrocities in suppressing the 1857 Indian rebellion. The conquest of the rest of India was in large part an effort to gain a monopoly in the opium trade for Britain's huge narcotrafficking enterprise, by far the largest in world history and designed primarily to compel China to accept Britain's manufactured goods.[30]

Similarly, there is no reason to doubt the sincerity of Japanese militarists in the 1930s who were bringing an "earthly paradise" to China under benign Japanese tutelage as they carried out the Rape of Nanking and their "burn all, loot all, kill all" campaigns in rural northern China. History is replete with similar glorious episodes.[31]

As long as such "exceptionalist" theses remain firmly implanted, however, the occasional revelations of the "abuse of history" can backfire, serving only to efface terrible crimes. In South Vietnam, for instance, the My Lai massacre was a mere footnote to the vastly greater atrocities of Washington's post–Tet Offensive pacification programs, ignored while indignation in this country was largely focused on this single crime.

Watergate was doubtless criminal, but the furor over it displaced incomparably worse crimes at home and abroad, including the FBI-organized assassination of black organizer Fred Hampton as part of the infamous COINTELPRO repression and the bombing of Cambodia, to mention just two egregious examples. Torture is hideous enough; the invasion of Iraq was a far worse crime. Quite commonly, selective atrocities have this function.

Historical amnesia is a dangerous phenomenon not only because it undermines moral and intellectual integrity but also because it lays the groundwork for crimes that still lie ahead.

4

The Invisible Hand of Power

The democratic uprising in the Arab world has been a spectacular display of courage, dedication, and commitment by popular forces—coinciding, fortuitously, with a remarkable uprising of tens of thousands in support of working people and democracy in Madison, Wisconsin, and other U.S. cities. If the trajectories of revolt in Cairo and Madison intersected, however, they were headed in opposite directions: in Cairo toward gaining elementary rights denied by the Egyptian dictatorship, in Madison toward defending rights that had been won in long and hard struggles and are now under severe attack.

Each is a microcosm of tendencies in global society, following varied courses. There are sure to be far-reaching consequences of what is taking place both in the decaying industrial heartland of the richest and most powerful country in human history and in what President Dwight Eisenhower called "the most strategically important area in the world"—"a stupendous source of strategic power" and "probably the richest economic prize in the world in the field of foreign investment," in the words of the State Department in the 1940s, a prize that the United States intended to keep for itself and its allies in the unfolding new world order of that day.[1]

Despite all the changes since, there is every reason to suppose that today's policymakers basically adhere to the judgment of President Franklin Delano Roosevelt's influential adviser Adolf A. Berle that control of the incomparable energy reserves of the Middle East would yield "substantial control of the world."[2] And correspondingly, they believe that loss of control would threaten the project of American global dominance that was clearly articulated during World War II and that has been sustained in the face of major changes in world order since that day.

From the outset of the war, in 1939, Washington anticipated that it would end with the United States in a position of overwhelming power. High-level State Department officials and foreign policy specialists met through the wartime years to lay out plans for the postwar world. They delineated a "Grand Area" that the United States was to dominate, including the western hemisphere, the Far East, and the former British Empire, with its Middle East energy resources. As Russia began to grind down Nazi armies after Stalingrad, the Grand Area goals extended to as much of Eurasia as possible—at least its economic core, in Western Europe. Within the Grand Area, the United States would maintain "unquestioned power" with "military and economic supremacy," while ensuring the "limitation of any exercise of sovereignty" by states that might interfere with its global designs.[3]

These careful wartime plans were soon implemented.

It was always recognized that Europe might choose to follow an independent course; the North Atlantic Treaty Organization (NATO) was partially intended to counter this threat. As soon as the official pretext for NATO dissolved in 1989, it was expanded to the east, in violation of verbal pledges to Soviet leader Mikhail Gorbachev. It has since become a U.S.-run intervention force with far-ranging scope, as spelled out by NATO Secretary General Jaap de Hoop Scheffer, who informed a NATO conference that "NATO troops have to guard pipelines that transport oil and gas that is directed for the West," and more generally protect sea routes used by tankers and other "crucial infrastructure" of the energy system.[4]

Grand Area doctrines license military intervention at will. That conclusion was articulated clearly by the Clinton administration, which declared that the United States has the right to use military force to ensure "uninhibited access to key markets, energy supplies, and strategic resources," and must maintain huge military forces "forward deployed" in Europe and Asia "in order to shape people's opinions about us" and "to shape events that will affect our livelihood and our security."[5]

The same principles governed the invasion of Iraq. As the United States' failure to impose its will in Iraq was becoming unmistakable, the actual goals of the invasion could no longer be concealed behind pretty rhetoric. In November 2007, the White House issued a "declaration of principles" demanding that U.S. forces must remain indefinitely in Iraq and committing Iraq to privilege American investors.[6] Two months later, President Bush informed Congress that he would reject legislation that might limit the permanent stationing of U.S. forces in Iraq or "United States control of the oil resources of Iraq"—demands that the United States had to abandon shortly after in the face of Iraqi resistance.[7]

In Tunisia and Egypt, the popular uprisings of 2011 have won impressive victories, but as the Carnegie Endowment reported, while names have changed, the regimes remain: "A change in ruling elites and system of governance is still a distant goal."[8] The report discusses internal barriers to democracy, but ignores the external ones, which as always are significant.

The United States and its Western allies are sure to do whatever they can to prevent authentic democracy in the Arab world. To understand why, it is only necessary to look at the studies of Arab opinion conducted by U.S. polling agencies. Though barely reported, they are certainly known to planners. They reveal that by overwhelming majorities, Arabs regard the United States and Israel as the major threats they face: the United States is so regarded by 90 percent of Egyptians and by over 75 percent of the inhabitants of the region generally. By way of contrast, 10 percent of Arabs regard Iran as a threat. Opposition to U.S. policy is so strong that a majority believes security would be improved if Iran had nuclear weapons—in Egypt, 80 percent.[9] Other figures are similar. If public opinion were to influence policy, the United States not only would not control the region but would be expelled from it, along with its allies, undermining fundamental principles of global dominance.

THE MUASHER DOCTRINE

Support for democracy is the province of ideologists and propagandists. In the real world, elite dislike of democracy is the norm. The evidence is overwhelming that democracy is supported only insofar as it contributes to social and economic objectives, a conclusion reluctantly conceded by the more serious scholarship.

Elite contempt for democracy was revealed dramatically in the reaction to the WikiLeaks exposures. Those that received the most attention, with euphoric commentary, were cables reporting that Arabs support the U.S. stand on Iran. The reference was to the ruling dictators of Arab nations; the attitude of the public went unmentioned.

The operative principle was described by Marwan Muasher, former Jordanian official and later director of Middle East research for the Carnegie Endowment: "The traditional argument put forward in and out of the Arab world is that there is nothing wrong, everything is under control. With this line of thinking, entrenched forces argue that opponents and outsiders calling for reform are exaggerating the conditions on the ground."[10]

Adopting that principle, if the dictators support us, what else could matter?

The Muasher doctrine is rational and venerable. To mention just one case that is highly relevant today, in internal discussions in 1958, President Eisenhower expressed concern about "the campaign of hatred" against us in the Arab world, not by governments, but by the people. The National Security Council (NSC) explained to Eisenhower that there is a perception in the Arab world that the United States supports dictatorships and blocks democracy and development so as to ensure control over the resources of the region. Furthermore, the perception is basically accurate, the NSC concluded, and that is exactly what we should be doing, relying on the Muasher doctrine. Pentagon studies conducted after 9/11 confirmed that the same perception holds today.[11]

It is normal for the victors to consign history to the trash can and for victims to take it seriously. Perhaps a few brief observations on this important matter may be useful. Today is not the first occasion when Egypt and the United States are facing similar problems and moving in opposite directions. That was also true in the early nineteenth century.

Economic historians have argued that Egypt was well placed to undertake rapid economic development at the same time that the United States was in this period.[12] Both had rich agriculture, including cotton, the fuel of the early industrial revolution—though unlike Egypt, the United States had to develop cotton production and a workforce through conquest, extermination, and slavery, with consequences that are evident now in the reservations for the survivors and the prisons that have rapidly expanded since the Reagan years to house the superfluous population left by deindustrialization.

One fundamental difference between the two nations was that the United States had gained independence and was therefore free to ignore the prescriptions of economic theory, delivered at the time by Adam Smith in terms rather like those preached to developing societies today. Smith urged the liberated colonies to produce primary products for export and to import superior British manufactured goods, and certainly not to attempt to monopolize crucial goods, particularly cotton. Any other path, Smith warned, "would retard instead of accelerating the further increase in the value of their annual produce, and would obstruct instead of promoting the progress of their country towards real wealth and greatness."[13]

Having gained their independence, the colonies simply dismissed his advice and followed England's own course of independent state-guided development, with high tariffs to protect industry from British exports (first textiles, later steel and others), and adopted numerous other devices to accelerate industrial development. The independent republic also sought to gain a monopoly over cotton so as to "place all other nations at our feet," particularly the British enemy, as the Jacksonian presidents announced when conquering Texas and half of Mexico.[14]

For Egypt, a comparable course was barred by British power. Lord Palmerston declared that "no ideas of fairness [toward Egypt] ought to stand in the way of such great and paramount interests" of Britain as preserving its economic and political hegemony, expressing his "hate" for the "ignorant barbarian" Muhammad Ali, who dared to seek an independent course, and deploying Britain's fleet and financial power to terminate Egypt's quest for independence and economic development.[15]

After World War II, when the United States displaced Britain as global hegemon, Washington adopted the same stand, making it clear that the United States would provide no aid to Egypt unless it adhered to the standard rules for the weak—which the United States continued to violate, imposing high tariffs to bar Egyptian cotton and causing a debilitating dollar shortage, as per the usual interpretation of market principles.

It is small wonder that the "campaign of hatred" against the United States that concerned Eisenhower was based on the recognition that the United States supports dictators and blocks democracy and development, as do its allies.

In Adam Smith's defense, it should be added that he recognized what would happen if Britain followed the rules of sound economics, now called "neoliberalism." He warned that if British manufacturers, merchants, and investors turned abroad, they might profit but England would suffer. But he felt that they would be guided by a home bias, so that as if by an "invisible hand" England would be spared the ravages of economic rationality.

The passage is hard to miss. It is the one occurrence of the famous phrase "invisible hand" in *The Wealth of Nations*. The other leading founder of classical economics, David Ricardo, drew similar conclusions, hoping that what is called "home bias" would lead men of property to "be satisfied with the low rate of profits in their own country, rather than seek a more advantageous employment for their wealth in foreign nations"—feelings that, he added, "I should be sorry to see weakened."[16] Their predictions aside, the instincts of the classical economists were sound.

THE IRANIAN AND CHINESE "THREATS"

The democratic uprising in the Arab world is sometimes compared to Eastern Europe in 1989, but on dubious grounds. In 1989, the democratic uprising was tolerated by the Russians, and supported by Western power in accord with standard doctrine: it plainly conformed to economic and strategic objectives, and was therefore a noble achievement, greatly honored, unlike the struggles at the same time "to defend the people's fundamental human rights" in Central America, in the words of the assassinated archbishop of El Salvador, one of the hundreds of thousands of victims of the military forces armed and trained by Washington.[17] There was no Mikhail Gorbachev in the West throughout those horrendous years, and there is none today. And Western power remains hostile to democracy in the Arab world for good reasons.

Grand Area doctrines continue to apply to contemporary crises and confrontations. In Western policymaking circles and political commentary, the Iranian threat is considered to pose the greatest danger to world order and hence must be the primary focus of U.S. foreign policy, with Europe trailing along politely.

Years ago, Israeli military historian Martin van Creveld wrote that "the world has witnessed how the United States attacked Iraq for, as it turned out, no reason at all. Had the Iranians not tried to build nuclear weapons, they would be crazy," particularly when they are under constant threat of attack, in violation of the UN Charter.[18]

The United States and Europe are united in punishing Iran for its threat to "stability"—in the technical sense of the term, meaning conformity to U.S. demands—but it is useful to recall how isolated they are; the nonaligned countries have vigorously supported Iran's right to enrich uranium. The major regional power, Turkey, voted against a U.S.-

initiated sanctions motion in the Security Council, along with Brazil, the most admired country of the global South. Their disobedience led to sharp censure, not for the first time: Turkey had been bitterly condemned in 2003 when the government followed the will of 95 percent of its population and refused to participate in the invasion of Iraq, thus demonstrating its weak grasp of democracy, Western-style.

While the United States can tolerate Turkish disobedience—though with dismay—China is harder to ignore. The press warns that "China's investors and traders are now filling a vacuum in Iran as businesses from many other nations, especially in Europe, pull out," and in particular, that China is expanding its dominant role in Iran's energy industries.[19] Washington is reacting with a touch of desperation. The State Department warned China that if it wants to be accepted in the "international community"—a technical term referring to the United States and whoever happens to agree with it—then it must not "skirt and evade international responsibilities, [which] are clear": namely, follow U.S. orders.[20] China is unlikely to be impressed.

There is also much concern about the growing Chinese military threat. A recent Pentagon study warned that China's military budget is approaching "one-fifth of what the Pentagon spent to operate and carry out the wars in Iraq and Afghanistan"—a fraction of the U.S. military budget, of course. China's expansion of military forces might "deny the ability of American warships to operate in international waters off its coast," the *New York Times* added.[21]

Off the coast of China, that is; it has yet to be proposed that the U.S. should eliminate military forces that deny the Caribbean to Chinese warships. China's lack of understanding of the rules of international civility is further illustrated by its objections to plans for the advanced nuclear-powered aircraft carrier *George Washington* to join naval exercises a few miles off China's coast, giving it the alleged capacity to strike Beijing.

In contrast, the West understands that such U.S. operations are all undertaken to defend "stability" and its own security. The liberal *New Republic* expresses its concern that "China sent ten warships through international waters just off the Japanese island of Okinawa."[22] That is indeed a provocation—unlike the fact, unmentioned, that Washington has converted the island into a major military base in defiance of vehement protests by the people of Okinawa. That is not a provocation, on the standard principle that we own the world.

Deep-seated imperial doctrine aside, there is good reason for China's neighbors to be concerned about its growing military and commercial power.

While Grand Area doctrine still prevails, the capacity to implement it has declined. The peak of U.S. power was after World War II, when it had literally half the world's wealth. But that naturally declined, as other industrial economies recovered from the devastation of the war and decolonization took its agonizing course. By the early 1970s, the U.S. share of global wealth had fallen to about 25 percent, and the industrial world had become tripolar: North America, Europe, and East Asia (then Japan-based).

There was also a sharp change in the U.S. economy in the 1970s, toward financialization and export of production. A variety of factors converged to create a vicious cycle of radical concentration of wealth, primarily in the top fraction of one percent of the population—mostly CEOs, hedge-fund managers, and the like. That leads to the concentration of political power, hence state policies to increase economic concentration: fiscal policies, rules of corporate governance, deregulation, and much more. Meanwhile the costs of electoral campaigns skyrocketed, driving the parties into the pockets of concentrated capital, increasingly financial: the Republicans reflexively, the Democrats—by now what used to be moderate Republicans—not far behind.

Elections have become a charade, run by the public relations industry. After his 2008 victory, Obama won an award from the industry for the best marketing campaign of the year. Executives were euphoric. In the business press they explained that they had been marketing candidates like other commodities since Ronald Reagan, but 2008 was their greatest achievement and would change the style in corporate boardrooms. The 2012 election cost over $2 billion, mostly in corporate funding, and the 2016 election is expected to cost twice that.[23] Small wonder that

Obama selected business leaders for top positions in his administration. The public is angry and frustrated, but as long as the doctrine described by Muasher prevails, that doesn't matter.

While wealth and power have narrowly concentrated, for most of the population real incomes have stagnated and people have been getting by with increased work hours, debt, and asset inflation, regularly destroyed by the financial crises that began as the regulatory apparatus was dismantled starting in the 1980s.

None of this is problematic for the very wealthy, who benefit from the "too big to fail" government insurance policy. That government insurance is no small matter. Considering just the ability of banks to borrow at lower rates, thanks to the implicit taxpayer subsidy, Bloomberg News, citing an International Monetary Fund working paper, estimates that "taxpayers give big banks $83 billion a year"—virtually their entire profit, a matter that is "crucial to understanding why the big banks present such a threat to the global economy."[24] Furthermore, the banks and investment firms can make risky transactions, with rich rewards, and when the system inevitably crashes, they can run to the nanny state for a taxpayer bailout, clutching their copies of F. A. Hayek and Milton Friedman.

That has been the regular process since the Reagan years, each crisis more extreme than the last—for the public population, that is. Real unemployment is at depression levels for much of the population, while Goldman Sachs, one of the main architects of the current crisis, is richer than ever. It quietly announced $17.5 billion in compensation for 2010, with CEO Lloyd Blankfein receiving a $12.6 million bonus, while his base salary more than tripled.[25]

It wouldn't do to focus attention on such facts as these. Accordingly, propaganda must seek to blame others, like public sector workers, with their fat salaries and exorbitant pensions: all fantasy, on the model of Reaganite imagery of black mothers being driven in their limousines to pick up welfare checks, and other models that need not be mentioned. We all must tighten our belts—almost all, that is.

Teachers are a particularly good target, as part of the deliberate effort to destroy the public education system from kindergarten through the universities by privatization—again, a policy that is good for the wealthy, but a disaster for the population as well as the long-term health of the economy, though that is one of the externalities that is put to the side insofar as market principles prevail.

Another fine target, always, is immigrants. That has been true throughout U.S. history, even more so at times of economic crisis, and exacerbated now by a sense that our country is being taken away from us: the white population will soon become a minority. One can understand the anger of aggrieved individuals, but the cruelty of the policy is shocking.

Who are the immigrants targeted? In eastern Massachusetts, where I live, many are Mayans fleeing the aftermath of the virtual genocide in the Guatemalan highlands carried out by Reagan's favorite killers. Others are Mexican victims of Clinton's North American Free Trade Agreement (NAFTA), one of those rare government agreements that managed to harm working people in all three of the participating countries. As NAFTA was rammed through Congress over popular objection in 1994, Clinton also initiated the militarization of the U.S.-Mexican border, previously fairly open. It was presumably understood that Mexican campesinos cannot compete with highly subsidized U.S. agribusiness, and that Mexican businesses would not survive competition with U.S. multinationals, which must be granted "national treatment" under the mislabeled "free-trade" agreements—a privilege granted only to corporate persons, not those of flesh and blood. Not surprisingly, these measures led to a flood of desperate refugees and to rising anti-immigrant hysteria on the part of the victims of state-corporate policies at home.

Much the same appears to be happening in Europe, where racism is probably more rampant than in the United States. One can only watch with wonder as Italy complains about the flow of refugees from Libya, the scene of the first post–World War I genocide, in the newly liberated east, at the hands of Italy's Fascist government. Or when France, still today the main protector of the brutal dictatorships in its former colonies, manages to overlook its hideous atrocities in Africa while French president Nicolas Sarkozy warns grimly of the "flood of immigrants" and Marine Le Pen objects that he is doing nothing to prevent it. I need not mention Belgium, which may win the prize for what Adam Smith called "the savage injustice of the Europeans."

The rise of neofascist parties in much of Europe would be a frightening phenomenon even if we were not to recall what happened on the continent in the recent past. Just imagine the reaction if Jews were being expelled from France to misery and oppression, and then witness the nonreaction when the same is happening to the Roma, also victims of the Holocaust and Europe's most brutalized population.

In Hungary, the neofascist party Jobbik gained 21 percent of the vote in national elections, perhaps unsurprising when three-quarters of the population feels that they are worse off than under Communist rule.[26] We might be relieved that in Austria the ultraright Jörg Haider won only 10 percent of the vote in 2008, were it not for the fact that the Freedom Party, outflanking him from the right, won more than 17 percent.[27] (It is chilling to recall that, in 1928, the Nazis won less than 3 percent of the vote in Germany.[28]) In England, the British National Party and the English Defence League, on the ultraracist right, are major forces.

In Germany, Thilo Sarrazin's book-length lament that immigrants are destroying the country was a runaway best seller, while Chancellor Angela Merkel, though she condemned the book, declared that multiculturalism had "utterly failed": the Turks imported to do the dirty work in Germany are failing to become blond and blue-eyed true Aryans.[29]

Those with a sense of irony may recall that Benjamin Franklin, one of the leading figures of the Enlightenment, warned that the newly liberated colonies should be wary of allowing Germans to immigrate because they were too swarthy, and Swedes as well. Into the twentieth century, ludicrous myths of Anglo-Saxon purity were common in the United States, including among presidents and other leading figures. Racism in our literary culture has been a rank obscenity. It has been much easier to eradicate polio than this horrifying plague, which regularly becomes more virulent in times of economic distress.

I do not want to end without mentioning another externality that is dismissed in market systems: the fate of the species. Systemic risk in the financial system can be remedied by the taxpayer, but no one will come to the rescue if the environment is destroyed. That it must be destroyed is close to an institutional imperative. Business leaders who are conducting propaganda campaigns to convince the population that anthropogenic global warming is a liberal hoax understand full well how grave is the threat, but they must maximize short-term profit and market share. If they don't, someone else will.

This vicious cycle could well turn out to be lethal. To see how grave the danger is, simply have a look at Congress in the United States, propelled into power by business funding and propaganda. Almost all the Republicans are climate deniers. They have already begun to cut funding for measures that might mitigate environmental catastrophe. Worse, some are true believers; take for example the new head of a subcommittee on the environment who explained that global warming cannot be a problem because God promised Noah that there will not be another flood.[30]

If such things were happening in some small and remote country, we might laugh, but not when they are happening in the richest and most powerful country in the world. And before we laugh, we might also bear in mind that the current economic crisis is traceable in no small measure to the fanatic faith in such dogmas as the efficient market hypothesis, and in general to what Nobel laureate Joseph Stiglitz, fifteen years ago, called the "religion" that markets know best—which prevented the central bank and the economics profession, with a few honorable exceptions, from taking notice of an $8 trillion housing bubble that had no basis at all in economic fundamentals, and that devastated the economy when it burst.[31]

All of this, and much more, can proceed as long as the Muasher doctrine prevails. As long as the general population is passive, apathetic, and diverted to consumerism or hatred of the vulnerable, then the powerful can do as they please, and those who survive will be left to contemplate the outcome.

5

American Decline: Causes and Consequences

"It is a common theme" that the United States, which "only a few years ago was hailed to stride the world as a colossus with unparalleled power and unmatched appeal . . . is in decline, ominously facing the prospect of its final decay."[1] This theme, articulated in the summer 2011 issue of the journal of the Academy of Political Science, is indeed widely believed—and with some reason, though a number of qualifications are in order. The decline has in fact been underway since the high point of U.S. power shortly after World War II, and the remarkable rhetoric of the decade of triumphalism after the Soviet Union imploded was mostly self-delusion. Furthermore, the commonly drawn corollary— that power will shift to China and India—is highly dubious. They are poor countries with severe internal problems. The world is surely becoming more diverse, but despite America's decline, in the foreseeable future there is no competitor for global hegemonic power.

To recall briefly some of the relevant history, during World War II U.S. planners recognized that the country would emerge from the war in a position of overwhelming power. It is quite clear from the documentary record that "President Roosevelt was aiming at United States hegemony in the postwar world," to quote the assessment of diplomatic historian Geoffrey Warner, one of the leading specialists on the topic.[2] Plans were developed, along lines discussed above, for the United States to control what was called a "Grand Area" spanning the globe. These doctrines still prevail, though their reach has declined.

The wartime plans, soon to be carefully implemented, were not unrealistic. The United States had long been by far the richest country in the world. The war ended the Great Depression, and American industrial capacity almost quadrupled, while rivals were decimated. At war's end the United States had half the world's wealth and unmatched security.[3] Each region of the Grand Area was assigned its "function" within the global system. The ensuing "Cold War" consisted largely of efforts by the two superpowers to enforce order in their own domains: for the Soviet Union, Eastern Europe; for the United States, most of the world.

By 1949 the Grand Area that the United States planned to control was already seriously eroding with "the loss of China," as it is routinely called.[4] The phrase is interesting: one can only "lose" what one possesses, and it is taken for granted that the United States owns most of the world by right. Shortly after, Southeast Asia began to slip free from Washington's control, leading to horrendous wars in Indochina and huge massacres in Indonesia in 1965 as U.S. dominance was restored. Meanwhile, subversion and massive violence continued elsewhere in an effort to maintain what is called "stability."

But decline was inevitable, as the industrial world reconstructed itself and decolonization pursued its agonizing course. By 1970, the U.S. share of world wealth had declined to about 25 percent.[5] The industrial world was becoming "tripolar," with major centers in the United States, Europe, and Asia, then Japan-centered and already becoming the globe's most dynamic region.

Twenty years later, the USSR collapsed. Washington's reaction teaches us a good deal about the reality of the Cold War. The first Bush administration, then in office, immediately declared that its policies would remain essentially unchanged, although with different pretexts; the huge military establishment would be maintained not for defense against the Russians but to confront the "technological sophistication" of Third World powers. Similarly, it would be necessary to maintain "the defense industrial base," a euphemism for advanced industry highly reliant on government subsidy and initiative. Intervention forces still had to be aimed at the Middle East, where serious problems "could not be laid at the Kremlin's door," contrary to half a century of deceit. It was quietly conceded that the problem had always been "radical nationalism," that is, attempts by countries to pursue an independent course in violation of Grand Area principles.[6] These principles were not to be modified in any fundamental way, as the Clinton doctrine (under which the United States could unilaterally use military power to further its economic interests) and the global expansion of NATO would soon make clear.

There was a period of euphoria after the collapse of the superpower enemy, replete with excited tales about "the end of history" and awed acclaim for President Bill Clinton's foreign policy, which had entered a "noble phase" with a "saintly glow," as for the first time in history a nation would be guided by "altruism" and dedicated to "principles and values." Nothing now stood in the way of an "idealistic New World bent on ending inhumanity" which could at last carry forward, unhindered, the emerging international norm of humanitarian intervention. And that's to sample just a few of the impassioned accolades of prominent intellectuals at the time.[7]

Not all were so enraptured. The traditional victims, the global South, bitterly condemned "the so-called 'right' of humanitarian intervention," recognizing it to be nothing but the old "right" of imperial domination tricked out in new clothing.[8] Meanwhile, more sober voices among the policy elite at home saw that, for much of the world, the United States was "becoming the rogue superpower," "the single greatest external threat to their societies," and that "the prime rogue state today is the United States," to quote Samuel P. Huntington, Harvard professor of the science of government, and Robert Jervis, president of the American Political Science Association.[9] After George W. Bush took over, increasingly hostile world opinion could scarcely be ignored; in the Arab world in particular, Bush's approval ratings plummeted. Obama has achieved the impressive feat of sinking still lower, down to 5 percent approval in Egypt and not much higher elsewhere in the region.[10]

Meanwhile, decline continued. In the past decade, South America has also been "lost." That is serious enough; as the Nixon administration was planning the destruction of Chilean democracy—the U.S.-backed military coup on "the first 9/11" that installed the dictatorship of General Augusto Pinochet—the National Security Council ominously warned that if the United States could not control Latin America, it could not expect "to achieve a successful order elsewhere in the world."[11] Far more serious, however, would be moves toward independence in the Middle East, for reasons recognized clearly in early post–World War II planning.

A further danger: there might be meaningful moves toward democracy. *New York Times* executive editor Bill Keller wrote movingly of Washington's "yearning to embrace the aspiring democrats across North Africa and the Middle East."[12] But polls of Arab opinion revealed very clearly that it would be a disaster for Washington if there were steps toward the creation of functioning democracies, where public opinion would influence policy: as we have seen, the Arab population regards the United States as a major threat, and would expel it and its allies from the region if given a choice.

While long-standing U.S. policies remain largely stable, with tactical adjustments, under Obama there have been some significant changes. Military analyst Yochi Dreazen and his coauthors observed in the *Atlantic* that while Bush's policy was to capture (and torture) suspects, Obama simply assassinates them, rapidly increasing the use of terror weapons (drones) and Special Forces personnel, many of them assassination teams.[13] Special Forces units have been deployed in 147 countries.[14] Now as large as Canada's entire military, these soldiers are, in effect, a private army of the president, a matter discussed in detail by American investigative journalist Nick Turse on the website *TomDispatch*.[15] The team that Obama sent to assassinate Osama bin Laden had already carried out perhaps a dozen similar missions in Pakistan. As these and many other developments illustrate, though U.S. hegemony has declined, its ambition has not.

Another common theme, at least among those who are not willfully blind, is that American decline is in no small measure self-inflicted. The comic opera in Washington centering around whether or not to "shut down" the government, which disgusts the country (a large majority of which thinks that Congress should just be disbanded) and bewilders the world, has few analogues in the annals of parliamentary democracy. The spectacle is even coming to frighten the sponsors of the charade. Corporate powers are now concerned that the extremists they helped put in office may choose to bring down the edifice on which their own wealth and privilege relies, the powerful "nanny state" that caters to their interests.

The eminent American social philosopher John Dewey once described politics as "the shadow cast on society by big business," warning that "attenuation of the shadow will not change the substance."[16] Since the 1970s, that shadow has become a dark cloud enveloping society and the political system. Corporate power, by now largely made up of financial capital, has reached a point where both political organizations—which by now barely resemble traditional parties—are far to the right of the population on the major issues under debate.

For the public, the primary domestic concern is the severe crisis of unemployment. Under prevailing circumstances, that critical problem could have been overcome only by a significant government stimulus, well beyond the one Obama initiated in 2009, which barely matched declines in state and local spending, though it still did probably save millions of jobs. For financial institutions, the primary concern is the deficit. Therefore, only the deficit is under discussion. A large majority of the population (72 percent) favor addressing the deficit by taxing the very rich.[17] Cutting health programs is opposed by overwhelming majorities (69 percent in the case of Medicaid, 78 percent for Medicare).[18] The likely outcome is therefore the opposite.

Reporting the results of a study of how the public would eliminate the deficit, Steven Kull, director of the Program for Public Consultation, which conducted the study, writes that "clearly both the administration and the Republican-led House are out of step with the public's values and priorities in regard to the budget . . . The biggest difference in spending is that the public favored deep cuts in defense spending, while the administration and the House propose modest increases . . . The public also favored more spending on job training, education, and pollution control than did either the administration or the House."[19]

The costs of the Bush-Obama wars in Iraq and Afghanistan are now estimated to run as high as $4.4 trillion—a major victory for Osama bin Laden, whose announced goal was to bankrupt America by drawing it into a trap.[20] The 2011 U.S. military budget—almost matching that of the rest of the world combined—was higher in real (inflation-adjusted) terms than at any time since World War II, and slated go even higher. There is much loose talk about projected cuts, but such reporting fails to mention that if they take place at all, they will be from projected future Pentagon growth rates.

The deficit crisis has largely been manufactured as a weapon to destroy hated social programs on which a large part of the population relies. The highly respected economics correspondent Martin Wolf, of the *Financial Times*, writes, "It is not that tackling the US fiscal position is urgent. . . . The US is able to borrow on easy terms, with yields on 10-year bonds close to 3 per cent, as the few non-hysterics predicted. The fiscal challenge is long term, not immediate." Significantly, he adds: "The astonishing feature of the federal fiscal position is that revenues are forecast to be a mere 14.4 per cent of GDP in 2011, far below their postwar average of close to 18 per cent. Individual income tax is forecast to be a mere 6.3 per cent of GDP in 2011. This non-American cannot understand what the fuss is about: in 1988, at the end of Ronald Reagan's term, receipts were 18.2 per cent of GDP. Tax revenue has to rise substantially if the deficit is to close." Astonishing indeed, but deficit reduction is the demand of the financial institutions and the super-rich, and in a rapidly declining democracy, that's what counts. [21]

Though the deficit crisis has been manufactured for reasons of savage class war, the long-term debt crisis is serious, and has been ever since Ronald Reagan's fiscal irresponsibility turned the United States from the world's leading creditor to the world's leading debtor, tripling the national debt and raising threats to the economy that were rapidly escalated by George W. Bush. For now, however, it is the crisis of unemployment that is the gravest concern.

The final "compromise" on the crisis—or, more accurately, the capitulation to the far right—was the opposite of what the public wanted. Few serious economists would disagree with Harvard economist Lawrence Summers that "America's current problem is much more a jobs and growth deficit than an excessive budget deficit," and that the deal reached in Washington to raise the debt limit, though preferable to a (highly unlikely) default, is likely to cause further harm to a deteriorating economy.[22]

Not even mentioned is the possibility, discussed by economist Dean Baker, that the deficit might be eliminated if the dysfunctional privatized health care system were replaced by one similar to those in other industrial societies, which have half the per capita costs and at least comparable health outcomes.[23] The financial institutions and the pharmaceutical industry, however, are far too powerful for such options even to be considered, though the thought seems hardly Utopian. Off the agenda for similar reasons are other economically sensible options, such as a small financial transactions tax.

Meanwhile, new gifts are regularly lavished on Wall Street. The House Committee on Appropriations cut the budget request for the Securities and Exchange Commission, the prime barrier against financial fraud, and Congress wields other weapons in its battle against future generations. In the face of Republican opposition to environmental protection, "a major American utility is shelving the nation's most prominent effort to capture carbon dioxide from an existing coal-burning power plant, dealing a severe blow to efforts to rein in emissions responsible for global warming," the New York Times reports.[24]

Such self-inflicted blows, while increasingly powerful, are not a recent innovation. They trace back to the 1970s, when the national political economy underwent major transformations, bringing to an end what is commonly called "the golden age of [state] capitalism." Two major elements of this shift were financialization and the offshoring of production, both related to the decline in the rate of profit in manufacturing and the dismantling of the postwar Bretton Woods system of capital controls and regulated currencies. The ideological triumph of "free market doctrines," highly selective as always, administered further blows as these doctrines were translated into deregulation, rules of corporate governance linking huge CEO rewards to short-term profits, and other such policy decisions. The resulting concentration of wealth yielded greater political power, accelerating a vicious cycle that has led to extraordinary wealth for a tiny minority while for the large majority real incomes have virtually stagnated.

At the same time, the cost of elections skyrocketed, driving both parties ever deeper into corporate pockets. What remains of political democracy has been further undermined as both parties turned to auctioning off congressional leadership positions. Political economist Thomas Ferguson observes that "uniquely among legislatures in the developed world, US congressional parties now post prices for key slots in the lawmaking process." The legislators who fund the party get the posts, virtually compelling them to become servants of private capital even beyond the norm. The result, Ferguson adds, is that debates "rely heavily on the endless repetition of a handful of slogans that have been battle tested for their appeal to national investor blocs and interest groups that the leadership relies on for resources."[25]

The post–golden age economy is enacting a nightmare envisaged by the classical economists Adam Smith and David Ricardo. In the past thirty years, the "masters of mankind," as Smith called them, have abandoned any sentimental concern for the welfare of their own society. They have instead concentrated on short-term gain and huge bonuses, the country be damned.

A graphic illustration is on the front page of the *New York Times* as I write. Two major stories appear side by side. One discusses how Republicans fervently oppose any deal "that involves increased revenues"—a euphemism for taxes on the rich.[26] The other is headlined "Even Marked Up, Luxury Goods Fly Off Shelves."[27]

This developing picture is aptly described in a brochure for investors produced by Citigroup, the huge bank that is once again feeding at the public trough, as it has done regularly for thirty years in a cycle of risky loans, huge profits, crashes, and bailouts. The bank's analysts describe a world that is dividing into two blocs, the plutonomy and the rest, creating a global society in which growth is powered by the wealthy few and largely consumed by them. Left out of the gains of the plutonomy are the "non-rich," the vast majority, now sometimes called the "global precariat," the workforce living an unstable and increasingly penurious existence. In the United States, they are subject to "growing worker insecurity," the basis for a healthy economy, as Federal Reserve chair Alan Greenspan explained to Congress while lauding his own skills in economic management.[28] This is the real shift of power in global society.

The Citigroup analysts advise investors to focus on the very rich, where the action is. Their "Plutonomy Stock Basket," as they call it, has far outperformed the world index of developed markets since 1985, when the Reagan-Thatcher economic programs for enriching the very wealthy were really taking off.[29]

Before the 2008 crash for which they were largely responsible, the new post–golden age financial institutions had gained startling economic power, more than tripling their share of corporate profits. After the crash, a number of economists began to inquire into their function in purely economic terms. Nobel laureate in economics Robert Solow concludes that their general impact is likely to be negative, because "the successes probably add little or nothing to the efficiency of the real economy, while the disasters transfer wealth from taxpayers to financiers."[30]

By shredding the remnants of political democracy, these financial institutions lay the basis for carrying the lethal process forward—as long as their victims are willing to suffer in silence.

Returning to the "common theme" that the United States "is in decline, ominously facing the prospect of its final decay," while the laments are considerably exaggerated, they contain elements of truth.

American power in the world is, indeed, continuing its decline from its early post–World War II peak. While the United States remains the most powerful state in the world, nevertheless, global power is continuing to diversify, and the United States is increasingly unable to impose its will. But decline has many dimensions and complexities. The domestic society is also in decline in significant ways, and what is decline for some may be unimaginable wealth and privilege for others. For the plutonomy—more narrowly, a tiny fraction of it at the upper extreme—privilege and wealth abound, while for the great majority prospects are often gloomy, and many even face problems of survival in a country with unparalleled advantages.

6

Is America Over?

Some significant anniversaries are solemnly commemorated—Japan's attack on the U.S. naval base at Pearl Harbor, for example. Others are ignored, and we can often learn valuable lessons from them about what is likely to lie ahead.

There was no commemoration of the fiftieth anniversary of President John F. Kennedy's decision to launch the most destructive and murderous act of aggression of the post–World War II period: the invasion of South Vietnam, and later all of Indochina, leaving millions dead and four countries devastated, with casualties still mounting from the long-term effects of drenching South Vietnam with some of the most lethal carcinogens known, undertaken to destroy ground cover and food crops.

The prime target was South Vietnam. The aggression later spread to North Vietnam, then to the remote peasant society of northern Laos, and finally to rural Cambodia, which was bombed at a stunning level, equivalent to all Allied air operations in the Pacific region during World War II, including the two atom bombs dropped on Hiroshima and Nagasaki. In this case, National Security Advisor Henry Kissinger's orders were being carried out—"anything that flies on anything that moves," an open call for genocide that is rare in the historical record.[1] Little of this is remembered. Most was scarcely known beyond narrow circles of activists.

When the invasion was launched fifty years ago, concern was so slight that there were few efforts at justification, hardly more than the president's impassioned plea that "we are opposed around the world by a monolithic and ruthless conspiracy that relies primarily on covert means for expanding its sphere of influence," and if that conspiracy achieved its ends in Laos and Vietnam, "the gates will be opened wide."[2]

Elsewhere, he warned further that "the complacent, the self-indulgent, the soft societies are about to be swept away with the debris of history [and] only the strong . . . can possibly survive," in this case reflecting on the failure of U.S. aggression and terror to crush Cuban independence.[3]

By the time protest began to mount half a dozen years later, the respected Vietnam specialist and military historian Bernard Fall, no dove, forecast that "Vietnam as a cultural and historic entity . . . is threatened with extinction [as] the countryside literally dies under the blows of the largest military machine ever unleashed on an area of this size."[4] He was again referring to South Vietnam.

When the war ended, eight horrendous years later, mainstream opinion was divided between those who described the war as a "noble cause" that could have been won with more dedication and, at the opposite extreme, the critics, for whom it was "a mistake" that proved too costly. By 1977, President Carter aroused little notice when he explained that we owe Vietnam "no debt" because "the destruction was mutual."[5]

There are important lessons in all this for today, even apart from another reminder that only the weak and defeated are called to account for their crimes. One lesson is that to understand what is happening we should attend not only to critical events of the real world, often dismissed from history, but also to what leaders and elite opinion believe, however tinged with fantasy. Another lesson is that alongside the flights of fancy concocted to terrify and mobilize the public (and perhaps believed by some who are trapped in their own rhetoric), there is also geostrategic planning based on principles that are rational and stable over long periods because they are rooted in stable institutions and their concerns. I will return to that point, only stressing here that the persistent factors in state action are generally well concealed.

The Iraq war is an instructive case. It was marketed to a terrified public on the usual grounds of self-defense against an awesome threat to survival: the "single question," George W. Bush and Tony Blair declared, was whether Saddam Hussein would end his programs of developing weapons of mass destruction. When the single question received the wrong answer, government rhetoric shifted effortlessly to our "yearning for democracy," and educated opinion duly followed course.

Later, as the scale of the U.S. defeat in Iraq was becoming difficult to suppress, the government quietly conceded what had been clear all along. In 2007, the administration officially announced that a final settlement must grant the U.S. military bases and the right of combat operations, and must privilege U.S. investors in the country's rich energy system—demands only reluctantly abandoned in the face of Iraqi resistance, and all kept well hidden from the general population.[6]

GAUGING AMERICAN DECLINE

With such lessons in mind, it is useful to look at what is highlighted in the major journals of policy and opinion. Let us keep to the most prestigious of the establishment journals, *Foreign Affairs*. The headline on the cover of the November/December 2011 issue reads in boldface: "Is America Over?"

The essay motivating this headline calls for a "retrenchment" in the "humanitarian missions" abroad that are consuming the country's wealth, so as to arrest the American decline that is a major theme of international affairs discourse, usually accompanied by the corollary that power is shifting to the East, to China and (maybe) India.[7]

The two opening commentaries are on Israel-Palestine. The first, by two high Israeli officials, is entitled "The Problem Is Palestinian Rejectionism." It asserts that the conflict cannot be resolved because Palestinians refuse to recognize Israel as a Jewish state—thereby conforming to standard diplomatic practice: states are recognized, but not privileged sectors within them.[8] The demand for Palestinian recognition is hardly more than a new device to deter the threat of a political settlement that would undermine Israel's expansionist goals.

The opposing position, defended by an American professor, is encapsulated by its heading: "The Problem Is the Occupation."[9] The subtitle of the article is "How the Occupation Is Destroying the Nation." Which nation? Israel, of course. The paired articles appear on the cover under the heading "Israel Under Siege."

The January/February 2012 issue features yet another call to bomb Iran before it is too late. Warning of "the dangers of deterrence," the author suggests that "skeptics of military action fail to appreciate the true danger that a nuclear-armed Iran would pose to US interests in the Middle East and beyond. And their grim forecasts assume that the cure would be worse than the disease—that is, that the consequences of a US assault on Iran would be as bad as or worse than those of Iran achieving its nuclear ambitions. But that is a faulty assumption. The truth is that a military strike intended to destroy Iran's nuclear program, if managed carefully, could spare the region and the world a very real threat and dramatically improve the long-term national security of the United States." [10] Others argue that the costs would be too high, and at the extreme some even point out that such an attack would violate international law—as does the stand of the moderates, who regularly deliver threats of violence, in violation of the UN Charter.

Let us review these dominant concerns in turn.

American decline is real, though the apocalyptic version of it reflects the familiar ruling-class perception that anything short of total control amounts to total disaster. Despite the piteous laments, the United States remains the world's dominant power by a large margin, with no competitor in sight, and not only in the military dimension, in which, of course, the United States reigns supreme.

China and India have recorded rapid (though highly inegalitarian) growth, but remain very poor countries, with enormous internal problems not faced by the West. China is the world's major manufacturing center, but largely as an assembly plant for the advanced industrial powers on its periphery and for Western multinationals. That is likely to change over time. Manufacturing regularly provides the basis for innovation, often even breakthroughs, as is now sometimes happening in China. One example that has impressed Western specialists is China's takeover of the growing global solar panel market, not on the basis of cheap labor but by coordinated planning and, increasingly, innovation.

But the problems China faces are serious. Some are demographic, as reviewed in *Science*, the leading U.S. science weekly. Its study shows that mortality sharply decreased in China during the Maoist years, "mainly a result of economic development and improvements in education and health services, especially the public hygiene movement that resulted in a sharp drop in mortality from infectious diseases." But this progress ended with the initiation of capitalist reforms thirty years ago, and the death rate has since increased.

Furthermore, China's recent economic growth has relied substantially on a "demographic bonus," a very large working-age population. "But the window for harvesting this bonus may close soon," with a "profound impact on development. . . . Excess cheap labor supply, which is one of the major factors driving China's economic miracle, will no longer be available."[11]

Demography is only one of many serious problems ahead. And for India, the problems are even more severe.

Not all prominent voices foresee American decline. Among international media, there is none more serious and responsible than the *Financial Times*. It recently devoted a full page to the optimistic expectation that new technology for extracting North American fossil fuels might allow the United States to become energy independent, hence retaining its global hegemony for a century.[12] There is no mention of the kind of world the United States would rule over in this happy event, but not for lack of evidence.

At about the same time, the International Energy Agency (IEA) reported that, with rapidly increasing carbon emissions from fossil fuel use, the limit of safety with regard to climate change will be reached by 2017 if the world continues on its present course. "The door is closing," the IEA's chief economist said, and very soon it "will be closed forever."[13]

Shortly before that, the U.S. Department of Energy reported its annual carbon dioxide emissions figures, which "jumped by the biggest amount on record," to a level higher than the worst-case scenario anticipated by the Intergovernmental Panel on Climate Change (IPCC).[14] That came as no surprise to many scientists, including the Massachusetts Institute of Technology (MIT)'s program on climate change, which for years has warned that the IPCC's predictions are too conservative.

Such critics of the IPCC predictions receive virtually no public attention, unlike the fringe climate change denialists who are supported by the corporate sector, along with huge propaganda campaigns that have driven many Americans off the international spectrum in their dismissal of the threats of climate change. Business support also translates directly into political power. Denialism is part of the catechism that must be intoned by Republican candidates in the farcical election campaigns now endlessly underway, and in Congress denialists are powerful enough to abort even efforts to inquire into the effects of global warming, let alone do anything serious about it.

In brief, American decline can perhaps be stemmed if we abandon hope for decent survival, a prospect that is all too real given the balance of forces in the world.

"LOSING" CHINA AND VIETNAM

Putting such unpleasant thoughts aside, a close look at American decline shows that China indeed plays a large role in it, as has been true for the last sixty years. The decline that now elicits such concern is not a recent phenomenon. It traces back to the end of World War II, when the United States had half the world's wealth and incomparable security and global reach. Planners were naturally well aware of the enormous disparity of power, and intended to keep it that way.

The basic viewpoint was outlined with admirable frankness in a major state paper of 1948. The author was one of the architects of the new world order of the day: the chair of the State Department's policy planning staff, respected statesman and scholar George Kennan, a moderate dove within the planning spectrum. He observed that the central policy goal of the United States should be to maintain the "position of disparity" that separated our enormous wealth from the poverty of others. To achieve that goal, he advised, "We should cease to talk about vague and . . . unreal objectives such as human rights, the raising of the living standards, and democratization," and must "deal in straight power concepts" and not be "hampered by idealistic slogans" about "altruism and world-benefaction."[15]

Kennan was referring specifically to the situation in Asia, but his observations can be generalized, with exceptions, to participants in the U.S.-run global system. It was well understood, however, that the "idealistic slogans" were to be displayed prominently when addressing others, including the intellectual classes, who were expected to promulgate them.

The plans that Kennan helped formulate and implement took for granted that the United States would control the western hemisphere, the Far East, the former British Empire (including the incomparable energy resources of the Middle East), and as much of Eurasia as possible, crucially its commercial and industrial centers. These were not unrealistic objectives, given the distribution of power at that moment. But decline set in at once.

In 1949, China declared independence—resulting, in the United States, in bitter recriminations and conflict over who was responsible for that "loss." The tacit assumption was that the United States "owned" China by right, along with most of the rest of the world, much as postwar planners assumed.

The "loss of China" was the first significant step in "America's decline." It had major policy consequences. One was the immediate decision to support France's effort to reconquer its former colony of Indochina, so that it, too, would not be "lost." Indochina itself was not a major concern, despite claims made by President Eisenhower and others about its rich resources. Rather, the concern was the "domino theory." Often ridiculed when dominoes don't fall, it remains a leading principle of policy because it is quite rational. To adopt Henry Kissinger's version, a region that falls out of U.S. control can become a "virus" that will "spread contagion," inducing others to follow the same path.

In the case of Vietnam, the concern was that the virus of independent development might infect Indonesia, which really does have rich resources. And that might lead Japan—the "superdomino," as it was called by the prominent Asia historian John Dower—to "accommodate" to an independent Asia, becoming its technological and industrial center in a system that would escape the reach of U.S. power.[16] That would have meant, in effect, that the United States had lost the Pacific phase of World War II, fought to prevent Japan's attempt to establish such a new order in Asia.

The way to deal with such a problem is clear: destroy the virus and "inoculate" those who might be infected. In the case of Vietnam, the rational choice was to destroy any hope of successful independent development and impose brutal dictatorships in the surrounding regions. Those tasks were successfully carried out—though history has its own cunning, and something similar to what was feared has nonetheless since been developing in East Asia, much to Washington's dismay.

The most important victory of the Indochina wars was in 1965, when a U.S.-backed military coup in Indonesia led by General Suharto carried out massive crimes that were compared by the CIA to those of Hitler, Stalin, and Mao. The "staggering mass slaughter," as the *New York Times* described it, was reported accurately across the mainstream, and with unrestrained euphoria.[17]

It was "a gleam of light in Asia," as the noted liberal commentator James Reston wrote in the *Times*.[18] The coup ended the threat of democracy by demolishing the mass-based political party of the poor, established a dictatorship that went on to compile one of the worst human rights records in the world, and threw the riches of the country open to Western investors. Small wonder that, after many other horrors, including the near-genocidal invasion of East Timor, Suharto was welcomed by the Clinton administration in 1995 as "our kind of guy."[19]

Years after the great events of 1965, Kennedy-Johnson National Security Advisor McGeorge Bundy reflected that it would have been wise to end the Vietnam War at that time, with the "virus" virtually destroyed and the primary domino solidly in place, buttressed by other U.S.-backed dictatorships throughout the region. Similar procedures have been routinely followed elsewhere; Kissinger was referring specifically to the threat of socialist democracy in Chile—a threat ended on "the first 9/11" with the vicious dictatorship of General Pinochet subsequently imposed on the country. Viruses have aroused deep concern elsewhere as well, including the Middle East, where the threat of secular nationalism has often concerned British and U.S. planners, inducing them to support radical Islamic fundamentalism to counter it.

THE CONCENTRATION OF WEALTH AND AMERICAN DECLINE

Despite such victories, American decline continued. Around the 1970s, it entered a new phase: conscious self-inflicted decline, as planners both private and state shifted the U.S. economy toward financialization and the offshoring of production, driven in part by the declining rate of profit in domestic manufacturing. These decisions initiated a vicious cycle in which wealth became highly concentrated (dramatically so in the top 0.1 percent of the population), yielding a concentration of political power, and hence legislation to carry the cycle further: revised taxation and other fiscal policies, deregulation, changes in the rules of corporate governance allowing huge gains for executives, and so on.

Meanwhile, for the majority, real wages largely stagnated, and people were able to get by only by sharply increased workloads (far beyond those of Europe), unsustainable debt, and, since the Reagan years, repeated bubbles, creating paper wealth that inevitably disappeared when they burst, after which their perpetrators were often bailed out by the taxpayer. In parallel, the political system has been increasingly shredded as both parties are driven deeper into corporate pockets with the escalating cost of elections—the Republicans to the level of farce, the Democrats not far behind.

A recent book-length study by the Economic Policy Institute, which has been the major source of reputable data on these developments for years, is entitled *Failure by Design*. The phrase "by design" is accurate; other choices were certainly possible. And as the study points out, the "failure" is class based. There is no failure for the designers—far from it. The policies are only a failure for the large majority—the 99 percent, in the imagery of the Occupy movements—and for the country, which has declined and will continue to do so under these policies.

One factor is the offshoring of manufacturing. As the Chinese solar panel example mentioned earlier illustrates, manufacturing capacity provides the basis and stimulus for innovation, leading to higher stages of sophistication in production, design, and invention. Those benefits too are being outsourced—not a problem for the "money mandarins" who increasingly design policy, but a serious problem for working people and the middle classes, and a real disaster for the most oppressed: African-Americans, who have never escaped the legacy of slavery and its ugly aftermath, and whose meager wealth virtually disappeared after the collapse of the housing bubble in 2008, setting off the most recent financial crisis, the worst so far.

STIRRINGS ABROAD

While conscious, self-inflicted decline went on at home, "losses" continued to mount elsewhere. In the past decade, for the first time in five hundred years, South America has taken successful steps to free itself from Western domination. The region has moved toward integration,

and has begun to address some of the terrible internal problems of societies ruled by mostly Europeanized elites, tiny islands of extreme wealth
in a sea of misery. These nations have also rid themselves of all U.S. military bases and of International Monetary Fund controls. A newly
formed organization, the Community of Latin American and Caribbean States (CELAC), includes all countries of the hemisphere apart
from the U.S. and Canada. If it actually functions, that will be another
step in American decline, in this case in what has always been regarded
as "the backyard."

Even more serious would be the loss of the MENA countries—
Middle East/North Africa—which have been regarded by planners
since the 1940s as "a stupendous source of strategic power, and one of the
greatest material prizes in world history."[20] To be sure, if the projections of
a century of U.S. energy independence based on North American energy
resources turn out to be realistic, the significance of controlling MENA
would decline somewhat, though probably not by much. The main concern has always been control more so than access. However, the likely
consequences to the planet's equilibrium are so ominous that discussion may be largely an academic exercise.

The Arab Spring, another development of historic importance, might
portend at least a partial "loss" of MENA. The United States and its allies
have tried hard to prevent that outcome—so far, with considerable success. Their policy toward the popular uprisings has kept closely to the
standard guidelines: support the forces most amenable to U.S. influence
and control.

Favored dictators must be supported as long as they can maintain
control (as in the major oil states). When that is no longer possible, dis-
card them and try to restore the old regime as fully as possible (as in
Tunisia and Egypt). The general pattern is familiar from elsewhere in
the world: Somoza, Marcos, Duvalier, Mobutu, Suharto, and many
others. In the case of Libya, the three traditional imperial powers, violating the UN Security Council resolution they had just sponsored,
became the air force of the rebels, sharply increasing civilian casualties

and creating a humanitarian disaster and political chaos as the country descended into civil war and weapons poured out to jihadis in western Africa and elsewhere.[21]

ISRAEL AND THE REPUBLICAN PARTY

Similar considerations carry over directly to the second major concern addressed in the November/December 2011 issue of *Foreign Affairs* cited above: the Israel-Palestine conflict. In this arena the United States' fear of democracy could hardly be more clearly exhibited. In January 2006, an election took place in Palestine, pronounced free and fair by international monitors. The instant reaction of the United States (and, of course, Israel), with Europe following along politely, was to impose harsh penalties on Palestinians for voting the wrong way.

That is no innovation. It is quite in keeping with the general principle recognized by mainstream scholarship: the United States supports democracy if, and only if, the outcomes accord with its strategic and economic objectives—the rueful conclusion of neo-Reaganite Thomas Carothers, the most careful and respected scholarly analyst of "democracy promotion" initiatives.

More broadly, for forty years the United States has led the rejectionist camp on Israel-Palestine, blocking an international consensus calling for a political settlement on terms too well-known to require repetition. The Western mantra is that Israel seeks negotiations without preconditions, while the Palestinians refuse such terms. The opposite is more accurate: the United States and Israel demand strict preconditions, which are, furthermore, designed to ensure that negotiations will lead either to Palestinian capitulation on crucial issues or nowhere.

The first precondition is that the negotiations must be supervised by Washington, which makes about as much sense as demanding that Iran supervise the negotiation of Sunni-Shiite conflicts in Iraq. Serious negotiations would have to take place under the auspices of some neutral party, preferably one that commands some international respect—

perhaps Brazil. These negotiations would seek to resolve the conflicts between the two antagonists: the United States and Israel on one side, most of the world on the other.

The second precondition is that Israel must be free to expand its illegal settlements in the West Bank. Theoretically, the United States opposes these actions, but with a very light tap on the wrist, while continuing to provide economic, diplomatic, and military support. When the United States does have some limited objections, it very easily bars Israel's actions, as in the case of the E1 project linking Greater Jerusalem to the town of Ma'aleh Adumim, virtually bisecting the West Bank—a very high priority for Israeli planners across the political spectrum, but one that raised some objections in Washington, so that Israel has had to resort to devious measures to chip away at the project.[22]

The pretense of opposition reached the level of farce in February 2011, when Obama vetoed a UN Security Council resolution calling for implementation of official U.S. policy (and also adding the uncontroversial observation that the settlements themselves are illegal, quite apart from their expansion). Since that time there has been little talk about ending settlement expansion, which continues with studied provocation.

Thus, as Israeli and Palestinian representatives prepared to meet in Jordan in January 2011, Israel announced new construction in Pisgat Ze'ev and Har Homa, West Bank areas that it has declared to be within the greatly expanded area of Jerusalem, already annexed, settled, and constructed as Israel's capital, all in violation of direct Security Council orders.[23] Other moves carry forward the grander design of separating whatever West Bank enclaves will be left to Palestinian administration from the cultural, commercial, and political center of Palestinian life in the former Jerusalem.

It is understandable that Palestinian rights should be marginalized in U.S. policy and discourse. Palestinians have no wealth or power. They offer virtually nothing to benefit U.S. policy concerns; in fact, they have negative value, as a nuisance that stirs up "the Arab street."

Israel, in contrast, is a rich society with a sophisticated, largely militarized high-tech industry. For decades, it has been a highly valued military and strategic ally, particularly since 1967, when it performed a great service to the United States and its ally Saudi Arabia by destroying the Nasserite "virus," establishing its "special relationship" with Washington in the form that has persisted since.[24] It is also a growing center for U.S. high-tech investment. In fact, high-tech—and particularly military—industries in the two countries are closely linked.[25]

Apart from such elementary considerations of great-power politics, there are cultural factors that should not be ignored. Christian Zionism in Britain and the United States long preceded Jewish Zionism, and has been a significant elite phenomenon with clear policy implications (including the Balfour Declaration, which drew from it). When General Edmund Allenby conquered Jerusalem during World War I, he was hailed in the American press as Richard the Lion-Hearted, who had at last won the Crusades and driven the pagans out of the Holy Land.

The next step was for the Chosen People to return to the land promised to them by the Lord. Articulating a common elite view, President Franklin Roosevelt's secretary of the interior, Harold Ickes, described Jewish colonization of Palestine as an achievement "without comparison in the history of the human race."[26] Such attitudes find their place easily within the Providentialist doctrines that have been a strong element in popular and elite culture since the country's origins, the belief that God has a plan for the world and the United States is carrying it forward under divine guidance, as articulated by a long list of leading figures.

Moreover, evangelical Christianity is a major popular force in the United States. Further toward the extreme, End Times evangelical Christianity also has enormous popular outreach, invigorated by the establishment of Israel in 1948 and revitalized even more by the conquest of the rest of Palestine in 1967—all signs, in this view, that End Times and the Second Coming are approaching.

These forces have become particularly significant since the Reagan years, as the Republicans have abandoned the pretense of being a political party in the traditional sense while devoting themselves in virtual lockstep uniformity to servicing a tiny percentage of the superrich and the corporate sector. However, the small constituency that is primarily served by the reconstructed party cannot provide votes, so they have to turn elsewhere. The only choice is to mobilize social tendencies that have always been present, though rarely as an organized political force: primarily nativists trembling in fear and hatred and religious elements that are extremist by international standards but not in the United States. One outcome is reverence for alleged Biblical prophecies; hence not only support for Israel and its conquests and expansion but a passionate love for Israel—another core part of the catechism that must be intoned by Republican candidates (with Democrats, again, not too far behind).

These factors aside, it should not be forgotten that the "Anglosphere"—Britain and its offshoots—consists of settler-colonial societies, which rose on the ashes of indigenous populations suppressed or virtually exterminated. Past practices must have been basically correct—in the case of the United States, even ordained by divine providence. Accordingly, there is often an intuitive sympathy for the children of Israel when they follow a similar course. But primarily, geostrategic and economic interests prevail, and policy is not graven in stone.

THE IRANIAN "THREAT" AND THE NUCLEAR ISSUE

Let us turn finally to the third of the leading issues addressed in the establishment journals cited earlier, the "threat of Iran." Among elites and the political class this is generally taken to be the primary threat to world order—though not among populations. In Europe, polls show that Israel is regarded as the leading threat to peace.[27] In the MENA countries, that status is shared with the United States, to the extent that in Egypt, on the eve of the Tahrir Square uprising, 80 percent of the population felt that the region would be more secure if Iran had nuclear weapons.[28] The same polls found that only 10 percent of Egyptians regard Iran as a threat—unlike the ruling dictators, who have their own concerns.[29]

In the United States, before the massive propaganda campaigns of the past few years, a majority of the population agreed with most of the world that, as a signatory to the Non-Proliferation Treaty, Iran has a right to carry out uranium enrichment. Even today, a significant majority favors peaceful means for dealing with Iran. There is even strong opposition to military engagement if Iran and Israel are at war. Only a quarter of Americans regard Iran as an important concern for the United States.[30] But it is not unusual for there to be a gap—often a chasm—dividing public opinion and policy.

Why exactly is Iran regarded as such a colossal threat? The question is rarely discussed, but it is not hard to find a serious answer—though not, as usual, in the fevered pronouncements of the political elite. The most authoritative answer is provided by the Pentagon and the intelligence services in their regular reports to Congress on global security, which note that "Iran's nuclear program and its willingness to keep open the possibility of developing nuclear weapons is a central part of its deterrent strategy."[31]

This survey comes nowhere near being exhaustive, needless to say. Among major topics not addressed is the shift of U.S. military policy toward the Asia-Pacific region, with new additions to the huge military base system underway on Jeju Island off South Korea and in northwest Australia, all elements of the policy of "containment of China." Closely related is the issue of U.S. bases in Okinawa, bitterly opposed by the population for many years and a continual crisis in U.S.-Tokyo-Okinawa relations.[32]

Revealing how little fundamental assumptions have changed, U.S. strategic analysts describe the result of China's military programs as a "classic 'security dilemma,' whereby military programs and national strategies deemed defensive by their planners are viewed as threatening by the other side," writes Paul Godwin of the Foreign Policy Research Institute.[33] The security dilemma arises over control of the seas off China's coasts. The United States regards its policy of controlling these waters as "defensive," while China regards it as threatening; correspondingly, China regards its actions in nearby areas as "defensive," while the

United States regards them as threatening. No such debate is even imaginable concerning U.S. coastal waters. This "classic security dilemma" makes sense, again, on the assumption that the United States has a right to control most of the world, and that U.S. security requires something approaching absolute global control.

While the principles of imperial domination have undergone little change, our capacity to implement them has markedly declined as power has become more broadly distributed in a diversifying world. The consequences are many. It is, however, important to bear in mind that—unfortunately—none of them lift the two dark clouds that hover over all consideration of global order: nuclear war and environmental catastrophe, both literally threatening the decent survival of the species.

Quite the contrary: both threats are ominous and increasing.

7

Magna Carta, Its Fate, and Ours

Down the road only a few generations, the millennium of Magna Carta, one of the great events in the establishment of civil and human rights, will arrive. Whether it will be celebrated, mourned, or ignored is not at all clear.

That should be a matter of serious, immediate concern. What we do right now, or fail to do, will determine what kind of world will greet that event. It is not an attractive prospect if present tendencies persist—not least because the Great Charter is being shredded before our eyes.

The first scholarly edition of Magna Carta was published by the eminent jurist William Blackstone. It was not an easy task; there was no good text available. As he wrote, "the body of the charter has been unfortunately gnawn by rats"—a comment that carries grim symbolism today as we take up the task the rats left unfinished.[1]

Blackstone's edition, entitled *The Great Charter and the Charter of the Forest*, actually includes two charters. The first, the Charter of Liberties, is widely recognized to be the foundation of the fundamental rights of the English-speaking peoples—or as Winston Churchill put it, more expansively, "the charter of every self-respecting man at any time in any land."[2] Churchill was referring specifically to the reaffirmation of the charter by Parliament in the Petition of Right, imploring King Charles I to recognize that the law is sovereign, not the king. Charles agreed briefly, but soon violated his pledge, setting the stage for the murderous English Civil War.

After a bitter conflict between king and Parliament, the power of royalty in the person of Charles II was restored. In defeat, Magna Carta was not forgotten. One of the leaders of Parliament, Henry Vane the Younger, was beheaded; on the scaffold, he tried to read a speech denouncing the sentence as a violation of Magna Carta but was drowned out by trumpets to ensure that such scandalous words would not be heard by the cheering crowds. His major crime had been to draft a petition calling the people "the original of all just power" in civil society—not the king, not even God.[3] That was the position that had been strongly advocated by Roger Williams, the founder of the first free society in what is now the state of Rhode Island. His heretical views influenced Milton and Locke, though Williams went much farther, founding the modern doctrine of separation of church and state—still much contested even in the liberal democracies.

As often is the case, apparent defeat nevertheless carried the struggle for freedom and rights forward. Shortly after Vane's execution, King Charles II granted a royal charter to the Rhode Island plantations, declaring that "the form of government is Democratical," and furthermore that the government could affirm freedom of conscience for Papists, atheists, Jews, Turks—even Quakers, one of the most feared and brutalized of the many sects that were appearing in those turbulent days.[4] All of this was astonishing in the climate of the times.

A few years later, the Charter of Liberties was enriched by the Habeas Corpus Act of 1679, formally entitled "an Act for the better securing the liberty of the subject, and for prevention of imprisonment beyond the seas." The U.S. Constitution, borrowing from English common law, affirms that "the Writ of Habeas Corpus shall not be suspended" except in case of rebellion or invasion. In a unanimous decision, the U.S. Supreme

Court held that the rights guaranteed by this act were "considered by the Founders [of the American Republic] as the highest safeguard of liberty." All of these words should resonate today.

THE SECOND CHARTER AND THE COMMONS

The significance of the companion charter, the Charter of the Forest, is no less profound and perhaps even more pertinent today—as explored in depth by Peter Linebaugh in his richly documented and stimulating history of Magna Carta and its later trajectory.[5] The Charter of the Forest demanded protection of the commons from external power. The commons were the source of sustenance for the general population: their fuel, their food, their construction materials, whatever was essential for life. The forest was no primitive wilderness. It had been carefully developed over generations, maintained in common, its riches available to all, and preserved for future generations—practices found today primarily in traditional societies that are under threat throughout the world.

The Charter of the Forest imposed limits on privatization. The Robin Hood myths capture the essence of its concerns (it is not too surprising that the popular TV series of the 1950s, *The Adventures of Robin Hood*, was written anonymously by Hollywood screenwriters blacklisted for leftist convictions).[6] By the seventeenth century, however, this charter had fallen victim to the rise of the commodity economy and capitalist practice and morality.

With the commons no longer protected for cooperative nurturing and use, the rights of the common people were restricted to what could not be privatized, a category that continues to shrink to virtual invisibility. In Bolivia, the attempt to privatize water was, in the end, beaten back by an uprising that brought the indigenous majority to power for the first time in history.[7] The World Bank has ruled that the mining multinational Pacific Rim can proceed with a case against El Salvador for trying to preserve lands and communities from highly destructive gold mining. Environmental constraints threaten to deprive the company of future profits, a crime that can be punished under the rules of the investor-rights regime mislabeled as "free trade."[8] And this is only a tiny sample of struggles underway over much of the world, some involving extreme violence, as in the eastern Congo, where millions have been killed in recent years to ensure an ample supply of minerals for cell phones and other uses, and, of course, ample profits.[9]

The rise of capitalist practice and morality brought with it a radical revision of how the commons are treated, and also how they are conceived of. The prevailing view today is captured by Garrett Hardin's influential argument that "freedom in a commons brings ruin to us all," the famous "tragedy of the commons": what is not owned will be destroyed by individual avarice.[10]

An international counterpart was the concept of terra nullius, employed to justify the expulsion of indigenous populations in the settler-colonial societies of the Anglosphere, or their "extermination," as the founding fathers of the American republic described what they were doing, sometimes with remorse, after the fact. According to this useful doctrine, the Indians had no property rights since they were just wanderers in an untamed wilderness. The hardworking colonists could therefore create value where there was none by turning that same wilderness to commercial use.

In reality, the colonists knew better, and there were elaborate procedures of purchase and ratification undertaken by crown and Parliament, later annulled by force when the evil creatures resisted extermination. The doctrine of terra nullius is often attributed to John Locke, but that is dubious. As a colonial administrator, he understood what was happening, and there is no basis for the attribution in his writings, as contemporary scholarship has shown convincingly, notably the work of the Australian scholar Paul Corcoran. (It was in Australia, in fact, that the doctrine has been most brutally employed.)[11]

The grim forecasts of the tragedy of the commons are not without challenge. The late Elinor Ostrom won the Nobel Prize in economics in 2009 for her work showing the superiority of user-managed fish stocks, pastures, woods, lakes, and groundwater basins. But the conventional doctrine has force if we accept its unstated premise: that humans are blindly driven by what American workers, at the dawn of the industrial revolution, bitterly called "the New Spirit of the Age, Gain Wealth forgetting all but Self."[12]

Like peasants and workers in England before them, American workers denounced this new spirit that was being imposed upon them, regarding it as demeaning and destructive, an assault on the very nature of free men and women. And I stress "women": among those most active and vocal in condemning the destruction of the rights and dignity of free people by the capitalist industrial system were the "factory girls," young women from the farms. They, too, were driven into the regime of supervised and controlled wage labor, which was regarded at the time as different from chattel slavery only in that it was temporary. That stand was considered so natural that it became a slogan of the Republican Party, and a banner under which northern workers carried arms during the American Civil War.[13]

CONTROLLING THE DESIRE FOR DEMOCRACY

That was 150 years ago—in England, earlier. Huge efforts have been devoted since to inculcating the New Spirit of the Age. Major industries are devoted to the task: public relations, advertising, and marketing generally, all of which add up to a very large component of the gross domestic product. They are dedicated to what the great political economist Thorstein Veblen called "fabricating wants."[14] In the words of business leaders themselves, the task is to direct people to "the superficial things" of life, like "fashionable consumption." That way people can be atomized, separated from one another, seeking personal gain alone, diverted from dangerous efforts to think for themselves and challenge authority.

The process of shaping opinions, attitudes, and perceptions was termed the "engineering of consent" by one of the founders of the modern public relations industry, Edward Bernays. He was a respected Wilson-Roosevelt-Kennedy progressive, much like his contemporary, journalist

Walter Lippmann, the most prominent public intellectual of twentieth-century America, who praised "the manufacture of consent" as a "new art" in the practice of democracy.

Both recognized that the public must be "put in its place," marginalized and controlled—for its own interest, of course. People were too "stupid and ignorant" to be allowed to run their own affairs. That task was to be left to the "intelligent minority," who must be protected from "the trampling and the roar of [the] bewildered herd," the "ignorant and meddlesome outsiders"—the "rascal multitude," as they were termed by their seventeenth-century predecessors. The role of the general population was to be "spectators," not "participants in action," in a properly functioning democratic society.[15]

And the spectators must not be allowed to see too much. President Obama has set new standards in safeguarding this principle. He has, in fact, punished more whistle-blowers than all previous presidents combined, a real achievement for an administration that came to office promising transparency.

Among the many topics that are not the business of the bewildered herd is foreign affairs. Anyone who has studied declassified secret documents will have discovered that, to a large extent, their classification was meant to protect public officials from public scrutiny. Domestically, the rabble should not hear the advice given by the courts to major corporations: that they should devote some highly visible efforts to good works, so that an "aroused public" will not discover the enormous benefits provided to them by the nanny state.[16]

More generally, the U.S. public should not learn that "state policies are overwhelmingly regressive, thus reinforcing and expanding social inequality," though designed in ways that lead "people to think that the government helps only the undeserving poor, allowing politicians to mobilize and exploit anti-government rhetoric and values even as they continue to funnel support to their better-off constituents"—I'm quoting here from the main establishment journal, *Foreign Affairs*, not from some radical rag.[17]

Over time, as societies became freer and the resort to state violence more constrained, the urge to devise sophisticated methods of control of attitudes and opinion has only grown. It is natural that the immense PR industry should have been created in the freest of societies, the United States and Great Britain. The first modern propaganda agency was the British Department of Information during World War I. Its U.S. counterpart, the Committee on Public Information, was formed by Woodrow Wilson to drive a pacifist population to violent hatred of all things German—with remarkable success. American commercial advertising deeply impressed others; Joseph Goebbels admired it and adapted it to Nazi propaganda, all too successfully.[18] The Bolshevik leaders tried as well, but their efforts were clumsy and ineffective.

A primary domestic task has always been "to keep [the public] from our throats," as essayist Ralph Waldo Emerson described the concerns of political leaders when the threat of democracy was becoming harder to suppress in the mid-nineteenth century.[19] More recently, the activism of the 1960s elicited elite concerns about "excessive democracy" and calls for measures to impose "more moderation" in democracy.

One particular concern was to introduce better controls over the institutions "responsible for the indoctrination of the young": the schools, the universities, and the churches, which were seen as failing that essential task. I'm quoting reactions from the left-liberal end of the mainstream ideological spectrum, the liberal internationalists who later staffed the Carter administration and their counterparts in other industrial societies.[20] The right wing was much harsher. One of many manifestations of this urge has been the sharp rise in college tuition—not on economic grounds, as is easily shown. The device does, however, trap and control young people through debt, often for the rest of their lives, thus contributing to more effective indoctrination.

THE THREE-FIFTHS PEOPLE

Pursuing these important topics further, we see that the destruction of the Charter of the Forest and its obliteration from memory relate rather closely to the continuing efforts to constrain the promise of the Charter of Liberties. The New Spirit of the Age cannot tolerate the precapitalist conception of the forest as the shared endowment of the community at large, cared for communally for its own use and for future generations, and protected from privatization, from transfer to the hands of private power for service to wealth, not needs. Inculcating the New Spirit is an essential prerequisite for achieving this end, and for preventing the Charter of Liberties from being misused to enable free citizens to determine their own fate.

Popular struggles to bring about a freer and more just society have been resisted by violence and repression and massive efforts to control opinion and attitudes. Over time, however, they have met with considerable success, even though there is a long way to go and there is often regression.

The most famous part of the Charter of Liberties is Article 39, which declares that "no free man" shall be punished in any way, "nor will We proceed against or prosecute him, except by the lawful judgment of his peers and by the law of the land."

Through many years of struggle, the principle has come to hold more broadly. The U.S. Constitution provides that no "person [shall] be deprived of life, liberty, or property, without due process of law [and] a speedy and public trial" by peers. The basic principle is "presumption of innocence"—what legal historians describe as "the seed of contemporary Anglo-American freedom," referring to Article 39 and, with the Nuremberg tribunal in mind, a "particularly American brand of legalism: punishment only for those who could be proved to be guilty through a fair trial with a panoply of procedural protections"—even if their guilt for some of the worst crimes in history is not in doubt.[21]

The founders, of course, did not intend the term "person" to apply to all persons: Native Americans were not persons. Their rights were virtually nil. Women were scarcely persons; wives were understood to be "covered" under the civil identity of their husbands in much the same way as children were subject to their parents. Blackstone's principles held that "the very being or legal existence of the woman is suspended during the marriage, or at least is incorporated and consolidated into that of the husband: under whose wing, protection, and cover, she performs every thing."[22] Women are thus the property of their fathers or husbands. This principle remains in force up to very recent years; until a Supreme Court decision of 1975, women did not even have a legal right to serve on juries. They were not peers.

Slaves, of course, were not persons. They were three-fifths human under the Constitution, so as to grant their owners greater voting power. The protection of slavery was no slight concern to the founders: it was one factor that led to the American Revolution. In the 1772 Somerset case, Lord Mansfield determined that slavery is so "odious" that it could not be tolerated in England, though it continued in British possessions for many years.[23] American slave owners could see the handwriting on the wall if the colonies remained under British rule. And it should be recalled that the slave states, including Virginia, had the greatest power and influence in the colonies. One can easily appreciate Dr. Johnson's famous quip that "we hear the *loudest yelps* for liberty among the drivers of negroes."[24]

Post–Civil War amendments extended the concept of personhood to African-Americans, ending slavery—in theory, at least. After about a decade of relative freedom, a condition akin to slavery was reintroduced by a North-South compact permitting the effective criminalization of black life. A black male standing on a street corner could be arrested for vagrancy, or for attempted rape if accused of looking at a white woman the wrong way. And once imprisoned, he had few chances of ever escaping the system of "slavery by another name," the term used by then *Wall Street Journal* bureau chief Douglas Blackmon in an arresting study.[25]

This new version of the "peculiar institution" provided much of the basis for the American industrial revolution, creating a perfect workforce for the steel industry and mining, along with agricultural production in the famous chain gangs: docile, obedient, disinclined to strike, and with no demand for employers even to sustain their workers, an improvement over the slavery system. The new system lasted in large measure until World War II, when free labor was needed for war production.

The postwar boom offered employment; a black man could get a job in a unionized auto plant, earn a decent salary, buy a house, and maybe send his children to college. That lasted for about twenty years, until the 1970s, when the economy was radically redesigned on newly dominant neoliberal principles, with the rapid growth of financialization and the offshoring of production. The black population, now largely superfluous, has been recriminalized.

Until Ronald Reagan's presidency, incarceration in the United States was within the spectrum of other industrial societies. By now it is far beyond. It targets primarily black males, but increasingly also black women and Latinos, largely guilty of victimless crimes in the fraudulent "drug wars." Meanwhile, the wealth of African-American families was virtually obliterated by the latest financial crisis, in no small measure thanks to the criminal behavior of financial institutions, enacted with impunity for the perpetrators, now richer than ever.

Looking over the history of African-Americans from the first arrival of slaves four hundred years ago to the present, it is evident they have enjoyed the status of authentic persons for only a few decades. There is a long way to go to realize the promise of Magna Carta.

SACRED PERSONS AND UNDONE PROCESS

The post–Civil War Fourteenth Amendment granted the rights of persons to former slaves, though mostly in theory. At the same time, it created a new category of persons with rights: corporations. In fact, almost all the cases subsequently brought to the courts under the Fourteenth Amendment had to do with corporate rights, and by a century ago, the courts had determined that these collectivist legal fictions, established and sustained by state power, had the full rights of persons of flesh and blood—in fact, far greater rights, thanks to their scale, their immortality, and the protections of limited liability. The rights of corporations by now far transcend those of mere humans. Under the "free-trade agreements," the mining company Pacific Rim can, for example, sue El Salvador for seeking to protect its environment; individuals cannot do the same. General Motors can claim national rights in Mexico. There is no need to dwell on what would happen if a Mexican person demanded national rights in the United States.

Domestically, recent Supreme Court rulings greatly enhance the already enormous political power of corporations and the superrich, striking further blows against the tottering relics of functioning political democracy.

Meanwhile, Magna Carta is under more direct assault. Recall the Habeas Corpus Act of 1679, which barred "imprisonment beyond the seas," and certainly the far more vicious procedure of imprisonment abroad for the purpose of torture—what is now more politely called "rendition," as when Tony Blair rendered Libyan dissident Abdel Hakim Belhaj to the mercies of Muammar al-Qaddafi; or when U.S. authorities deported Canadian citizen Maher Arar to his native Syria for imprisonment and torture, only later conceding that there was never any case against him.[26] The same has happened to many others, often transported through Shannon Airport, leading to courageous protests in Ireland.

The concept of due process has been extended under the Obama administration's international drone assassination campaign in a way that makes this core element of the Charter of Liberties (and the Constitution) null and void. The Justice Department explained that the constitutional guarantee of due process, tracing to Magna Carta, is now satisfied by internal deliberations in the executive branch alone.[27] The constitutional lawyer in the White House agreed. King John might have nodded with satisfaction.

The issue arose after the presidentially ordered assassination by drone of Anwar al-Awlaki, accused of inciting jihad in speech, writing, and unspecified actions. A headline in the New York Times captured the general elite reaction when he was murdered in a drone attack, along with the usual "collateral damage." It read, in part: "The West Celebrates a Cleric's Death."[28] Some eyebrows were lifted, however, because Awlaki was an American citizen, which raised questions about due process—considered irrelevant when noncitizens are murdered at the whim of the chief executive. And now irrelevant for citizens, too, under the Obama administration's due-process legal innovations.

Presumption of innocence has also been given a new and useful interpretation. As the *New York Times* later reported, "Mr. Obama embraced a disputed method for counting civilian casualties that did little to box him in. It in effect counts all military-age males in a strike zone as combatants, according to several administration officials, unless there is explicit intelligence posthumously proving them innocent." [29] So post-assassination determination of innocence maintains the sacred principle of presumption of innocence.

It would be ungracious to recall (as the *Times* avoids doing in its report) the Geneva Conventions, the foundation of modern humanitarian law: they bar "the carrying out of executions without previous judgment pronounced by a regularly constituted court, affording all the judicial guarantees which are recognized as indispensable by civilized peoples."[30]

The most famous recent case of executive assassination was that of Osama bin Laden, murdered after he was apprehended by seventy-nine Navy SEALs, defenseless and accompanied only by his wife. Whatever one thinks of him, he was a suspect and nothing more than that. Even the FBI agreed on this point.

The celebrations in the United States were overwhelming, but there were a few questions raised about the bland rejection of the principle of presumption of innocence, particularly when trial was hardly impossible. These were met with harsh condemnations. The most interesting was that of a respected left-liberal political commentator, Matthew Yglesias, who explained that "one of the main functions of the international institutional order is precisely to *legitimate* the use of deadly military force by western powers," so it is "amazingly naïve" to suggest that the United States should obey international law or other conditions that we righteously demand of the weak.[31]

Only tactical objections, it seems, can be raised to aggression, assassination, cyberwar, or other actions that the Holy State undertakes in the service of mankind. If the traditional victims see matters somewhat differently, that merely reveals their moral and intellectual backwardness. And the occasional Western critic who fails to comprehend these fundamental truths can be dismissed as "silly," Yglesias explains—incidentally, he is referring specifically to me, and I cheerfully confess my guilt.

EXECUTIVE TERRORIST LISTS

Perhaps the most striking assault on the foundations of traditional liberties is a little-known case brought to the Supreme Court by the Obama administration, *Holder v. Humanitarian Law Project*. The Project was condemned for providing "material assistance" to the guerrilla organization Kurdistan Workers' Party (PKK), which has fought for Kurdish rights in Turkey for many years and is listed as a terrorist group by the state executive. The "material assistance" was legal advice. The wording of the ruling would appear to apply quite broadly, for example, to discussions and research inquiry—even to advice to the PKK to keep to nonviolent means. Again, there was a marginal fringe of criticism, but even those critiques generally accepted the legitimacy of the state terrorist list—of, that is, arbitrary decisions by the executive, with no legal recourse. [32]

The record of the terrorist list is of some interest. One of the ugliest examples of the use of the terrorist list has to do with the tortured people of Somalia. Immediately after 9/11, the United States closed down the Somali charitable network Al-Barakaat on grounds that it was financing terror.[33] This achievement was hailed as one of the great successes of the "war on terror." In contrast, Washington's withdrawal of its charges as without merit a year later aroused little notice.

Al-Barakaat was responsible for about half the $500 million in remittances sent back to Somalia annually, "more than [Somalia] earns from any other economic sector and 10 times the amount of foreign aid it receives," a UN review determined.[34] The charity also ran major businesses in Somalia, all of which were destroyed. The leading academic scholar of Bush's "financial war on terror," Ibrahim Warde, concludes that apart from devastating the economy, this frivolous attack on a very fragile society "may have played a role in the rise . . . of Islamic fundamentalists," another familiar consequence of the "war on terror."[35]

The very idea that the state should have the authority to make such judgments unchecked is a serious offense against the Charter of Liberties, as is the fact that it is considered uncontentious. If the charter's fall from grace continues on the path of the past few years, the future of rights and liberties looks dim.

WHO WILL HAVE THE LAST LAUGH?

A few final words on the fate of the Charter of the Forest. Its goal was to protect the source of sustenance for the population, the commons, from external power—in the early days, from royalty, over the years, from enclosures and other forms of privatization by predatory corporations and the state authorities who cooperate with them, which have only accelerated and are properly rewarded. The damage is very broad.

If we listen to voices from the global South today we can learn that "the conversion of public goods into private property through the privatization of our otherwise commonly held natural environment is one way neoliberal institutions remove the fragile threads that hold African nations together. Politics today has been reduced to a lucrative venture where one looks out mainly for returns on investment rather than on what one can contribute to rebuild highly degraded environments, communities, and a nation. This is one of the benefits that structural adjustment programmes inflicted on the continent—the enthronement of corruption." I'm quoting Nigerian poet and activist Nnimmo Bassey, chair of Friends of the Earth International, in his searing exposé of the ravaging of Africa's wealth, *To Cook a Continent*, which examines the latest phase of the Western torture of Africa.[36]

A torture that has always been planned at the highest level, and should be recognized as such. At the end of World War II, the United States held a position of unprecedented global power. Not surprisingly, careful and sophisticated plans were developed for organizing the world. Each region was assigned its "function" by State Department planners, headed by the distinguished diplomat George Kennan. He determined that the United States had no special interest in Africa, so it should be handed over to Europe to "exploit"—his word—for its reconstruction.[37] In the light of history, one might have imagined a different relationship between Europe and Africa, but there is no indication that that was ever considered.

More recently, the United States has recognized that it, too, must join the game of exploiting Africa, alongside new entrants like China, which is busily at work compiling one of the worst records in destruction of the environment and oppression of hapless victims.

It should be unnecessary to dwell on the extreme dangers posed by one central element of the predatory obsessions that are producing calamities all over the world: the reliance on fossil fuels, which courts global disaster, perhaps in the not-too-distant future. Details may be debated, but there is little doubt that the problem is serious, if not awesome, and that the longer we delay in addressing it, the more awful will be the legacy left to generations to come. There are some efforts afoot to face reality, but they are far too minimal.

Meanwhile, power concentrations are charging in the opposite direction, led by the richest and most powerful country in world history. Congressional Republicans are dismantling the limited environmental protections initiated by Richard Nixon, who would be something of a dangerous radical in today's political scene.[38] The major business lobbies openly announce their propaganda campaigns to convince the public that there is no need for undue concern—with some effect, as polls show.[39]

The media cooperate by barely reporting the increasingly dire climate change forecasts of international agencies and even the U.S. Department of Energy. The standard presentation is a debate between alarmists and skeptics: on one side virtually all qualified scientists, on the other a few holdouts. Not part of the debate are a very large number of experts, including those in the climate change program at MIT, among others, who criticize the scientific consensus because it is too conservative and cautious, arguing that the truth when it comes to climate change is far more dire. Not surprisingly, the public is confused.

In his 2012 State of the Union speech, President Obama hailed the bright prospects of a century of energy self-sufficiency, thanks to new technologies that permit extraction of hydrocarbons from Canadian tar sands, shale, and other previously inaccessible sources.[40] Others agree; the *Financial Times* forecasts a century of energy independence for the US.[41] Unasked in these optimistic forecasts is the question of what kind of a world will survive the rapacious onslaught.

In the lead in confronting the crisis throughout the world are indigenous communities, those who have always upheld the Charter of the Forests. The strongest stand has been taken by the one country they govern, Bolivia, the poorest country in South America and for centuries a victim of Western destruction of the rich resources of one of the most advanced of the developed societies in the hemisphere, pre-Columbus.

After the ignominious collapse of the Copenhagen global climate change summit in 2009, Bolivia organized a World People's Conference on Climate Change with thirty-five thousand participants from 140 countries—not just representatives of governments but also members of civil society and activists. It produced a People's Agreement, which called for very sharp reductions in emissions, and a Universal Declaration on the Rights of Mother Earth.[42] Establishing the rights of the planet is a key demand of indigenous communities all over the world. It is ridiculed by sophisticated Westerners, but unless we can acquire some of the indigenous sensibility, they are likely to have the last laugh—a laugh of grim despair.

8

The Week the World Stood Still

The world stood still some fifty years ago during the last week of October, from the moment when it learned that the Soviet Union had placed nuclear-armed missiles in Cuba until the crisis was officially ended—though, unknown to the public, only officially.

The image of the world standing still is the turn of phrase of Sheldon Stern, former historian at the John F. Kennedy Presidential Library, who published the authoritative version of the tapes of the meetings of the Executive Committee of the National Security Council (ExComm) in which Kennedy and a close circle of advisers debated how to respond to the crisis. Those meetings were secretly recorded by the president, which might bear on the fact that his stand throughout the recorded sessions is relatively temperate compared to those of other participants, who were unaware that they were speaking to history.

Stern has now published an accessible and accurate review of this critically important documentary record, finally declassified in the late 1990s. I will keep to that version here. "Never before or since," he concludes, "has the survival of human civilization been at stake in a few short weeks of dangerous deliberations," culminating in "the week the world stood still."[1]

There was good reason for the global concern. A nuclear war was all too imminent, a war that might "destroy the Northern Hemisphere," as President Dwight Eisenhower had warned.[2] Kennedy's own judgment was that the probability of war might have been as high as 50 percent.[3] Estimates became higher as the confrontation reached its peak and the "secret doomsday plan to ensure the survival of the government was put into effect" in Washington, as described by journalist Michael Dobbs in his well-researched best seller on the crisis (though he doesn't explain why there would be much point in doing so, given the likely nature of nuclear war).[4]

Dobbs quotes Dino Brugioni, "a key member of the CIA team monitoring the Soviet missile buildup," who saw no way out except "war and complete destruction" as the clock moved to "one minute to midnight," the title of Dobbs's book.[5] Kennedy's close associate the historian Arthur M. Schlesinger Jr. described the events as "the most dangerous moment in human history."[6] Defense Secretary Robert McNamara wondered aloud whether he "would live to see another Saturday night," and later recognized that "we lucked out"—barely.[7]

"THE MOST DANGEROUS MOMENT"

A closer look at what took place adds grim overtones to these judgments, with reverberations to the present moment.

There are several candidates for "the most dangerous moment." One is October 27, 1962, when U.S. destroyers enforcing a quarantine around Cuba were dropping depth charges on Soviet submarines. According to Soviet accounts, reported by the National Security Archive, submarine commanders were "rattled enough to talk about firing nuclear torpedoes, whose 15 kiloton explosive yields approximated the bomb that devastated Hiroshima in August 1945."[8]

In one case, a reported decision to assemble a nuclear torpedo for battle readiness was aborted at the last minute by Second Captain Vasili Arkhipov, who may have saved the world from nuclear disaster.[9] There is little doubt what the U.S. reaction would have been had the torpedo been fired, or how the Russians would have responded as their country was going up in smoke.

Kennedy had already declared the highest nuclear alert short of launch, DEFCON 2, which authorized "NATO aircraft with Turkish pilots . . . [or others] . . . to take off, fly to Moscow, and drop a bomb," according to the well-informed Harvard University strategic analyst Graham Allison, writing in *Foreign Affairs*.[10]

Another candidate is October 26. That day has been selected as "the most dangerous moment" by B-52 pilot Major Don Clawson, who piloted one of those NATO aircraft and provides a hair-raising description of details of the Chrome Dome (CD) missions during the crisis— "B-52s on airborne alert" with nuclear weapons "on board and ready to use."

October 26 was the day when "the nation was closest to nuclear war," he writes in his "irreverent anecdotes of an air force pilot." On that day, Clawson himself was in a good position to set off a likely terminal cataclysm. He concludes, "We were damned lucky we didn't blow up the world—and no thanks to the political or military leadership of this country."

The errors, confusions, near accidents, and miscomprehension of the leadership that Clawson reports are startling enough, but nothing like the operative command-and-control rules—or lack of them. As Clawson recounts his experiences during the fifteen twenty-four-hour CD missions he flew, the maximum possible, the official commanders "did not possess the capability to prevent a rogue crew or crew-member from arming and releasing their thermonuclear weapons," or even from broadcasting a mission that would have sent off "the entire Airborne Alert force without possibility of recall." Once the crew was airborne carrying thermonuclear weapons, he writes, "it would have been possible to arm and drop them all with no further input from the ground. There was no inhibitor on any of the systems."[11]

About one-third of the total force was in the air, according to General David Burchinal, director of plans on the air staff at air force headquarters. The Strategic Air Command (SAC), technically in charge, appears to have had little control. And according to Clawson's account, the civilian National Command Authority was kept in the dark by SAC, which means that the ExComm "deciders" pondering the fate of the world knew even less. General Burchinal's oral history is no less hair-raising, and reveals even greater contempt for the civilian command. According to him, Russian capitulation was never in doubt. The CD operations were designed to make it crystal clear to the Russians that they were hardly even competing in the military confrontation, and could quickly have been destroyed.[12]

From the ExComm records, Sheldon Stern concludes that, on October 26, President Kennedy was "leaning towards military action to eliminate the missiles" in Cuba, to be followed by invasion, according to Pentagon plans.[13] It was evident then that the act might have led to terminal war, a conclusion fortified by much later revelations that tactical nuclear weapons had been deployed and that Russian forces were far greater than U.S. intelligence had reported.

As the ExComm meetings were drawing to a close at 6:00 p.m. on the 26th, a letter arrived from Soviet prime minister Nikita Khrushchev, sent directly to President Kennedy. His "message seemed clear," Stern writes. "The missiles would be removed if the US promised not to invade Cuba."[14]

The next day, at 10:00 a.m., the president again turned on the secret tape recorder. He read aloud a wire service report that had just been handed to him: "Premier Khrushchev told President Kennedy in a message today he would withdraw offensive weapons from Cuba if the United States withdrew its rockets from Turkey"—Jupiter missiles with nuclear warheads.[15] The report was soon authenticated.

Though received by the committee as an unexpected bolt from the blue, it had actually been anticipated: "We've known this might be coming for a week," Kennedy informed them. To refuse public acquiescence would be difficult, he realized: these were obsolete missiles, already slated for withdrawal, soon to be replaced by far more lethal and effectively invulnerable submarine-based Polaris missiles. Kennedy recognized that he would be in an "*insupportable* position if this becomes [Khrushchev's] proposal," both because the Turkish missiles were useless and were being withdrawn anyway, and because to any man at the United Nations or any other *rational* man, it will look like a very fair trade."[16]

KEEPING U.S. POWER UNRESTRAINED

The planners therefore faced a serious dilemma. They had in hand two somewhat different proposals from Khrushchev to end the threat of catastrophic war, and each would seem to any "rational man" to be a fair trade. How then to react?

One possibility would have been to breathe a sigh of relief that civilization could survive and to eagerly accept both offers; to announce that the United States would adhere to international law and remove any threat to invade Cuba; and to carry forward the withdrawal of the obsolete missiles in Turkey, proceeding as planned to upgrade the nuclear threat against the Soviet Union to a far greater one—only part, of course, of the global encirclement of Russia. But that was unthinkable.

The basic reason why no such thought could be contemplated was spelled out by National Security Advisor McGeorge Bundy, a former Harvard dean and reputedly the brightest star in the Camelot firmament. The world, he insisted, must come to understand that "the current threat to peace is *not* in Turkey, it is in *Cuba*," where missiles were directed against the United States.[17] A vastly more powerful U.S. missile force trained on the much weaker and more vulnerable Soviet enemy could not possibly be regarded as a threat to peace, because we are Good, as a great many people in the western hemisphere and beyond could testify—among numerous others, the victims of the ongoing terrorist war that the United States was then waging against Cuba, or those swept up in the "campaign of hatred" in the Arab world that so puzzled Eisenhower, though not the National Security Council, which explained it clearly.

In subsequent colloquy, the president stressed that we would be "in a bad position" if we chose to set off an international conflagration by rejecting proposals that would seem quite reasonable to survivors (if any cared). This "pragmatic" stance was about as far as moral considerations could reach.[18]

In a review of recently released documents on Kennedy-era terror, Harvard University Latin Americanist Jorge Domínguez observes, "Only once in these nearly thousand pages of documentation did a U.S. official raise something that resembled a faint moral objection to U.S.-government sponsored terrorism": a member of the National Security Council staff suggested that raids that are "haphazard and kill innocents . . . might mean a bad press in some friendly countries."[19]

The same attitudes prevailed throughout the internal discussions during the missile crisis, as when Robert Kennedy warned that a full-scale invasion of Cuba would "kill an awful lot of people, and we're going to take an awful lot of heat on it."[20] And they prevail to the present, with only the rarest of exceptions, as easily documented.

We might have been "in even a worse position" if the world had known more about what the United States was doing at the time. Only recently was it learned that, six months earlier, the United States had secretly deployed missiles in Okinawa virtually identical to those the Russians would send to Cuba.[21] These were surely aimed at China at a moment of elevated regional tensions. To this day, Okinawa remains a major offensive U.S. military base over the bitter objections of its inhabitants.

AN INDECENT DISRESPECT FOR THE OPINIONS OF HUMANKIND

The deliberations that followed are revealing, but I will put them aside here. They did reach a conclusion. The United States pledged to withdraw the obsolete missiles from Turkey, but would not do so publicly or put the offer in writing: it was important that Khrushchev be seen to capitulate. An interesting justification was offered, and is accepted as reasonable by scholarship and commentary. As Michael Dobbs puts it, "If it appeared that the United States was dismantling the missile bases unilaterally, under pressure from the Soviet Union, the [NATO] alliance might crack"—or, to rephrase a little more accurately, if the United States replaced useless missiles with a far more lethal threat, as already planned, in a trade with Russia that any "rational man" would regard as very fair, then the NATO alliance might crack.[22]

To be sure, when Russia withdrew Cuba's only deterrent against an ongoing U.S. attack—with a severe threat to proceed to direct invasion still in the air—and quietly departed from the scene, the Cubans would be infuriated (as, in fact, they understandably were). But that is an unfair comparison for the standard reasons: we are human beings who matter, while they are merely "unpeople," to adopt George Orwell's useful phrase.

Kennedy also made an informal pledge not to invade Cuba, but with conditions: not just the withdrawal of the missiles, but also termination, or at least "a great lessening," of any Russian military presence. (Unlike Turkey, on Russia's borders, where nothing of the kind from our military could be contemplated.) When Cuba was no longer an "armed camp," then "we probably wouldn't invade," in the president's words. He added that if it hoped to be free from the threat of U.S. invasion, Cuba must end its "political subversion" (Sheldon Stern's phrase) in Latin America.[23] "Political subversion" had been a constant theme in U.S. rhetoric for years, invoked for example when Eisenhower overthrew the parliamentary government of Guatemala and plunged that tortured country into an abyss from which it has yet to emerge. This theme remained alive and well right through Ronald Reagan's vicious terror wars in Central America in the 1980s. Cuba's "political subversion" consisted of support for those resisting the murderous assaults of the United States and its client regimes, and sometimes even perhaps— horror of horrors—providing arms to the victims.

Though these assumptions are so deeply embedded in prevailing doctrine as to be virtually invisible, they are occasionally articulated in the internal record. In the case of Cuba, the State Department Policy Planning Staff explained that "the primary danger we face in Castro is . . . in the impact the very existence of his regime has upon the leftist movement in many Latin American countries. . . . The simple fact is that Castro represents a successful defiance of the US, a negation of our whole hemispheric policy of almost a century and a half," since the Monroe Doctrine announced Washington's intention, then unrealizable, to dominate the western hemisphere.[24]

The right to dominate is a leading principle of U.S. foreign policy found almost everywhere, though typically concealed in defensive terms: during the Cold War years, routinely by invoking the "Russian threat," even when Russians were nowhere in sight. An example of great contemporary import is revealed in Iran scholar Ervand Abrahamian's important book on the U.S.-UK coup that overthrew the parliamentary regime of Iran in 1953. With scrupulous examination of internal records, he shows convincingly that standard accounts cannot be sustained. The primary causes were not Cold War concerns, nor Iranian irrationality that undermined Washington's "benign intentions," nor even access to oil or profits, but rather the way the U.S. demand for "overall control"—with its broader implications for global dominance— was threatened by independent nationalism.[25]

That is what we discover over and over by investigating particular cases, including Cuba (not surprisingly), though the fanaticism in that particular case might merit examination. U.S. policy toward Cuba is harshly condemned throughout Latin America and indeed most of the world, but "a decent respect for the opinions of mankind" is understood to be meaningless rhetoric intoned mindlessly on the Fourth of July. Ever since polls have been taken on the matter, a considerable majority of the U.S. population has favored normalization of relations with Cuba, but that too is insignificant.[26]

Dismissal of public opinion is, of course, quite normal. What is interesting in this case is dismissal of powerful sectors of U.S. economic power which also favor normalization and are usually highly influential in setting policy: energy, agribusiness, pharmaceuticals, and others.

That suggests that, in addition to the cultural factors revealed in the hysteria of the Camelot intellectuals, there is a powerful state interest involved in punishing Cubans.

SAVING THE WORLD FROM THE THREAT OF NUCLEAR DESTRUCTION

The missile crisis officially ended on October 28. The outcome was not obscure. That evening, in a special CBS News broadcast, Charles Collingwood reported that the world had come out "from under the most terrible threat of nuclear holocaust since World War II" with a "humiliating defeat for Soviet policy."[27] Dobbs comments that the Russians tried to pretend that the outcome was "yet another triumph for Moscow's peace-loving foreign policy over warmongering imperialists," and that "the supremely wise, always reasonable Soviet leadership had saved the world from the threat of nuclear destruction."[28]

Extricating the basic facts from the fashionable ridicule, Khrushchev's agreement to capitulate had indeed "saved the world from the threat of nuclear destruction."

The crisis, however, was not over. On November 8, the Pentagon announced that all known Soviet missile bases had been dismantled.[29] On the same day, Stern reports, "a sabotage team carried out an attack on a Cuban factory," though Kennedy's terror campaign, Operation Mongoose, had been formally curtailed at the peak of the crisis.[30] The November 8 terror attack lends support to McGeorge Bundy's observation that the threat to peace was Cuba, not Turkey, where the Russians were not continuing a lethal assault—though it was certainly not what Bundy had in mind or could have understood.

More details are added by the respected scholar Raymond Garthoff, who also had rich experience within the government, in his careful 1987 account of the missile crisis. On November 8, he writes, "a Cuban covert action sabotage team dispatched from the United States successfully blew up a Cuban industrial facility," killing four hundred workers, according to a Cuban government letter to the UN secretary-general.

Garthoff comments: "The Soviets could only see [the attack] as an effort to backpedal on what was, for them, the key question remaining: American assurances not to attack Cuba," particularly since the terrorist attack was launched from the United States. These and other "third party actions" reveal again, he concludes, "that the risk and danger to both sides could have been extreme, and catastrophe not excluded." Garthoff also reviews the murderous and destructive operations of Kennedy's terrorist campaign, which we would certainly regard as more than ample justification for war if the United States or its allies or clients were its victims, not its perpetrators.[31]

From the same source we learn further that, on August 23, 1962, the president had issued National Security Action Memorandum (NSAM) No. 181, "a directive to engineer an internal revolt that would be followed by US military intervention," involving "significant US military plans, maneuvers, and movement of forces and equipment" that were surely known to Cuba and Russia.[32] Also in August, terrorist attacks were intensified, including speedboat strafing attacks on a Cuban seaside hotel "where Soviet military technicians were known to congregate, killing a score of Russians and Cubans"; attacks on British and Cuban cargo ships; the contamination of sugar shipments; and other atrocities and sabotage, mostly carried out by Cuban exile organizations permitted to operate freely in Florida. Shortly after came "the most dangerous moment in human history," not exactly out of the blue.

Kennedy officially renewed the terrorist operations after the crisis ebbed. Ten days before his assassination he approved a CIA plan for "destruction operations" by U.S. proxy forces "against a large oil refinery and storage facilities, a large electric plant, sugar refineries, railroad bridges, harbor facilities, and underwater demolition of docks and ships." A plot to assassinate Castro was apparently initiated on the day of the Kennedy assassination. The terrorist campaign was called off in 1965, but, reports Garthoff, "one of Nixon's first acts in office in 1969 was to direct the CIA to intensify covert operations against Cuba."[33]

We can, at last, hear the voices of the victims in Canadian historian Keith Bolender's *Voices From the Other Side*, the first oral history of the terror campaign—one of many books unlikely to receive more than casual notice, if that, in the West because its contents are too revealing.[34]

In the *Political Science Quarterly*, the professional journal of the American Political Science Association, Montague Kern observes that the Cuban Missile Crisis is one of those "full-bore crises . . . in which an ideological enemy (the Soviet Union) is universally perceived to have gone on the attack, leading to a rally-'round-the-flag effect that greatly expands support for a president, increasing his policy options."[35]

Kern is right that it is "universally perceived" that way, apart from those who have escaped sufficiently from their ideological shackles to pay some attention to the facts; Kern is, in fact, one of them. Another is Sheldon Stern, who recognizes what has long been known to such deviants. As he writes, we now know that "Khrushchev's original explanation for shipping missiles to Cuba had been fundamentally true: the Soviet leader had never intended these weapons as a threat to the security of the United States, but rather considered their deployment a defensive move to protect his Cuban allies from American attacks and as a desperate effort to give the USSR the appearance of equality in the nuclear balance of power."[36] Dobbs, too, recognizes that "Castro and his Soviet patrons had real reasons to fear American attempts at regime change, including, as a last resort, a US invasion of Cuba . . . [Khrushchev] was also sincere in his desire to defend the Cuban revolution from the mighty neighbor to the north."[37]

"TERRORS OF THE EARTH"

The American attacks are often dismissed in U.S. commentary as silly pranks, CIA shenanigans that got out of hand. That is far from the truth. The best and the brightest had reacted to the failure of the Bay of Pigs invasion with near hysteria, including the president, who solemnly informed the country: "The complacent, the self-indulgent, the soft societies are about to be swept away with the debris of history. Only the strong . . . can possibly survive." And they could only survive, he evidently believed, by massive terror—though that addendum was kept secret, and is still not known to loyalists who perceive the ideological enemy as having "gone on the attack" (the near-universal perception, as Kern observes). After the Bay of Pigs defeat, historian Piero Gleijeses writes, JFK launched a crushing embargo to punish the Cubans for defeating a U.S.-run invasion, and "asked his brother, Attorney General Robert Kennedy, to lead the top-level interagency group that oversaw Operation Mongoose, a program of paramilitary operations, economic warfare, and sabotage he launched in late 1961 to visit the 'terrors of the earth' on Fidel Castro and, more prosaically, to topple him."[38]

The phrase "terrors of the earth" is Arthur Schlesinger's, in his quasi-official biography of Robert Kennedy, who was assigned responsibility for conducting the terrorist war and who informed the CIA that the Cuban problem carries "the top priority in the United States Government—all else is secondary—no time, no effort, or manpower is to be spared" in the effort to overthrow the Castro regime.[39] The Mongoose operations were run by Edward Lansdale, who had ample experience in "counterinsurgency"—a standard term for terrorism that we direct. He provided a timetable leading to "open revolt and overthrow of the Communist regime" in October 1962. The "final definition" of the program recognized that "final success will require decisive US military intervention" after terrorism and subversion had laid the basis for it. The implication was that U.S. military intervention would take place in October 1962—when the missile crisis erupted. The events just reviewed help explain why Cuba and Russia had good reason to take such threats seriously.

Years later, Robert McNamara recognized that Cuba was justified in fearing an attack. "If I were in Cuban or Soviet shoes, I would have thought so, too," he observed at a major conference on the missile crisis on its fortieth anniversary.[40]

As for Russia's "desperate effort to give the USSR the appearance of equality," to which Stern refers, recall that Kennedy's very narrow victory in the 1960 election relied heavily on a fabricated "missile gap" concocted to terrify the country and to condemn the Eisenhower administration as soft on national security.[41] There was indeed a "missile gap," but strongly in favor of the United States.

The first "public, unequivocal administration statement" on the true facts, according to strategic analyst Desmond Ball in his authoritative study of the Kennedy missile program, was in October 1961, when Deputy Secretary of Defense Roswell Gilpatric informed the Business Council that "the US would have a larger nuclear delivery system left after a surprise attack than the nuclear force which the Soviet Union could employ in its first strike."[42] The Russians, of course, were well aware of their relative weakness and vulnerability. They were also aware of Kennedy's reaction when Khrushchev offered to sharply reduce offensive military capacity and proceeded to do so unilaterally: the president failed to respond, undertaking instead a huge armaments program.

OWNING THE WORLD, THEN AND NOW

The two most crucial questions about the missile crisis are: How did it begin? And how did it end? It began with Kennedy's terrorist attack against Cuba, with a threat of invasion in October 1962. It ended with the president's rejection of Russian offers that would seem fair to a "rational" person, but were unthinkable because they would have undermined the fundamental principle that the United States has the unilateral right to deploy nuclear missiles anywhere, aimed at China or Russia or anyone else, even on their borders, and the accompanying principle that Cuba had no right to have missiles for defense against what appeared to be an imminent U.S. invasion. To establish these principles firmly, it was entirely proper to face a high risk of a war of unimaginable destruction and to reject simple and admittedly fair ways to end the threat.

Garthoff observes that "in the United States, there was almost universal approbation for President Kennedy's handling of the crisis."[43] Dobbs writes, "The relentlessly upbeat tone was established by the court historian, Arthur M. Schlesinger, Jr., who wrote that Kennedy had 'dazzled the world' through a 'combination of toughness and restraint, of will, nerve and wisdom, so brilliantly controlled, so matchlessly calibrated.'"[44] Rather more soberly, Stern partially agrees, noting that Kennedy repeatedly rejected the militant advice of his advisers and associates who called for military force and the dismissal of peaceful options. The events of October 1962 are widely hailed as Kennedy's finest hour. Graham Allison joins many others in presenting them as "a guide for how to defuse conflicts, manage great-power relationships, and make sound decisions about foreign policy in general."[45]

In a very narrow sense, that judgment seems reasonable. The ExComm tapes reveal that the president stood apart from others, sometimes almost all others, in rejecting premature violence. There is, however, a further question: How should JFK's relative moderation in the management of the crisis be evaluated against the background of the broader considerations just reviewed? But that question does not arise in a disciplined intellectual and moral culture, which accepts without question the basic principle that the United States effectively owns the world by right and is by definition a force for good despite occasional errors and misunderstandings, a principle in which it is plainly entirely proper for the United States to deploy massive offensive force all over the world while it is an outrage for others (allies and clients apart) to make even the slightest gesture in that direction or even to think of deterring the threatened use of violence by the benign global hegemon.

That doctrine is the primary official charge against Iran today: it might pose a deterrent to U.S. and Israeli force. This was a consideration during the missile crisis as well. In internal discussion, the Kennedy brothers expressed their fears that Cuban missiles might deter a U.S. invasion of Venezuela then under consideration. So "the Bay of Pigs was really right," JFK concluded.[46]

These principles still contribute to the constant risk of nuclear war. There has been no shortage of severe dangers since the missile crisis. Ten years later, during the 1973 Israeli-Arab war, National Security Advisor

Henry Kissinger called a high-level nuclear alert (DEFCON 3) to warn the Russians to keep their hands off while he was secretly authorizing Israel to violate the cease-fire imposed by the United States and Russia.[47] When Ronald Reagan came into office a few years later, the United States launched operations probing Russian defenses and simulating air and naval attacks, while placing Pershing missiles in Germany that had a five- to ten-minute flight time to Russian targets, providing what the CIA called a "super-sudden first strike" capability.[48] Naturally this caused great alarm in Russia, which unlike the United States has repeatedly been invaded and virtually destroyed. That led to a major war scare in 1983. There have also been hundreds of cases when human intervention aborted a first strike minutes before launch after automated systems gave false alarms. We don't have Russian records, but there's no doubt that their systems are far more accident-prone.

Meanwhile, India and Pakistan have come close to nuclear war several times, and the sources of their conflict remain. Both have refused to sign the Non-Proliferation Treaty, along with Israel, and have received U.S. support for development of their nuclear weapons programs.

In 1962, war was avoided by Khrushchev's willingness to accept Kennedy's hegemonic demands. But we can hardly count on such sanity forever. It's a near miracle that nuclear war has so far been avoided. There is more reason than ever to attend to the warning of Bertrand Russell and Albert Einstein, almost sixty years ago, that we must face a choice that is "stark and dreadful and inescapable: Shall we put an end to the human race; or shall mankind renounce war?"[49]

9

The Oslo Accords: Their Context, Their Consequences

In September 1993, President Clinton presided over a handshake between Israeli prime minister Yitzhak Rabin and PLO chairman Yasser Arafat on the White House lawn—capping off a "day of awe," as the press described it with reverence.[1] The occasion was the announcement of the Declaration of Principles (DOP) for political settlement of the Israel-Palestine conflict, which resulted from secret meetings in Oslo sponsored by the Norwegian government.

Independent negotiations had been underway between Israel and the Palestinians since November 1991, initiated by the United States during the glow of success after the first Iraq war, which established that "what we say goes," in the triumphant words of President George H. W. Bush.[2] The negotiations opened with a brief conference in Madrid and contin- ued under the guiding hand of the United States (and technically, the fading Soviet Union, to provide the illusion of international auspices). The Palestinian delegation, consisting of Palestinians within the Occu- pied Territories (henceforth the "internal Palestinians"), was led by the dedicated and incorruptible left nationalist Haidar Abdul Shafi, prob- ably the most respected figure in Palestine. The "external Palestinians"— the PLO, based in Tunis and headed by Yasser Arafat—were excluded, though they had an unofficial observer, Faisal Husseini. The huge number of Palestinian refugees were totally excluded, with no regard for their rights, even those accorded them by the UN General Assembly.

To appreciate the nature and significance of the Oslo Accords and the consequences that flowed from them, it is important to understand the background and the context in which the Madrid and Oslo negotiations took place. I will begin by reviewing highlights of the immediate background that set the context for the negotiations, then turn to the DOP and the consequences of the Oslo process, which extend to the present, and finally add a few words on lessons that should be learned.

The PLO, Israel, and the United States had recently released formal positions on the basic issues that were the topic of the Madrid and Oslo negotiations. The PLO position was presented in a November 1988 declaration of the Palestinian National Council, carrying forward a long series of diplomatic initiatives that had been dismissed. It called for a Palestinian state to be established in the territories occupied by Israel since 1967 and requested the UN Security Council "to formulate and guarantee arrangements for security and peace between all the states concerned in the region, including the Palestinian state" alongside Israel.[3] The PNC declaration, which accepted the overwhelming international consensus on a diplomatic settlement, was virtually the same as the two-state resolution brought to the Security Council in January 1976 by the Arab "confrontation states" (Egypt, Syria, and Jordan). It was vetoed by the United States then, and again in 1980. For forty years the United States has blocked the international consensus, and it still does, diplomatic pleasantries aside.

By 1988, Washington's rejectionist stance was becoming difficult to sustain. By December, the outgoing Reagan administration had become an international laughingstock with its increasingly desperate efforts to pretend that, alone in the world, it could not hear the accommodating proposals of the PLO and the Arab states. Grudgingly, Washington decided to "declare victory," claiming that at last the PLO had been compelled to utter Secretary of State George Shultz's "magic words" and express its willingness to pursue diplomacy.[4] As Shultz makes clear in his memoirs, the goal was to ensure maximum humiliation of the PLO while admitting that peace offers could no longer be denied. He informed President Reagan that Arafat was saying in one place "'Unc, unc, unc,' and in another he was saying, 'cle, cle, cle,' but nowhere will he yet bring himself to say 'Uncle,'" conceding total capitulation in the humble style expected of the lower orders. Low-level discussions with the PLO would therefore be allowed, but on the understanding that they would be meaningless: specifically, it was stipulated that the PLO must abandon its request for an international conference, so that the United States would maintain control.[5]

In May 1989, Israel's Likud-Labor coalition government formally responded to Palestinian acceptance of a two-state settlement, declaring that there could be no "additional Palestinian state" between Jordan and Israel (Jordan already being a Palestinian state by Israeli dictate, whatever Jordanians and Palestinians might think), and that "there will be no change in the status of Judea, Samaria and Gaza [the West Bank and Gaza] other than in accordance with the basic guidelines of the [Israeli] Government."[6] Furthermore, Israel would conduct no negotiations with the PLO, though it would permit "free elections" under Israeli military rule, with much of the Palestinian leadership in prison without charge or expelled from Palestine.

In the plan proposed by Secretary of State James A. Baker, the new Bush administration endorsed this proposal without qualifications in December 1989. Those were the three formal positions on the eve of the Madrid negotiations, with Washington mediating as the "honest broker."

When Arafat went to Washington to take part in the "day of awe" in September 1993, the lead story in the *New York Times* celebrated the handshake as a "dramatic image" that "will transform Mr. Arafat into a statesman and peacemaker" who finally renounced violence under Washington's tutelage.[7] At the extreme critical end of the mainstream, *New York Times* columnist Anthony Lewis wrote that until that moment Palestinians had always "rejected compromise" but now at last they were willing to "make peace possible."[8] Of course, it was the United States

and Israel that had rejected diplomacy and the PLO that had been offering compromise for years, but Lewis's reversal of the facts was quite normal and unchallenged in the mainstream.

There were other crucial developments in the immediate pre-Madrid/
pre-Oslo years. In December 1987, the Intifada erupted in Gaza and
quickly spread throughout the Occupied Territories.[9] This broad-based
and remarkably restrained uprising was as much of a surprise to the
PLO in Tunis as it was to the occupying Israeli forces with their extensive system of military and paramilitary forces, surveillance, and col-
laborators. The Intifada was not limited to opposing the occupation. It
was also a social revolution within Palestinian society, breaking patterns of subordination of women, authority by notables, and other
forms of hierarchy and domination.

Though the timing of the Intifada was a surprise, the uprising itself
was not, at least to those who paid any attention to Israel's U.S.-backed
operations within the territories. Something was bound to happen;
there is only so much that people can endure. For the preceding twenty
years, Palestinians under military occupation had been subjected to
harsh repression, brutality, and cruel humiliation while watching what
remained of their country disappear before their eyes as Israel conducted its programs of settlement, implemented huge infrastructure
developments designed to integrate valuable parts of the territories
within Israel, robbed them of resources, and put into place other measures to bar independent development—always with crucial U.S. military, economic, and diplomatic support, as well as ideological backing
in shaping how the issues were framed.

To take just one of the many cases that elicited no notice or concern
in the West: shortly before the outbreak of the Intifada, a Palestinian
girl, Intissar al-Atar, was shot and killed in a school yard in Gaza by a
resident of a nearby Jewish settlement.[10] He was one of the several thousand Israelis who settled in Gaza with substantial state subsidies, protected by a huge army presence as they took over much of the land and
the scarce water of the Strip while living "lavishly in twenty-two settle-

ments in the midst of 1.4 million destitute Palestinians," as the crime is described by Israeli scholar Avi Raz.[11]

The murderer of the schoolgirl, Shimon Yifrah, was arrested, but quickly released on bail when the court determined that "the offense is not severe enough" to warrant detention. The judge commented that Yifrah only intended to shock the girl by firing his gun at her in a school yard, not to kill her, so "this is not a case of a criminal person who has to be punished, deterred, and taught a lesson by imprisoning him." Yifrah was given a seven-month suspended sentence while settlers in the courtroom broke out in song and dance. And the usual silence reigned. After all, it was routine.

And so it was: as Yifrah was freed, the Israeli press reported that an army patrol fired into the yard of a school in a West Bank refugee camp, wounding five children, likewise intending only "to shock them." There were no charges, and the event again attracted no attention. It was just another episode in a program of "illiteracy as punishment," as the Israeli press termed it, including the closing of schools, the use of gas bombs, the beating of students with rifle butts, and the barring of medical aid for victims. Beyond the schools, a reign of even more severe brutality that became yet more savage during the Intifada was enacted under the orders of Defense Minister Yitzhak Rabin. After two years of violent and sadistic repression, Rabin informed Peace Now leaders that "the inhabitants of the territories are subject to harsh military and economic pressure. In the end, they will be broken," and would accept Israel's terms—as they did, when Arafat restored control through the Oslo process.[12]

The Madrid negotiations between Israel and internal Palestinians continued inconclusively from 1991, primarily because Abdul Shafi insisted on an end to the expansion of Israeli settlements. The settlements were all illegal, as had repeatedly been determined by international authorities, including the UN Security Council (among other resolutions, in UNSC 446, passed 12-0, with the United States, the United Kingdom, and Norway abstaining).[13] The illegality of the settlements was later affirmed by the International Court of Justice. It had also been recognized by Israel's highest legal authorities and government officials in late 1967 when the settlement projects were beginning. The criminal enterprise included the vast expansion and annexation of Greater Jerusalem, in explicit violation of repeated Security Council orders.[14]

Israel's position as the Madrid conference opened was summarized accurately by Israeli journalist Danny Rubinstein, one of the best-informed analysts on the topic of the Occupied Territories.[15] He wrote that, at Madrid, Israel and the United States would agree to some form of Palestinian "autonomy," as required by the 1978 Camp David Accords, but it would be "autonomy as in a POW camp, where the prisoners are 'autonomous' to cook their meals without interference and to organize cultural events."[16] Palestinians would be granted little more than what they already had—control over local services—and the Israeli settlement programs would continue.

While the Madrid negotiations and the secret Oslo negotiations were underway, these programs expanded rapidly, under first Yitzhak Shamir and then Yitzhak Rabin, who became prime minister in 1992 and "boasted that more housing in the territories is being built during his tenure than at any time since 1967." Rabin explained the guiding principle succinctly: "What is important is what is within the boundaries, and it is less important where the boundaries are, as long as the State [of Israel] covers most of the territory of the Land of Israel [Eretz Israel, the former Palestine], whose capital is Jerusalem."

Israeli researchers reported that the aim of the Rabin government was to radically expand "the greater Jerusalem zone of influence," extending from Ramallah to Hebron to the border of Ma'aleh Adumim, near Jericho, and to "finish creating circles of contiguous Jewish settlements in the greater Jerusalem zone of influence, so as to further surround the Palestinian communities, limit their development, and prevent any possibility that East Jerusalem could become a Palestinian capital." Furthermore, "a vast network of roads has been under construction, forming the backbone of the settlement pattern."[17]

The programs were expanded rapidly after the Oslo Accords, includ-

ing new settlements and the "thickening" of old ones, special induce-
ments to attract new settlers, and highway projects to cantonize the
territory. Excluding annexed East Jerusalem, building starts increased
by over 40 percent from 1993 to 1995, according to a Peace Now study.[18]
Government funding for settlements in the territories increased by
70 percent in 1994, the year following the accords.[19] *Davar*, the journal
of the governing Labor Party, reported that Rabin's administration was
maintaining the priorities of the ultraright Shamir government it
replaced. While pretending to freeze settlements, Labor "helped them
financially even more than the Shamir government had ever done,"
enlarging settlements "everywhere in the West Bank, even in the most
provocative spots."[20] This policy was carried forward in the following
years, and is the basis for the current programs of the Netanyahu government. It is designed to leave Israel in control of some 40 to 50 percent
of the West Bank, with the rest cantonized, imprisoned as Israel takes
over the Jordan Valley, and separated from Gaza, in explicit violation of
the Oslo Accords, thus ensuring that any potential Palestinian entity
will have no access to the outside world.

The Intifada was initiated and carried out by the internal Palestinians. The PLO, in Tunis, tried to exert some control over the events but
with little success. The programs of the early 1990s while negotiations
were in process deepened the alienation of the internal Palestinians
from the PLO leadership abroad.

Under these circumstances, it was not surprising that Arafat sought
a way to reestablish PLO authority. The opportunity was offered by the
secret negotiations between Arafat and Israel under Norwegian auspices
that undercut the local leadership. As they were concluded in August
1993, the growing PLO estrangement was reviewed by Lamis Andoni,
one of the few journalists who was keeping a close watch on what was
happening among the Palestinians under occupation and in refugee
camps in neighboring countries.

Andoni reported that the PLO is "facing the worst crisis since its
inception [as] Palestinian groups—except for Fatah—and independents

are distancing themselves from the PLO [and the] shrinking clique around Yasir Arafat." She reported further that "two top PLO executive committee members, Palestinian poet Mahmoud Darwish and Shafiq al-Hout, have resigned from the PLO executive committee," while Palestinian negotiators were offering their resignations, and even groups that remained inside were distancing themselves from Arafat. The leader of Fatah in Lebanon called on Arafat to resign, while opposition to him personally and to PLO corruption and autocracy were mounting in the territories. Along with "the rapid disintegration of the mainstream group and Arafat's loss of support within his own movement . . . the speedy disintegration of the PLO's institutions and the steady erosion of the Organisation's constituency could render any breakthrough at the peace talks meaningless."

"At no point in the PLO's history has opposition to the leadership, and to Arafat himself, been as strong," Andoni observed, "while for the first time there is a growing feeling that safeguarding Palestinian national rights no longer hinges on defending the PLO's role. Many believe that it is the leadership's policies that are destroying Palestinian institutions and jeopardising Palestinian national rights."

For such reasons, she observed, Arafat was pursuing the Jericho-Gaza option offered by the Oslo agreement, which he hoped would "assert the PLO's authority, especially amid signs that the Israeli government could go the extra ten miles by talking directly to the PLO, thus salvaging for it the legitimacy it is losing internally."

Israeli authorities were surely aware of the developments within Palestine, and presumably came to appreciate that it made good sense to deal with those who were "destroying Palestinian institutions and jeopardising Palestinian national rights" before the population sought to realize its national goals and rights in some other way.

Reaction to the Oslo Accords among Palestinians within the territories was mixed. Some had high hopes. Others saw little to celebrate. "The provisions of the agreement have alarmed even the most moderate Palestinians, who worry that the accord consolidates Israeli control in the territories," Lamis Andoni reported. Saeb Erekat, a senior

Palestinian negotiator, commented that "apparently this agreement aims at reorganizing the Israeli occupation and not at a gradual termination."[21] Even Faisal Husseini, who was close to Arafat, said that the accord "is definitely not the beginning that our people were looking for." Haidar Abdul Shafi criticized the PLO leadership for accepting an agreement that permitted Israel to continue its settlement policies and land appropriation, as well as the "annexation and Judaization" of its expanded Jerusalem area and its "economic hegemony" over Palestinians—and refused to attend the celebration on the White House lawn.[22] Particularly grating to many was what they saw as "the shabby behavior of the P.L.O. leadership, including a pattern of ignoring Palestinians who have suffered through 27 years of Israeli occupation in favor of exiles coming from Tunis to take power," Youssef Ibrahim reported in the *New York Times*. He added that PLO representatives "were pelted with stones by Palestinian youths as they rode into [Jericho] in Israeli Army jeeps."[23] Arafat's provisional list for his governing authority revealed "that he is determined to stack it with loyalists and members of the Palestinian diaspora," Julian Ozanne reported from Jerusalem in the *Financial Times*, including only two Palestinian "insiders," Faisal Husseini and Zakaria al-Agha, both Arafat loyalists.[24] The rest came from Arafat's "loyal political factions" outside the territories.

A look at the actual contents of the Oslo Accords reveals that such reactions were, if anything, overly optimistic.

The Declaration of Principles was quite explicit about satisfying Israel's demands, but was silent on Palestinian national rights. It conformed to the conception articulated by Dennis Ross, President Clinton's main Middle East adviser and negotiator at Camp David in 2000 and later a key adviser for Obama as well. As Ross explained, Israel has *needs*, but Palestinians have only *wants*—obviously of lesser significance.[25]

Article I of the DOP states that the end result of the process is to be "a permanent settlement based on Security Council Resolutions 242 and 338." Those familiar with the diplomacy concerning the Israel-Palestine conflict should have had no difficulty understanding what this meant.

Resolutions 242 and 338 say nothing at all about Palestinian rights, apart from a vague reference to a "just settlement of the refugee problem."[26] Later resolutions referring to Palestinian national rights were ignored in the DOP. If the culmination of the "peace process" is implemented along such lines, then Palestinians could kiss goodbye their hopes for some limited degree of national rights in the former Palestine.

Further articles of the DOP spell all of this out more clearly. They stipulate that Palestinian authority extends over "West Bank and Gaza Strip territory, except for issues that will be negotiated in the permanent status negotiations: Jerusalem, settlements, military locations, and Israelis"—that is, except for every issue of significance.[27] Furthermore, "subsequent to the Israeli withdrawal, Israel will continue to be responsible for external security, and for internal security and public order of settlements and Israelis. Israeli military forces and civilians may continue to use roads freely within the Gaza Strip and the Jericho area," the two areas from which Israel was pledged to withdraw—eventually.[28] In short, there would be no meaningful changes. The DOP also did not have a word to say about the settlement programs at the heart of the conflict, which even before the vast expansion under the Oslo process were already undermining realistic prospects of achieving any meaningful Palestinian self-determination.

In brief, only by succumbing to what is sometimes called "intentional ignorance" could one believe that the Oslo process was a path to peace. Nevertheless, this belief became virtual dogma among Western commentators and intellectuals.

The Oslo Accords were followed by additional Israel–Arafat/PLO agreements. The first and most important of these was Oslo II, in 1995, shortly before Prime Minister Rabin was assassinated, a tragic event even if the illusions concocted about "Rabin the peace-maker" cannot sustain analysis.

The Oslo II agreement is what one would expect to be crafted by intelligent law students assigned the task of constructing a document that would give U.S. and Israeli authorities the option of doing as they pleased while leaving room for speculation about more acceptable outcomes. When these outcomes remain unrealized, the blame can be laid on the "extremists" who have undermined the promise.

To illustrate, the Oslo II agreement stipulated that settlers (illegally) in the Occupied Territories would remain under Israeli jurisdiction and legislation. In the official wording, "the Israeli military government [in the territories] shall retain the necessary legislative, judicial and executive powers and responsibilities, in accordance with international law"— which the United States and Israel have always interpreted as they chose, with tacit European acquiescence. Such latitude also granted these authorities effective veto power over Palestinian legislation. The agreement stated that any such "legislation which amends or abrogates existing [Israeli-imposed] laws or military orders . . . shall have no effect and shall be void *ab initio* if it exceeds the jurisdiction of the [Palestinian] Council"—which had no authority in most of the territories and authority elsewhere only conditional on Israeli approval—or is "otherwise inconsistent with this or any other agreement." Furthermore, "the Palestinian side shall respect the legal rights of Israelis (including corporations owned by Israelis) related to lands located in areas under the territorial jurisdiction of the Council"—that is, in the limited areas in which the Palestinian authorities were to have jurisdiction subject to Israeli approval; specifically, their rights related to government and so-called "absentee" land, a complex legal construction that effectively transfers to Israeli jurisdiction the land of Palestinians absent from territories taken by Israel. [29] The latter two categories constitute most of the region, though the government of Israel, which determines their boundaries unilaterally, provided no official figures. The Israeli press reported that "unsettled state lands" amounted to about half of the West Bank, and total state lands to about 70 percent.[30]

Oslo II thus rescinded the decision of virtually the entire world, and all relevant legal authorities, that Israel has no claim to the territories occupied in 1967 and that the settlements are illegitimate. The Palestinian side recognized their legality, along with unspecified other legal rights of Israelis throughout the territories, including Zones A and B (under conditional Palestinian control). Oslo II implanted more firmly the major accomplishment of Oslo I: all UN resolutions that have any bearing on Palestinian rights were abrogated, including those concerning the legality of settlements, the status of Jerusalem, and the right of return. That wiped out with a stroke virtually the entire record of Middle East diplomacy, apart from the version implemented in the unilateral U.S.-run "peace process." The basic facts were not just excised from history, at least in U.S. commentary, but were officially removed as well.

So matters have continued, to the present.

As noted, it is understandable that Arafat would leap at the opportunity to undercut the internal Palestinian leadership and to try to reassert his waning power in the territories. But what exactly did the Norwegian negotiators think they were accomplishing? The only serious scholarly study of the matter, to my knowledge, is the work of Hilde Henriksen Waage, who had been commissioned by the Norwegian Ministry of Foreign Affairs to research the topic and was granted access to internal files, only to make the remarkable discovery that the documentary record for the crucial period is missing.[31]

Waage observes that the Oslo Accords were certainly a turning point in the history of the Israel-Palestine conflict, while also establishing Oslo as the world's "capital of peace." The Oslo process was "expected to bring peace to the Middle East," Waage writes, but "for the Palestinians, it resulted in the parceling of the West Bank, the doubling of Israeli settlers, the construction of a crippling separation wall, a draconian closure regime, and an unprecedented separation between the Gaza Strip and the West Bank."[32]

Waage concludes plausibly that the "Oslo process could serve as the perfect case study for flaws" in the model of "third party mediation by a small state in highly asymmetrical conflicts"—and that, as she puts it starkly, "the Oslo process was conducted on Israel's premises, with Norway acting as Israel's helpful errand boy."

"The Norwegians," she writes, "believed that through dialogue and a gradual building of trust, an irreversible peace dynamic would be created that could push the process forward to solution. The problem with this entire approach is that the issue is not one of trust, but of power.

The facilitative process masks that reality. In the end, the results that can be achieved by a weak third-party facilitator are no more than the strong party will allow. . . . The question to be asked is whether such a model can ever be appropriate."[33]

A good question, worth pondering, particularly as educated Western opinion now adopts the ludicrous assumption that meaningful Israel-Palestine negotiations can be seriously conducted under the auspices of the United States as an "honest broker"—in reality a partner of Israel for forty years in blocking a diplomatic settlement that has near-universal support.

10

The Eve of Destruction

To ask what the future is likely to bring, a reasonable stance might be to try to look at the human species from the outside. So imagine that you're an extraterrestrial observer who is trying to take a neutral stance and figure out what's happening here, or, for that matter, imagine you're a historian a hundred years from now—assuming there are any historians a hundred years from now, which is not obvious—and you're looking back at what's happening today. You'd see something quite remarkable.

For the first time in the history of the human species, we have clearly developed the capacity to destroy ourselves. That's been true since 1945. It's now being finally recognized that there are more long-term processes like environmental destruction leading in the same direction—maybe not to total destruction, but at least to the destruction of the capacity for a decent existence.

And there are other dangers, like pandemics, which have to do with globalization and interaction. So there are processes underway and institutions right in place, like nuclear weapons systems, which could lead to a serious blow to, or maybe the termination of, an organized existence.

HOW TO DESTROY A PLANET WITHOUT REALLY TRYING

The question is: What are people doing about it? None of this is a secret. It's all perfectly open. In fact, you have to make an effort not to see it. And there has been a range of reactions. There are those who are trying hard to do something about these threats, and others who are acting to escalate them. If you, this future historian or extraterrestrial observer, looked at who is in each group, you would see something strange indeed: those trying to mitigate or overcome these threats are the least developed societies—the indigenous populations, or the remnants of them; tribal societies; and first nations in Canada. They're not talking about nuclear war but environmental disaster, and they're really trying to do something about it.

In fact, all over the world—Australia, India, South America—there are battles going on, sometimes wars. In India, it's a major war over direct environmental destruction, with tribal societies trying to resist resource-extraction operations that are extremely harmful locally but also in their general consequences. In societies where indigenous populations have influence, many are taking a strong stand. The strongest stance of any country with regard to global warming is that of Bolivia, which has an indigenous majority and constitutional requirements that protect the "rights of nature." Ecuador, which also has a large indigenous population, is the only oil exporter I know of whose government is seeking aid to help keep that oil in the ground instead of producing and exporting it—and the ground is where it ought to be.

Venezuelan President Hugo Chavez, who died recently, and who was the object of mockery, insult, and hatred throughout the Western world, attended a session of the UN General Assembly a few years ago where he elicited all sorts of ridicule for calling George W. Bush a "devil." He also gave a speech there that was quite interesting. Venezuela is a major oil producer; oil is practically their whole gross domestic product. In his speech, Chavez warned of the dangers of the overuse of fossil fuels and urged producer and consumer countries to get together and try to work out ways to reduce fossil-fuel use. That was pretty amazing on the part of an oil producer. Chavez was part Indian, of indigenous background. Unlike the funny things he did, this aspect of his actions at the United Nations was never even reported.[1]

So, at one extreme you have indigenous, tribal societies trying to stem the race to disaster. At the other extreme, the richest, most powerful societies in world history, like the United States and Canada, are racing full speed ahead to destroy the environment as quickly as possible. Unlike Ecuador and indigenous societies throughout the world, they want to extract every drop of hydrocarbons from the ground with all possible speed. Both political parties, President Obama, the media, and the international press seem to be looking forward with great enthusiasm to what they call "a century of energy independence" for the United States. "Energy independence" is an almost meaningless concept, but put that aside. What they mean is: we'll have a century in which to maximize the use of fossil fuels and contribute to the destruction of the world.

And that's pretty much the case everywhere. Admittedly, when it comes to alternative energy development, Europe's doing something. Meanwhile, the United States, the richest and most powerful country in world history, is the only nation among perhaps a hundred relevant ones that doesn't have a national policy for restricting the use of fossil fuels, that doesn't even have renewable energy targets. It's not because the population doesn't want it; Americans are pretty close to the international norm in their concern about global warming. It's institutional structures that block change. Business interests don't want it, and they're overwhelmingly powerful in determining policy, so you get a big gap between opinion and policy on lots of issues, including this one.

So that's what the future historian—if there is one—would see. He might also read today's scientific journals. Just about every one you open has a more dire prediction than the last.

The other issue is nuclear war. It's been known for a long time that if there were to be a first strike by a major power, even with no retaliation, it would probably destroy civilization just because of the nuclear-winter consequences that would follow. You can read about it in the *Bulletin of the Atomic Scientists*; it's well understood. So the danger has always been a lot worse than we thought it was.

We've recently passed the fiftieth anniversary of the Cuban Missile Crisis. It was a very close call, and not the only time either. In some ways, however, the worst aspect of these grim events is that their lessons haven't been learned. Ten years after those events, in 1973, Secretary of State Henry Kissinger called a high-level nuclear alert. It was his way of warning the Russians not to interfere in the ongoing Israeli–Arab war and, in particular, not to interfere after he had informed the Israelis that they could violate a cease-fire the United States and Russia had just agreed upon.[2] Fortunately, nothing happened.

Ten years after that, President Ronald Reagan was in office. Soon after he entered the Oval Office, he and his advisers had the U.S. Air Force start penetrating Russian airspace to try to elicit information about Russian warning systems; this was called Operation Able Archer.[3] Essentially, these were mock attacks. The Russians were uncertain how to respond, with some high-level officials fearing that this was a step toward a real first strike. Fortunately, they didn't react, though it was a close call. And it goes on like that.

WHAT TO MAKE OF THE IRANIAN AND NORTH KOREAN NUCLEAR CRISES

The nuclear issue is regularly front-page news in the cases of Iran and North Korea. There are ways to deal with these ongoing crises. Maybe they wouldn't work, but at least they could be tried. They are, however, not being considered, not even reported.

Take the case of Iran, which is considered in the West—not in the Arab world, not in Asia—the gravest threat to world peace. It's a Western obsession, and it's interesting to look into the reasons, but I'll put that aside here. Is there a way to deal with the supposed gravest threat to world peace? Actually, there are quite a few. One way, a pretty sensible one, was proposed at a meeting of the nonaligned countries in Tehran in 2013. In fact, they were just reiterating a proposal that's been around for decades, pressed particularly by Egypt, and has been approved by the UN General Assembly.

The proposal is to move toward establishing a nuclear weapons–free zone in the region. That wouldn't be the answer to everything, but it would be a pretty significant step forward. And there were ways to proceed: under UN auspices, there was to be an international conference in Finland in December 2012 to try to implement such a plan. What happened? You won't read about it in the newspapers, because it was only reported in specialist journals. In early November, Iran agreed to attend the meeting. A couple of days later Obama cancelled the meeting, saying the time wasn't right.[4] The European Parliament issued a statement calling for it to continue, as did the Arab states. Nothing resulted.

In Northeast Asia, it's the same sort of thing. North Korea may be the craziest country in the world; it's certainly a good competitor for that title. But it does make sense to try to figure out what's in the minds of people when they're acting in crazy ways. Why would they behave the way they do? Just imagine ourselves in their position. Imagine what it meant in the Korean War years of the early 1950s for your country to be totally leveled—everything destroyed by a huge superpower, which furthermore was gloating about what it was doing. Imagine the imprint that would leave behind.

Bear in mind that the North Korean leadership is likely to have read the public military journals of this superpower at that time explaining that since everything in North Korea had been destroyed, the air force was then sent to destroy North Korea's dams, huge dams that controlled the nation's water supply—a war crime, by the way, for which people had been hanged in Nuremberg. And these official journals were talking excitedly about how wonderful it was to see the water pouring down, digging out the valleys, and the "Asians" scurrying around trying to survive.[5] The journals exulted in what this meant to those Asians— horrors beyond our imagination. It meant the destruction of their rice crop, which in turn meant starvation and death. How magnificent! It's not in our memory bank, but it's in theirs.

Let's turn to the present. There's an interesting recent history: in 1993, Israel and North Korea were moving toward an agreement in which North Korea would stop sending any missiles or military technology to the Middle East and Israel would recognize that country. President Clinton intervened and blocked it.[6] Shortly after that, in retaliation, North Korea carried out a minor missile test. The United States and North Korea did then reach a framework agreement in 1994 that halted North Korean nuclear work and was more or less honored by both sides. When George W. Bush came into office, North Korea had maybe one nuclear weapon and verifiably wasn't producing any more.

Bush immediately launched his aggressive militarism, threatening North Korea ("Axis of Evil" and all that), so that country got back to work on its nuclear program. By the time Bush left office, it had eight to ten nuclear weapons and a missile system, another great neocon achievement.[7] In between, other things happened. In 2005, the United States and North Korea actually reached an agreement in which North Korea was to end all nuclear weapons and missile development; in return, the West—but mainly the United States—would provide a light-water reactor for its medical needs and end aggressive statements. They would then form a nonaggression pact and move toward accommodation.

The agreement was pretty promising, but almost immediately Bush undermined it. He withdrew the offer of the light-water reactor and initiated programs to compel banks to stop handling any North Korean transactions, even perfectly legal ones.[8] The North Koreans reacted by picking up their nuclear weapons program. And that's the way it's been going.

The pattern is well-known. You can read it in straight, mainstream American scholarship. What they say is: it's a pretty crazy regime, but it's also following a kind of tit-for-tat policy. You make a hostile gesture, and we'll respond with some crazy gesture of our own. You make an accommodating gesture, and we'll reciprocate in some way.

Lately, for instance, there have been South Korean–U.S. military exercises on the Korean peninsula which from North Korea's point of view have got to look threatening. We'd think they were threatening if they were going on, aimed at us, in Canada. In the course of these exercises, the most advanced bombers in history, stealth B-2s and B-52s, carried out simulated nuclear bombing attacks right on North Korea's borders.[9]

This surely set off alarm bells from the past. The North Koreans remember something from the past, so they're reacting in a very aggressive, extreme way. Well, what generally comes to the West from all this is how crazy and how awful the North Korean leaders are. Yes, they are—but that's hardly the whole story, and this is the way the world is going.

It's not that there are no alternatives. The alternatives just aren't being taken. That's dangerous. So if you ask what the world is going to look like, it's not a pretty picture. Unless people do something about it. We always can.

11

Israel-Palestine: The Real Options

On July 13, 2013, former Shin Bet chief Yuval Diskin issued a dire warning to the government of Israel: either it would reach some kind of two-state settlement or there would be a "shift to a nearly inevitable outcome of the one remaining reality—a state 'from the sea to the river.'" The near-inevitable outcome, "one state for two nations," will pose "an immediate existential threat of the erasure of the identity of Israel as a Jewish and democratic state," which would soon have a Palestinian-Arab majority.[1]

On similar grounds, in Britain's leading journal of international affairs two prominent Middle East specialists, Clive Jones and Beverly Milton-Edwards, write that "if Israel wishes to be both Jewish and democratic," it must embrace "the two-state solution."[2]

It is easy to cite many other examples, but unnecessary, because it is assumed almost universally that there are two options for mandatory Palestine: either two states—Palestinian and Jewish-democratic—or one state "from the sea to the river." Israeli commentators express concern about the "demographic problem": too many Palestinians in a Jewish state. Many Palestinians and their advocates support the "one-state solution," anticipating a civil-rights, anti-apartheid struggle that will lead to secular democracy. Other analysts also consistently pose the options in similar terms.

This analysis is almost universal, but crucially flawed. There is a third option—namely, the option that Israel is pursuing with constant U.S. support—and this third option is the only realistic alternative to the two-state settlement.

It makes sense, in my opinion, to contemplate a future binational secular democracy in the former Palestine, from the sea to the river. For what it's worth, that is what I have advocated for seventy years. But I stress "advocated." Advocacy, as distinct from mere proposal, requires sketching a path from here to there. The forms of true advocacy have changed with shifting circumstances. Since the mid-1970s, when Palestinian national rights became a salient issue, the only plausible form of advocacy has been as a staged process beginning with a two-state settlement. No other path has been suggested that has even a remote chance of success. Proposing a binational ("one state") settlement without moving on to advocacy in effect provides support for the third option, the realistic one taking shape before our eyes. Israel is systematically extending plans that were sketched and initiated shortly after the 1967 war, and institutionalized more fully with the accession to power of Menachem Begin's Likud party a decade later.

The first step was to create what Yonatan Mendel has called "a disturbing new city" still named "Jerusalem" but extending far beyond historic Jerusalem, incorporating dozens of Palestinian villages and surrounding lands, and now designated as a Jewish city and the capital of Israel.[3] All of this is in direct violation of explicit Security Council orders. A corridor to the east of this new Greater Jerusalem incorporates the town of Ma'aleh Adumim (established in the 1970s but built primarily after the 1993 Oslo Accords), with lands reaching virtually to Jericho, thus effectively bisecting the West Bank. Corridors to the north incorporating the settler towns of Ariel and Kedumim further divide what is to remain under some degree of Palestinian control.[4]

Meanwhile, Israel is incorporating the territory on the Israeli side of the illegal "separation wall" (in reality an annexation wall), taking arable land and water resources and many villages, strangling the town of Qalqilya, and separating Palestinian villagers from their fields. In what Israel calls "the seam" between the wall and the border, close to 10 percent of the West Bank, anyone is permitted to enter—except Palestinians. Those who live in the region have to go through an intricate bureaucratic procedure to gain temporary entry. Exiting—for example, in order to receive medical care—is hampered in the same way. The result, predictably, has been severe disruption of Palestinian lives and, according to UN reports, a decrease of more than 80 percent in the number of farmers who routinely cultivate their lands and a decline of 60 percent in the total yield of olive orchards, among other harmful effects.[5] The pretext for the wall was security, but that means security for illegal Jewish settlers; about 85 percent of the wall runs through the occupied West Bank.[6]

Israel is also taking over the Jordan Valley, thus fully imprisoning the cantons that remain. Huge infrastructure projects link settlers to Israel's urban centers, ensuring that they will see no Palestinians. Following a traditional neocolonial model, a modern center remains for Palestinian elites in Ramallah, while the remainder of the population mostly languishes.

To complete the separation of Greater Jerusalem from remaining Palestinian cantons, Israel would have to take over the E1 region. So far that action has been barred by Washington, and Israel has been compelled to resort to subterfuges, like building a police station there. Obama is the first U.S. president to have imposed no limits on Israeli actions. It remains to be seen whether he will permit Israel to take over E1—perhaps with expressions of discontent and a diplomatic wink to make it clear that these are not seriously intended.

There are regular expulsions of Palestinians. In the Jordan Valley alone, the population has been reduced from three hundred thousand in 1967 to sixty thousand today, and similar processes are under way elsewhere.[7] Following policies that go back a century, each action is limited in scope so as not to arouse too much international attention, but they have a cumulative effect and intent that are quite clear.

Furthermore, ever since the Oslo Accords declared that Gaza and the West Bank are an indivisible territorial unity, the U.S.–Israeli duo have been committed to separating the two regions. One significant effect is to ensure that any limited Palestinian entity will have no access to the outside world.

In the areas that Israel is taking over, the Palestinian population is small and scattered and is being reduced further by regular expulsions. The result will be a Greater Israel with a substantial Jewish majority. Under this third option, there will be no "demographic problem" and no civil-rights or anti-apartheid struggle—nothing more than what already exists within Israel's recognized borders, where the mantra "Jewish and democratic" is regularly intoned for the benefit of those who choose to believe, oblivious to the inherent contradiction, which is far more than merely symbolic.

Unless achieved in stages, the one-state option will prove to be an illusion. It has no international support, and there is no reason why Israel and its U.S. sponsor would accept it.

The question, often raised, of whether the hawkish prime minister Benjamin Netanyahu would accept a "Palestinian state" is misleading. In fact, his administration was the first to countenance this possibility when it came into office in 1996, following those of Yitzhak Rabin and Shimon Peres, which rejected it. Netanyahu's director of communications and policy planning, David Bar-Illan, explained that some areas would be left to Palestinians, and if they wanted to call them "a state," Israel would not object—or they could call them "fried chicken."[8] His response reflects the operative attitude of the U.S.-Israeli coalition to Palestinian rights.

The United States and Israel call for negotiations without preconditions. Commentary in both countries and elsewhere in the West typically claims that the Palestinians are imposing such preconditions and so hampering the "peace process." In reality, it is the United States and Israel that insist upon crucial preconditions. The first is that negotiations must be mediated by the United States, whereas any authentic negotiations would, of course, have to be in the hands of some neutral state with a degree of international respect. The second precondition is that illegal settlement expansion must be allowed to continue, as has happened without a break during the twenty years following the Oslo Accords.

In the early years of the occupation the United States joined the world in regarding the settlements as illegal, as confirmed by the UN Security Council and the International Court of Justice. Since the Reagan years, their status has been downgraded to "a barrier to peace." Obama has weakened the designation further, to "not helpful to peace."[9] Obama's extreme rejectionism did arouse some attention in February 2011, when he vetoed a Security Council resolution supporting official U.S. policy, which calls for the ending of settlement expansion.[10]

As long as these preconditions remain in force, diplomacy is likely to remain at a standstill. With brief and rare exceptions, that has been true since January 1976, when the United States vetoed a Security Council resolution, brought by Egypt, Jordan, and Syria, calling for a two-state settlement on the internationally recognized border, the Green Line, with guarantees for the security of all states within acknowledged and stable borders.[11] That is essentially the international consensus that is by now universal, with the two usual exceptions. The consensus has been modified to include "minor and mutual adjustments" on the Green Line, to borrow official U.S. wording before it had broken with the rest of the world.[12]

The same is true of any negotiations that may take place in Washington or take place elsewhere overseen by Washington. Given these preconditions, little can be achieved other than letting Israel carry forward its project of taking over whatever it finds valuable in the West Bank and the Syrian Golan Heights, annexed in violation of Security Council orders, while maintaining the siege of Gaza. One can, of course, hope for better, but it is hard to be optimistic.

Europe could play a role in advancing the world's aspirations for a peaceful diplomatic settlement if it were willing to pursue an independent path. The European Union decision to exclude West Bank settlements from any future deals with Israel might be a step in this direction. U.S. policies are also not graven in stone, though they have deep strategic, economic, and cultural roots. In the absence of such changes, there is every reason to expect that the picture from the river to the sea will conform to the third option. Palestinian rights and aspirations will be shelved, temporarily at least.

If the Israel-Palestine conflict is not resolved, a regional peace settlement is highly unlikely. That failure has far broader implications—in particular for what U.S. media call "the gravest threat to world peace": Iran's nuclear programs. The implications become clearer when we look at the most obvious ways to deal with the alleged threat and their fate. It is useful, first, to consider a few preliminary questions: Who regards the threat as being of such cosmic significance? And what is the perceived threat?

The Iran "threat" is overwhelmingly a Western obsession; the non-aligned countries—most of the world—have vigorously supported Iran's right, as a signer of the Non-Proliferation Treaty (NPT), to enrich uranium.[13] In Western discourse, it is commonly claimed that the Arabs support the U.S. position regarding Iran, but the reference is to Arab dictators, not the general population. Also standard is reference to "the standoff between the international community and Iran," to quote from the current scholarly literature. Here the phrase "international community" refers to the United States and whoever happens to go along with it—in this case, a small minority of the international community, but many more if political stands are weighted by power.

What then is the perceived threat? An authoritative answer is given by U.S. intelligence and the Pentagon in their regular reviews of global security. They conclude that Iran is not a military threat. It has low military expenditures even by the standards of the region and limited capacity to deploy force. Its strategic doctrine is defensive, designed to resist attack. The intelligence community reports no evidence that Iran is developing nuclear weapons, but if it is, they conclude, that would be part of Iran's deterrent strategy.

It is hard to think of a country in the world that needs a deterrent more than Iran. It has been tormented by the West without respite ever since its parliamentary regime was overthrown by a U.S.-British military coup in 1953, first under the harsh and brutal regime of the shah, then under murderous attack by Saddam Hussein with Western support.[14] It was largely U.S. intervention that induced Iran to capitulate in its war with Iraq, and shortly after, President George H. W. Bush invited Iraqi nuclear engineers to the United States for training in advanced weapons production, an extraordinary threat to Iran.[15]

Iraq soon became an enemy of the United States, but meanwhile Iran was subjected to harsh sanctions, intensifying under U.S. initiative. It was also constantly subjected to the threat of military attack by the United States and Israel—in violation of the UN Charter, if anyone cares.

It is, however, understandable that the United States and Israel would regard an Iranian deterrent as an intolerable threat. It would limit their ability to control the region, by violence if they choose, as they often have. That is the essence of the perceived Iranian threat.

That the clerical regime is a threat to its own people is hardly in doubt, though regrettably it is hardly alone in that regard. But it goes well beyond naïveté to believe that Iran's internal repression is much of a concern to the great powers.

Whatever one thinks of the threat, are there ways to mitigate it? Quite a few, in fact. One of the most reasonable, as I have said elsewhere, would be to move toward establishing a nuclear weapons–free zone in the region. Arab states and others call for immediate moves to eliminate weapons of mass destruction as a step toward regional security. The United States and Israel, in contrast, reverse the order, and demand regional security—meaning security for Israel—as a prerequisite to eliminating such weapons. In the not-very-remote background is the understanding that Israel, alone in the region, has an advanced nuclear weapons system and also refuses to join the NPT, along with India and Pakistan, both of whom similarly benefit from U.S. support for their nuclear arsenals.

The connection of the Israel-Palestine conflict to the alleged Iranian threat is therefore clear. As long as the United States and Israel persist in their rejectionist stance, blocking the international consensus on a two-state settlement, there will be no regional security arrangements, hence no moves toward establishing a nuclear weapons–free zone and mitigating, perhaps even ending, what the United States and Israel claim to be the gravest threat to peace—at least to do so in the most obvious and far-reaching way.

It should be noted that, along with Britain, the United States has a special responsibility to devote its efforts to establishing a Middle East nuclear weapons–free zone. When attempting to provide a thin legal cover for their invasion of Iraq in 2003, the two aggressors appealed to UN Security Council Resolution 687 of 1991, claiming that Saddam Hussein had violated the demand to end his nuclear weapons programs. The resolution also has another paragraph, calling for "steps towards the goal of establishing in the Middle East a zone free from weapons of mass destruction"—obligating the United States and United Kingdom even more than others to take this initiative seriously.[16]

These comments naturally leave out many urgent topics, among them the horrifying descent of Syria into suicide and ominous developments in Egypt, which are sure to have a regional impact. Nonetheless, this is how some of the core issues appear, to me at least.

12

"Nothing for Other People":
Class War in the United States

Norman Ware's classic study of the industrial worker appeared ninety years ago, the first of its kind.[1] It has lost none of its significance. The lessons Ware draws from his close investigation of the impact of the emerging industrial revolution on the lives of working people, and on society in general, are just as pertinent today as when he wrote, if not more so, in the light of the striking parallels between the 1920s and today.

It is important to remember the condition of working people when Ware wrote. The powerful and influential American labor movement that arose during the nineteenth century was being subjected to brutal attack, culminating in Woodrow Wilson's Red Scare after World War I. By the 1920s, the movement had largely been decimated; a classic study by the eminent labor historian David Montgomery is entitled *The Fall of the House of Labor*. The fall occurred in the 1920s. By the end of the decade, he writes, "corporate mastery of American life seemed secure. . . . Rationalization of business could then proceed with indispensable government support," with government largely in the hands of the corporate sector. [2] It was far from a peaceful process; American labor history is unusually violent. One scholarly study concludes that "the United

States had more deaths at the end of the nineteenth century due to labor violence—in absolute terms and in proportion to population size—than any other country except Czarist Russia."[3] The term "labor violence" is a polite way of referring to violence by state and private security forces targeting working people. That continued into the late 1930s; I can remember such scenes from my childhood.

As a result, Montgomery wrote, "modern America had been created over its workers' protests, even though every step in its formation had been influenced by the activities, organizations, and proposals that had sprung from working class life," not to speak of the hands and brains of those who did the work.[4]

The labor movement revived during the Great Depression, significantly influencing legislation and striking fear into the hearts of industrialists. In their publications the industrialists warned of the "hazard" facing them from labor action backed by "the newly realized political power of the masses."

Though violent repression did not end, it was no longer adequate to the task. It was necessary to devise more subtle means to ensure corporate rule, primarily a flood of sophisticated propaganda and "scientific methods of strike breaking," developed into a high art by the enterprises that specialize in the task.[5]

We should not forget Adam Smith's perspicuous observation that the "masters of mankind"—in his day, the merchants and manufacturers of England—never cease to pursue their "vile maxim": "All for ourselves, and nothing for other people."[6]

The business counterattack was put on hold during World War II, but quickly revived afterward, with harsh legislation passed restricting workers' rights and an extraordinary propaganda campaign aimed at factories, schools, churches, and every other form of association. Every available means of communication was employed. By the 1980s, with the bitterly antilabor Reagan administration, the attack was again underway in full force. President Reagan made it clear to the business world that the laws protecting labor rights, never very strong, would not be enforced. The illegal firing of union organizers skyrocketed, and the

United States returned to the use of scabs, outlawed almost everywhere in developed countries except South Africa. The liberal Clinton administration undermined labor in different ways. One highly effective means was the creation of the North American Free Trade Agreement (NAFTA) linking Canada, Mexico, and the United States.

For propaganda purposes, NAFTA was labeled a "free-trade agreement." It was nothing of the sort. Like other such agreements, it had strong protectionist elements and much of it was not about trade at all; it was an investors' rights agreement. And like other such "free-trade agreements," this one predictably proved harmful to working people in the participating countries. One effect was to undermine labor organizing: a study conducted under NAFTA auspices revealed that successful organizing declined sharply, thanks to such practices as management warnings that if an enterprise were unionized, it would be transferred to Mexico.[7] Such practices are, of course, illegal, but that is irrelevant as long as business can count on the "indispensable government support" to which Montgomery referred.

By such means, private sector unions were driven down to less than 7 percent of the workforce, despite the fact that most working people prefer unions.[8] The attack then turned to public-sector unions that had been somewhat protected by legislation. That unraveling is now fiercely under way, and not for the first time. We may recall that Martin Luther King Jr. was assassinated in 1968 while supporting a strike of public-sector workers in Memphis, Tennessee.

In many respects, the condition of working people when Ware wrote was similar to what we see today as inequality has again reached the astonishing heights of the late 1920s. For a tiny minority, wealth has accumulated beyond the dreams of avarice. In the past decade, 95 percent of growth has gone into the pockets of 1 percent of the population—mostly a fraction of these.[9] Median real income is below its level of twenty-five years ago. For males, median real income is below what it was in 1968.[10] The labor share of output has fallen to its lowest level since World War II.[11] This is not the result of the mysterious workings of the market or economic laws but, again, largely of the "indispensable" support and initiative of a government that is significantly in corporate hands.

The American industrial revolution, Ware observed, created "one of the major notes of American life" in the 1840s and 1850s. While its ultimate outcome may be "pleasing enough in modern eyes, it was repugnant to an astonishingly large section of the earlier American community." Ware reviews the hideous working conditions imposed on formerly independent craftsmen and farmers, as well as the "factory girls," young women from the farms working in the textile mills around Boston. But his primary focus is on more fundamental features of the revolution that persisted even as specific conditions were ameliorated in the course of dedicated struggles over many years.

Ware emphasized "the degradation suffered by the industrial worker," the loss "of status and independence" that had been their most treasured possession as free citizens of the republic, a loss that could not be compensated for even by material improvement. He explores the devastating impact of the radical capitalist "social revolution in which sovereignty in economic affairs passed from the community as a whole into the keeping of a special class" of masters, a group "alien to the producers" and generally remote from production. He shows that "for every protest against machine industry, there can be found a hundred against the new power of capitalist production and its discipline."

Workers were striking not just for bread but for roses, to borrow the traditional labor slogan. They sought dignity and independence, recognition of their rights as free men and women. They created a lively and independent labor press, written and produced by those who toiled in the mills. In their journals they condemned "the blasting influence of monarchical principles on democratic soil." They recognized that this assault on elementary human rights would not be overcome until "they who work in the mills own them," and sovereignty returns to free producers. Then working people will no longer be "menials or the humble subjects of a foreign despot, [the absentee owners], slaves in the strictest sense of the word [who] toil . . . for their masters." Rather, they will regain their status as "free American citizens."[12]

The capitalist revolution instituted a crucial change from price to wage. When the producer sold his product for a price, Ware writes, "he retained his person. But when he came to sell his labor, he sold himself," and lost his dignity as a person as he became a slave—a "wage slave," the term commonly used. Wage labor was considered similar to chattel slavery, though differing in that it was temporary—in theory. That understanding was so widespread that it became a slogan of the Republican Party, advocated by its leading figure, Abraham Lincoln.[13]

The concept that productive enterprises should be owned by the workforce was common coin in the mid-nineteenth century, not just by Marx and the left but also by the most prominent classical liberal figure of the day, John Stuart Mill. Mill held that "the form of association, however, which if mankind continue to improve, must be expected to predominate is . . . the association of the labourers themselves on terms of equality, collectively owning the capital with which they carry on their operations, and working under managers electable and removable by themselves."[14] The concept indeed has solid roots in insights that animated classical liberal thought. It is a short step to link it to control of other institutions and of communities within a framework of free association and federal organization, in the general style of a range of thought that includes, along with much of the anarchist tradition and left anti-Bolshevik Marxism, also G. D. H. Cole's guild socialism and much more recent theoretical work.[15] And still more significantly, it includes actions as workers in many walks of life seek to gain control over their lives and fate.

To undermine these subversive doctrines, it was necessary for the "masters of mankind" to try to change the attitudes and beliefs that foster them. As Ware reports, labor activists warned of the new "Spirit of the Age: Gain Wealth, forgetting all but Self"—the vile maxim of the masters, which they naturally sought to impose on their subjects as well, knowing that they would be able to gain very little of the available wealth. In sharp reaction to this demeaning spirit, the rising movements of working people and radical farmers, the most significant democratic popular movements in American history, were dedicated to solidarity and mutual aid.[16] They were defeated, mostly by force. But the battle is far from over, despite setbacks, often violent repression, and massive efforts to instill the vile maxim in the public mind, with the resources of educational systems, the huge advertising industry, and other propaganda institutions dedicated to the task.

There are serious barriers to overcome in the struggle for justice, freedom, and dignity, even beyond the bitter class war conducted ceaselessly by the highly class-conscious business world with the "indispensable support" of the governments they largely control. Ware discusses some of these insidious threats as they were understood by working people. He reports the thinking of skilled workers in New York 170 years ago, who repeated the common view that a daily wage is a form of slavery and warned perceptively that a day might come when wage slaves "will so far forget what is due to manhood as to glory in a system forced on them by their necessity and in opposition to their feelings of independence and self-respect."[17] They hoped that that day would be "far distant." Today, signs of it are common, but demands for independence, self-respect, personal dignity, and control of one's own work and life, like Marx's old mole, continue to burrow not far from the surface, ready to reappear when awakened by circumstances and militant activism.

13

Whose Security? How Washington Protects Itself and the Corporate Sector

The question of how foreign policy is determined is a crucial one in world affairs. In these comments, I can only provide a few hints as to how I think the subject can be productively explored, keeping to the United States for several reasons. First, the United States is unmatched in its global significance and impact. Second, it is an unusually open society, possibly uniquely so, which means we know more about it. Finally, it is plainly the most important case for Americans, who are able to influence policy choices in the United States—and indeed for others, insofar as their actions can influence such choices. The general principles, however, extend to the other major powers and well beyond.

There is a "received standard version," common to academic scholarship, government pronouncements, and public discourse. It holds that the prime commitment of governments is to ensure security, and that the primary concern of the United States and its allies from 1945 was the Russian threat.

There are a number of ways to evaluate this doctrine. One obvious question to ask is: What happened when the Russian threat disappeared in 1989? The answer: everything continued much as before.

The United States immediately invaded Panama, killing possibly thousands of people and installing a client regime. This was routine practice in U.S.-dominated domains—but in this case not quite as routine. For the first time, a major foreign policy act was not justified by an alleged Russian threat.

Instead, a series of fraudulent pretexts for the invasion were concocted that collapse instantly on examination. The media chimed in enthusiastically, lauding the magnificent achievement of defeating Panama, unconcerned that the pretexts were ludicrous, that the act itself was a radical violation of international law, and that it was bitterly condemned elsewhere, most harshly in Latin America. Also ignored was the U.S. veto of a unanimous Security Council resolution condemning crimes by U.S. troops during the invasion, with Britain alone abstaining.[1]

All routine. And all forgotten (which is also routine).

FROM EL SALVADOR TO THE RUSSIAN BORDER

The administration of George H. W. Bush issued a new national security policy and defense budget in reaction to the collapse of the global enemy. It was pretty much the same as before, although with new pretexts. It was, it turned out, necessary to maintain a military establishment almost as great as the rest of the world combined and far more advanced in technological sophistication—but not for defense against the disappearing Soviet Union. Rather, the excuse was the growing "technological sophistication" of Third World powers.[2] Disciplined intellectuals understood that it would have been improper to collapse in ridicule, so they maintained a proper silence.

The United States, the new policy insisted, must maintain its "defense industrial base." The phrase is a euphemism, referring to high-tech industry generally, which relies heavily on extensive state intervention for research and development, often under Pentagon cover, in what many economists continue to call the U.S. "free-market economy."

One of the most interesting provisions of the new plans had to do with the Middle East. There, it was declared, Washington must maintain intervention forces targeting a crucial region where the major problems "could not have been laid at the Kremlin's door." Contrary to fifty years of deceit, it was quietly conceded that the main concern in this region was not the Russians, but rather what is called "radical nationalism," meaning independent nationalism not under U.S. control.[3]

All of this has evident bearing on the received standard version, but it passed unnoticed—or, perhaps, *therefore* it passed unnoticed.

Other important events took place immediately after the fall of the Berlin Wall, ending the Cold War. One was in El Salvador, the leading recipient of U.S. military aid—apart from Israel and Egypt, a separate category—and with one of the worst human rights records anywhere. That is a familiar and very close correlation.

The Salvadoran high command ordered the Atlacatl Battalion to invade the Jesuit university and murder six leading Latin American intellectuals, all Jesuit priests, including the rector, Fr. Ignacio Ellacuría, and any witnesses, meaning their housekeeper and her daughter. The battalion had already left a bloody trail of thousands of the usual victims in the course of the U.S.-run state terror campaign in El Salvador, part of a broader terror and torture campaign throughout the region.[4] All routine, ignored and virtually forgotten in the United States and by its allies—again routine. But it tells us a lot about the factors that drive policy, if we care to look at the real world.

Another important event took place in Europe. Soviet president Mikhail Gorbachev agreed to allow the reunification of Germany and its membership in NATO, a hostile military alliance. In light of recent history, this was a most astonishing concession. There was a quid pro quo: President Bush and Secretary of State James Baker agreed that NATO would not expand "one inch to the East," meaning into East Germany. Instantly, they expanded NATO to East Germany.

Gorbachev was naturally outraged, but when he complained, he was instructed by Washington that this had only been a verbal promise, a gentleman's agreement, hence without force.[5] If he was naïve enough to accept the word of American leaders, it was his problem.

All of this, too, was routine, as was the silent acceptance and approval of the expansion of NATO in the United States and the West generally. President Bill Clinton then expanded NATO right up to Russia's borders. Today, the world faces a serious crisis that is in no small measure a result of these policies.

THE APPEAL OF PLUNDERING THE POOR

Another source of evidence is the declassified historical record. It contains revealing accounts of the actual motives of state policy. The story is rich and complex, but a few persistent themes play a dominant role. One was articulated clearly at a western hemispheric conference called by the United States in Mexico in February 1945, where Washington imposed an "Economic Charter of the Americas" designed to eliminate economic nationalism "in all its forms."[6] There was one unspoken exception: economic nationalism would be fine for the United States, whose economy relies heavily on massive state intervention.

The elimination of economic nationalism for others stood in sharp conflict with the Latin American stand of that moment, which State Department officials described as "the philosophy of the New Nationalism [that] embraces policies designed to bring about a broader distribution of wealth and to raise the standard of living of the masses."[7] As U.S. policy analysts added, "Latin Americans are convinced that the first beneficiaries of the development of a country's resources should be the people of that country."[8]

That, of course, will not do. Washington understands that the "first beneficiaries" should be U.S. investors, while Latin America fulfills its service function. It should not, as both the Truman and Eisenhower administrations would make clear, undergo "excessive industrial development" that might infringe on U.S. interests. Thus Brazil could produce low-quality steel that U.S. corporations did not want to bother with, but it would be "excessive" were it to compete with U.S. firms.

Similar concerns resonate throughout the post–World War II period. The global system that was to be dominated by the United States was threatened by what internal documents call "radical and nationalistic regimes" that responded to popular pressures for independent development.[9] That was the concern that motivated the overthrow of the parliamentary governments of Iran and Guatemala in 1953 and 1954, as well as numerous others. In the case of Iran, a major concern was the potential impact of Iranian independence on Egypt, then in turmoil over British colonial practices. In Guatemala, apart from the crime of the new democracy in empowering the peasant majority and infringing on possessions of the United Fruit Company—already offensive enough—Washington's concern was labor unrest and popular mobilization in neighboring U.S.-backed dictatorships.

In both cases the consequences reach to the present. Literally not a day has passed since 1953 when the United States has not been torturing the people of Iran. Guatemala remains one of the world's worst horror chambers; to this day, Mayans are fleeing from the effects of near-genocidal government military campaigns in the highlands backed by President Ronald Reagan and his top officials. As the country director of Oxfam, a Guatemalan doctor, reported in 2014, "There is a dramatic deterioration of the political, social and economic context. Attacks against [human rights] defenders have increased 300 percent during the last year. There is a clear evidence of a very well organized strategy by the private sector and Army, both have captured the government in order to keep the status quo and to impose the extraction economical model, pushing away dramatically Indigenous peoples from their own land, due to the mining industry, African Palm and sugar cane plantations. In addition the social movement defending their land and rights has been criminalized, many leaders are in jail and many others have been killed." [10]

Nothing is known about this in the United States, and the very obvious cause of it remains suppressed.

In the 1950s, President Eisenhower and Secretary of State John

Foster Dulles explained quite clearly the dilemma that the United States faced. They complained that the Communists had an unfair advantage: they were able to "appeal directly to the masses" and "get control of mass movements, something we have no capacity to duplicate. The poor people are the ones they appeal to and they have always wanted to plunder the rich."[11]

That causes problems. The United States somehow finds it difficult to appeal to the poor with its doctrine that the rich should plunder the poor.

THE CUBAN EXAMPLE

A clear illustration of the general pattern was Cuba, when it finally gained independence in 1959. Within months, military attacks on the island began. Shortly after, the Eisenhower administration made a secret decision to overthrow the government. John F. Kennedy then became president. He intended to devote more attention to Latin America and so, on taking office, he created a study group to develop policies that was headed by the historian Arthur M. Schlesinger Jr., who summarized its conclusions for the incoming president.

As Schlesinger explained, what was threatening in an independent Cuba was "the Castro idea of taking matters into one's own hands." It was an idea that unfortunately appealed to the mass of the population in Latin America, where "the distribution of land and other forms of national wealth greatly favors the propertied classes, and the poor and underprivileged, stimulated by the example of the Cuban revolution, are now demanding opportunities for a decent living."[12] Again, Washington's usual dilemma.

As the CIA explained, "The extensive influence of 'Castroism' is not a function of Cuban power . . . Castro's shadow looms large because social and economic conditions throughout Latin America invite opposition to ruling authority and encourage agitation for radical change," for which his Cuba provided a model.[13] Kennedy feared that Russian aid might make Cuba a "showcase" for development, giving the Soviets the upper hand throughout Latin America.[14]

The State Department Policy Planning Staff warned that "the primary danger we face in Castro is . . . in the impact the very existence of his regime has upon the leftist movement in many Latin American countries. . . . The simple fact is that Castro represents a successful defiance of the United States, a negation of our whole hemispheric policy of almost a century and a half"—that is, since the Monroe Doctrine of 1823, when the United States declared its intention of dominating the hemisphere.[15]

The immediate goal at the time of the doctrine was to conquer Cuba, but that could not be achieved because of the power of the British enemy. Still, that grand strategist John Quincy Adams, the intellectual father of the Monroe Doctrine and Manifest Destiny, informed his colleagues that over time Cuba would fall into our hands by "the laws of political gravitation," as an apple falls from the tree.[16] In brief, U.S. power would increase and Britain's would decline.

In 1898, Adams's prognosis was realized: the United States invaded Cuba in the guise of liberating it. In fact, it prevented the island's liberation from Spain and turned it into a "virtual colony," to quote historians Ernest May and Philip Zelikow.[17] Cuba remained a virtual U.S. colony until January 1959, when it gained independence. Since that time it has been subjected to major U.S. terrorist wars, primarily during the Kennedy years, and economic strangulation—and not because of the Russians.

The pretense all along was that we were defending ourselves from the Russian threat—an absurd explanation that generally went unchallenged. A simple test of the thesis, again, is what happened when any conceivable Russian threat disappeared: U.S. policy toward Cuba became even harsher, spearheaded by liberal Democrats, including Bill Clinton, who outflanked Bush from the right in the 1992 election. On the face of it, these events should have considerable bearing on the validity of the doctrinal framework for discussion of foreign policy and the factors that drive it. Once again, however, the impact is slight.

THE VIRUS OF NATIONALISM

Henry Kissinger caught the essence of the real foreign policy of the United States when he termed independent nationalism a "virus" that might "spread contagion."[18] Kissinger was referring to Salvador Allende's Chile; the virus was the idea that there might be a parliamentary path toward some kind of socialist democracy. The way to deal with such a threat was to destroy the virus and inoculate those who might be infected, typically by imposing murderous national-security states. That was achieved in the case of Chile, but it is important to recognize that the thinking held, and still holds, worldwide.

It was, for example, the reasoning behind the decision to oppose Vietnamese nationalism in the early 1950s and support France's effort to reconquer its former colony. It was feared that independent Vietnamese nationalism might be a virus that would spread contagion to the surrounding regions, including resource-rich Indonesia. That might even have led Japan to become the industrial and commercial center of an independent new order of the kind imperial Japan had so recently fought to establish. The remedy was clear—and largely achieved. Vietnam was virtually destroyed and ringed by military dictatorships that kept the "virus" from spreading contagion.

The same was true in Latin America in the same years: one virus after another was viciously attacked and either destroyed or weakened to the point of bare survival. From the early 1960s, a plague of repression was imposed on the continent that had no precedent in the violent history of the hemisphere, extending to Central America in the 1980s, a matter that there should be no need to review.

Much the same was true in the Middle East. The unique U.S. relations with Israel were established in their current form in 1967 when Israel delivered a smashing blow to Egypt, the center of secular Arab nationalism. By doing so, it protected U.S. ally Saudi Arabia, then engaged in military conflict with Egypt in Yemen. Saudi Arabia, of course, is the most extreme radical fundamentalist Islamic state, and also a missionary state, expending huge sums to establish its Wahhabi-

Salafi doctrines beyond its borders. It is worth remembering that the United States, like England before it, has tended to support radical fundamentalist Islam in opposition to secular nationalism, which has until recently been perceived as posing more of a threat of independence and contagion.

THE VALUE OF SECRECY

There is much more to say, but the historical record demonstrates very clearly that the standard doctrine has little merit. Security in the normal sense is not a prominent factor in policy formation.

To repeat: "in the normal sense." But in evaluating the standard doctrine we have to ask what is actually meant by "security": Security for whom?

One answer is: security for state power. There are many illustrations. In May 2014, for example, the United States agreed to support a UN Security Council resolution calling on the International Criminal Court to investigate war crimes in Syria, but with a proviso: there could be no inquiry into possible war crimes by Israel.[19] Or by Washington, though it was unnecessary to add that last condition; the United States is uniquely self-immunized from the international legal system. In fact, there is even congressional legislation authorizing the president to use armed force to "rescue" any American brought to the Hague for trial—the "Netherlands Invasion Act," as it is sometimes called in Europe.[20] That once again illustrates the importance of protecting the security of state power.

But protecting it from whom? There is, in fact, a strong case to be made that a prime concern of government is the security of state power from the population. As those who have spent time rummaging through archives should be aware, government secrecy is rarely motivated by a genuine need for security, but it definitely does serve to keep the population in the dark. And for good reasons, which were lucidly explained by prominent liberal scholar and government adviser Samuel Huntington.

In his words: "The architects of power in the United States must create a force that can be felt but not seen. Power remains strong when it remains in the dark; exposed to the sunlight it begins to evaporate."[21]

Huntington wrote that in 1981, when the Cold War was again heating up, and he explained further that "you may have to sell [intervention or other military action] in such a way as to create the misimpression that it is the Soviet Union that you are fighting. That is what the United States has been doing ever since the Truman Doctrine."[22]

These simple truths are rarely acknowledged, but they provide insight into state power and policy, with reverberations to the present moment.

State power has to be protected from its domestic enemy; in sharp contrast, the population is not secure from state power. A striking illustration is the radical attack on the Constitution by the Obama administration's massive surveillance program. It is, of course, justified by "national security." That is routine for virtually all actions of all states and so carries little information.

When the NSA's surveillance program was exposed by Edward Snowden's revelations, high officials claimed that it had prevented fifty-four terrorist acts. On inquiry, that was whittled down to a dozen. A high-level government panel then discovered that there was actually only one case: someone had sent $8,500 to Somalia. That was the total yield of the huge assault on the Constitution and, of course, on others throughout the world.[23]

Britain's attitude is interesting: in 2007, the British government called on Washington's colossal spy agency "to analyze and retain any British citizens' mobile phone and fax numbers, emails, and IP addresses swept up by its dragnet," the *Guardian* reported.[24] That is a useful indication of the relative significance, in government eyes, of the privacy of its own citizens and of Washington's demands.

Another concern is security for private power. One illustration is the huge trade agreements—the trans-Pacific and trans-Atlantic pacts—now being negotiated. These are being negotiated "in secret"—but not completely in secret. They are not secret from the hundreds of corporate lawyers who are drawing up the detailed provisions. It is not hard to guess what the results will be, and the few leaks about them suggest that the expectations are accurate. Like NAFTA and other such pacts, these are not free-trade agreements. In fact, they are not even trade agreements, but primarily investor-rights agreements.

Again, secrecy is critically important to protect the primary domestic constituency of the governments involved: the corporate sector.

THE FINAL CENTURY OF HUMAN CIVILIZATION?

There are other examples too numerous to mention, facts that are well established and would be taught in elementary schools in free societies.

There is, in other words, ample evidence that securing state power from the domestic population and securing concentrated private power are driving forces in policy formation. Of course, it is not quite that simple. There are interesting cases, some quite current, where these commitments conflict, but we can consider this to be a good first approximation, and one radically opposed to the received standard doctrine.

Let us turn to another question: What about the security of the population? It is easy to demonstrate that this is of marginal concern to policy planners. Take two prominent current examples, global warming and nuclear weapons. As any literate person is doubtless aware, these are dire threats to the security of the population. Turning to state policy, we find that it is committed to accelerating each of those threats—in the interests of its primary concerns, protection of state power and of the concentrated private power that largely determines state policy.

Consider global warming. There is now much exuberance in the United States about "a hundred years of energy independence" as we become "the Saudi Arabia of the next century"—perhaps the final century of human civilization if current policies persist.

That illustrates very clearly the nature of the concern for security—certainly not for the population. It also illustrates the moral calculus of contemporary state capitalism: the fate of our grandchildren counts as nothing when compared with the imperative of higher profits tomorrow.

These conclusions are fortified by a closer look at the propaganda system. There is a huge public relations campaign in the United States, organized quite openly by Big Energy and the business world, to try to convince the public that global warming is either unreal or not a result of human activity. And it has had some impact. The United States ranks lower than other countries in public concern about global warming, and the results are stratified: among Republicans, the party more fully dedicated to the interests of wealth and corporate power, it ranks far lower than the global norm.[25]

The premier journal of media criticism, the *Columbia Journalism Review*, had an interesting article on the subject attributing this outcome to the media doctrine of "fair and balanced."[26] In other words, if a journal publishes an opinion piece reflecting the conclusions of 97 percent of scientists, it must also run a counter-piece expressing the viewpoint of the energy corporations.

That indeed is what happens, but there certainly is no "fair and balanced" doctrine. Thus, if a journal runs an opinion piece denouncing Russian President Vladimir Putin for the criminal act of taking over the Crimea, it surely does not have to run a piece pointing out that, while the act is indeed criminal, Russia has a far stronger case today than the United States did more than a century ago in taking over southeastern Cuba, including Guantánamo, the country's major port—and rejecting the Cuban demand since independence to have it returned. And the same is true of many other cases. The actual media doctrine is "fair and balanced" when the concerns of concentrated private power are involved, but surely not elsewhere.

On the issue of nuclear weapons, the record is similarly interesting—and frightening. It reveals very clearly that, from the earliest days, the security of the population was a nonissue, and remains so. There is no need here to run through the shocking record, but there is little doubt that policymakers have been playing roulette with the fate of the species.

As we are all surely aware, we now face the most ominous decisions in human history. There are many problems that must be addressed, but two are overwhelming in their significance: environmental destruction and nuclear war. For the first time in history, we face the possibility of destroying the prospects for decent existence—and not in the distant future. For this reason alone, it is imperative to sweep away the ideological clouds and face honestly and realistically the question of how policy decisions are made, and what we can do to alter them before it is too late.

14

Outrage

Almost every day brings news of awful crimes, but some are so heinous, so horrendous and malicious, that they dwarf all else. One of those rare events took place when Malaysia Airlines Flight 17 was shot down in eastern Ukraine, killing 298 people.

The Guardian of Virtue in the White House denounced it as an "outrage of unspeakable proportions," which he attributed to "Russian support."[1] His UN ambassador thundered that "when 298 civilians are killed" in the "horrific downing" of a civilian plane, "we must stop at nothing to determine who is responsible and to bring them to justice." She also called on Vladimir Putin to end his shameful efforts to evade his very clear responsibility.[2]

True, the "irritating little man" with the "ratlike face"—as Timothy Garton Ash described him—had called for an independent investigation, but that could only have been because of sanctions from the one country courageous enough to impose them, the United States, while Europeans cowered in fear.[3]

On CNN, former U.S. ambassador to Ukraine William Taylor assured the world that the irritating little man "is clearly responsible . . . for the shoot down of this airliner."[4] For weeks, lead stories reported on the anguish of the families, the lives of the murdered victims, the international efforts to claim the bodies, and the fury over the horrific crime that "stunned the world," as the press reported daily in grisly detail.

Every literate person, and certainly every editor and commentator, should instantly have recalled another case when a plane was shot down with comparable loss of life: Iran Air Flight 655, with 290 killed, including 66 children, shot down in Iranian airspace on a clearly identified commercial air route. The agent of this act has always been known: it was the guided-missile cruiser USS *Vincennes*, operating in Iranian waters in the Persian Gulf.

The commander of a nearby U.S. vessel, David Carlson, wrote in the U.S. Naval Institute's magazine, *Proceedings*, that he "wondered aloud in disbelief" as "the *Vincennes* announced her intentions" to attack what was clearly a civilian aircraft. He speculated that "Robo Cruiser," as the *Vincennes* was called because of its aggressive behavior, "felt a need to prove the viability of Aegis (the sophisticated anti-aircraft system on the cruiser) in the Persian Gulf, and that they hankered for the opportunity to show their stuff."[5]

Two years later, the commander of the *Vincennes* and the officer in charge of anti–air warfare were given the U.S. Legion of Merit award for "exceptionally meritorious conduct in the performance of outstanding service" and for the "calm and professional atmosphere" maintained during the period around the downing of the Iranian Airbus. The airplane's destruction itself was not mentioned in the award.[6]

President Ronald Reagan blamed the Iranians for the disaster and defended the actions of the warship, which "followed standing orders and widely publicized procedures, firing to protect itself against possible attack."[7] His successor, George H. W. Bush, proclaimed that "I will never apologize for the United States—I don't care what the facts are . . . I'm not an apologize-for-America kind of guy."[8]

No evasions of responsibility here, unlike the barbarians in the East.

There was little reaction at the time: no outrage, no desperate search for victims, no passionate denunciations of those responsible, no eloquent laments by the U.S. ambassador to the United Nations about the "immense and heart-wrenching loss" when the airliner was downed. Iranian condemnations were occasionally noted, but dismissed as "boiler-plate attacks on the United States," as Philip Shenon of the *New York Times* put it.[9]

Small wonder, then, that this insignificant earlier event merited only a few scattered words in the U.S. media during the vast furor over a real crime, in which the demonic enemy might have been indirectly involved.

One exception was the London *Daily Mail*, where Dominic Lawson wrote that although "Putin's apologists" might bring up the Iran Air attack, the comparison actually demonstrates our high moral values as contrasted with those of the miserable Russians, who try to evade their responsibility for MH 17 with lies while Washington at once announced that the U.S. warship had shot down the Iranian aircraft—righteously.[10] What more powerful evidence could there be of our nobility and their depravity?

We know why Ukrainians and Russians are in their own countries, but one might ask what exactly the *Vincennes* was doing in Iranian waters. The answer is simple: it was defending Washington's great friend Saddam Hussein in his murderous aggression against Iran. For the victims, the shoot-down was no small matter. It was a major factor in Iran's recognition that it could not fight on any longer, according to historian Dilip Hiro.[11]

It is worth remembering the extent of Washington's devotion to its friend Saddam. Reagan removed him from the State Department's terrorist list so that aid could be sent to expedite his assault on Iran, and later both denied his terrible crimes against the Kurds, including the use of chemical weapons, and blocked congressional condemnations of those crimes. He also accorded Saddam a privilege otherwise granted only to Israel: there was no serious reaction when Iraq attacked the USS *Stark* with Exocet missiles, killing thirty-seven crewmen, much like the case of the USS *Liberty*, attacked repeatedly by Israeli jets and torpedo ships in 1967, killing thirty-four crewmen.[12]

Reagan's successor, George H. W. Bush, went on to provide further aid to Saddam, badly needed after the war with Iran that he had launched. Bush also invited Iraqi nuclear engineers to come to the United States for advanced training in weapons production. In April 1990, he dispatched a high-level Senate delegation, led by future Republican presidential candidate Bob Dole, to convey his warm regards to his friend Saddam and to assure him that he should disregard irresponsible criticism from the "haughty and pampered press," and that such miscreants had been removed from Voice of America.[13] The fawning before Saddam continued until he suddenly turned into a new Hitler a few months later when he disobeyed orders, or perhaps misunderstood them, and invaded Kuwait, with illuminating consequences that I must leave aside here.

Other precedents for MH 17 had long since been sent down the memory hole as being without significance. Take, for instance, the Libyan civilian airliner that was lost in a sandstorm in 1973 and shot down by U.S.-supplied Israeli jets, two minutes' flight time from Cairo, toward which it was heading.[14] The death toll was only 110 that time. Israel blamed the French pilot of the Libyan plane, with the endorsement of the *New York Times*, which added that the Israeli act was "at worst . . . an act of callousness that not even the savagery of previous Arab actions can excuse."[15] The incident was passed over quickly in the United States, with little criticism. When Israeli prime minister Golda Meir arrived in Washington four days later, she faced few embarrassing questions and returned home with new gifts of military aircraft. The reaction was much the same when Washington's favored Angolan terrorist organization, UNITA, claimed to have shot down two civilian airliners.

Returning to the sole authentic and truly horrific crime, the *New York Times* reported that UN ambassador Samantha Power "choked up as she spoke of infants who perished in the Malaysia Airlines crash in Ukraine [and] the Dutch foreign minister, Frans Timmermans, could barely contain his anger as he recalled seeing pictures of 'thugs' snatching wedding bands off the fingers of the victims."[16]

At the same session, the report continues, there was also "a long recitation of names and ages—all belonging to children killed in the latest Israeli offensive in Gaza." The only reported reaction was by

Palestinian envoy Riyad Mansour, who "grew quiet in the middle of" the recitation.[17]

The Israeli attack on Gaza in July did, however, elicit outrage in Washington. President Obama "reiterated his 'strong condemnation' of rocket and tunnel attacks against Israel by the militant group Hamas," *The Hill* reported. He "also expressed 'growing concern' about the rising number of Palestinian civilian deaths in Gaza," but without condemnation.[18] The Senate filled that gap, voting unanimously to support Israeli actions in Gaza while condemning "the unprovoked rocket fire at Israel" by Hamas and calling on "Palestinian Authority President Mahmoud Abbas to dissolve the unity governing arrangement with Hamas and condemn the attacks on Israel."[19]

As for Congress, perhaps it's enough to join the 80 percent of the public who disapprove of their performance, though the word "disapprove" is rather too mild in this case.[20] But in Obama's defense, it may be that he has no idea what Israel is doing in Gaza with the weapons that he is kind enough to supply to them. After all, he relies on U.S. intelligence, which may be too busy collecting phone calls and e-mail messages of citizens to pay much attention to such marginalia. It may be useful, then, to review what we all should know.

Israel's goal had long been a simple one: quiet for quiet, a return to the norm (though now it may demand even more). What then was the norm?

For the West Bank, the norm has been that Israel carries forward its illegal construction of settlements and infrastructure, so that whatever might be of value can be integrated into Israel, while the Palestinians are consigned to unviable cantons and subjected to intense repression and violence. For the past fourteen years, the norm has been that Israel kills more than two Palestinian children a week. One such recent Israeli rampage was set off on June 12, 2014, by the brutal murder of three Israeli boys from a settler community in the occupied West Bank. A month before, two Palestinian boys had been shot dead in the West Bank city of Ramallah. That elicited no attention, which is understandable, since it is routine. "The institutionalised disregard for Palestinian life in the West helps explain not only why Palestinians resort to violence," the respected Middle East analyst Mouin Rabbani reports, "but also Israel's latest assault on the Gaza Strip."[21]

Its quiet-for-quiet policy has also enabled Israel to carry forward its program of separating Gaza from the West Bank. That program has been pursued vigorously, always with U.S. support, ever since the United States and Israel accepted the Oslo Accords, which declare the two regions to be an inseparable territorial unity. A look at the map explains the rationale. Gaza provides Palestine's only access to the outside world, so once the two are separated, any autonomy that Israel might grant to Palestinians in the West Bank would leave them effectively imprisoned between hostile states, Israel and Jordan. The imprisonment will become even more severe as Israel continues its systematic program of expelling Palestinians from the Jordan Valley and constructing Israeli settlements there.

The norm in Gaza was described in detail by the heroic Norwegian trauma surgeon Mads Gilbert, who has worked in Gaza's main hospital through Israel's most grotesque crimes and returned again for the current onslaught. In June 2014, immediately before it began, he submitted a report on the Gaza health sector to UNRWA, the UN agency that tries desperately, on a shoestring, to care for refugees.

"At least 57 percent of Gaza households are food insecure and about 80 percent are now aid recipients," Gilbert reported. "Food insecurity and rising poverty also mean that most residents cannot meet their daily caloric requirements, while over 90 percent of the water in Gaza has been deemed unfit for human consumption," a situation that became even worse when Israel again attacked water and sewage systems, leaving over a million people with even more severe disruptions of the barest necessities of life.[22]

Gilbert further reported that "Palestinian children in Gaza are suffering immensely. A large proportion are affected by the man-made malnourishment regime caused by the Israeli imposed blockage. Prevalence of anaemia in children <2yrs in Gaza is at 72.8 percent, while prevalence of wasting, stunting, underweight have been documented at

34.3 percent, 31.4 percent, 31.45 percent respectively."[23] And it gets worse as the report proceeds.

The distinguished human rights lawyer Raji Sourani, who has remained in Gaza through years of Israeli brutality and terror, reports that "the most common sentence I heard when people began to talk about ceasefire: everybody says it's better for all of us to die and not go back to the situation we used to have before this war. We don't want that again. We have no dignity, no pride; we are just soft targets, and we are very cheap. Either this situation really improves or it is better to just die. I am talking about intellectuals, academics, ordinary people: everybody is saying that."[24]

For Gaza, the plans for the norm were explained forthrightly by Dov Weisglass, a confidant of Ariel Sharon and the person who negotiated the withdrawal of Israeli settlers from Gaza in 2005. Hailed as a grand gesture in Israel and among acolytes, the withdrawal was in reality a carefully staged "national trauma," ridiculed by informed Israeli commentators, among them the country's leading sociologist, the late Baruch Kimmerling. What actually happened is that Israeli hawks, led by Sharon, realized that it made good sense to transfer the illegal settlers from their subsidized communities in devastated Gaza, where they were sustained at exorbitant cost, to subsidized settlements in the other occupied territories, which Israel intends to keep. Instead of simply transferring them, as would have been simple enough, it was clearly more useful to present the world with images of little children pleading with soldiers not to destroy their homes, amid cries of "Never Again," with the implication obvious. What made the farce even more transparent was that it was a replica of the staged trauma when Israel had to evacuate the Egyptian part of the Sinai Peninsula in 1982. But it played very well for the intended audience at home and abroad.

Weisglass provided his own description of the transfer of settlers from Gaza to other occupied territories: "What I effectively agreed to with the Americans was that [the major settlement blocs in the West Bank] would not be dealt with at all, and the rest will not be dealt with until the Palestinians turn into Finns"—but a special kind of Finns, who would quietly accept rule by a foreign power. "The significance is the freezing of the political process," Weisglass continued. "And when you freeze that process you prevent the establishment of a Palestinian state and you prevent a discussion about the refugees, the borders and Jerusalem. Effectively, this whole package that is called the Palestinian state, with all that it entails, has been removed from our agenda indefinitely. And all this with [President Bush's] authority and permission and the ratification of both houses of Congress."[25]

Weisglass explained that Gazans would remain "on a diet, but not to make them die of hunger" (which would not help Israel's fading reputation).[26] With their vaunted technical efficiency, Israeli experts determined precisely how many calories a day Gazans needed for bare survival, while also depriving them of medicines and other means of a decent life. Israeli military forces confined them by land, sea, and air to what British prime minister David Cameron accurately described as a prison camp. The Israeli withdrawal left them in total control of Gaza, hence the occupying power under international law. And to close the prison walls even more tightly, Israel excluded Palestinians from a large region along the border, including a third or more of Gaza's scarce arable land. The justification was security for Israelis, which could have been just as well achieved by establishing the security zone on the Israeli side of the border, or by ending the savage siege and other punishments.

The official story is that after Israel graciously handed Gaza over to the Palestinians in the hope that they would construct a flourishing state, they revealed their true nature by subjecting Israel to unremitting rocket attacks and forcing the captive population to become martyrs so that Israel would be pictured in a bad light. Reality is rather different.

A few weeks after Israeli troops withdrew, leaving the occupation intact, Palestinians committed a major crime. In January 2006, they voted the wrong way in a carefully monitored free election, handing control of their parliament to Hamas. The Israeli media constantly intoned that Hamas was dedicated to the destruction of the country. In reality, Hamas's leaders have repeatedly made it clear that they would accept a two-state settlement in accord with the international consensus that has been blocked by the United States and Israel for forty years. In contrast, Israel is dedicated to the destruction of Palestine, apart from some occasional meaningless words, and is implementing that commitment.

True, Israel accepted the "road map" for reaching a two-state settlement initiated by President Bush and adopted by the "quartet" that was supposed to supervise it: the United States, the European Union, the United Nations, and Russia. But as he accepted the road map, Prime Minister Sharon at once added fourteen reservations that effectively nullified it. The facts were known to activists, but only revealed to the general public for the first time in Jimmy Carter's book *Palestine: Peace Not Apartheid*.[27] They remain under wraps in media reporting and commentary.

The (unrevised) 1999 platform of Israel's governing party, Benjamin Netanyahu's Likud, "flatly rejects the establishment of a Palestinian Arab state west of the Jordan river."[28] And for those who like to obsess about meaningless charters, the core component of Likud, Menachem Begin's Herut party, has yet to abandon its founding doctrine that the territory on both sides of the Jordan is part of the Land of Israel.

The crime of the Palestinians in January 2006 was punished at once. The United States and Israel, with Europe shamefully trailing behind, imposed harsh sanctions on the errant population, and Israel stepped up its violence. By June, when the attacks sharply escalated, Israel had already fired more than 7,700 shells at northern Gaza.[29]

The United States and Israel quickly initiated plans for a military coup to overthrow the elected government. When Hamas had the effrontery to foil these plans, the Israeli assaults and the siege became far more severe, justified by the claim that Hamas had taken over the Gaza Strip by force.

There should be no need to review again the horrendous record since. The relentless siege and savage attacks have been punctuated by episodes of "mowing the lawn," to borrow Israel's cheery expression for its periodic exercises of shooting fish in a pond in what it calls a "war of defense."

Once the lawn is mowed and the desperate population seeks to reconstruct somehow from the devastation and the murders, there is a cease-fire agreement. These have been regularly observed by Hamas, as Israel concedes, until Israel violates them with renewed violence.

The most recent cease-fire was established after Israel's October 2012 assault. Though Israel maintained its devastating siege, Hamas observed the cease-fire, as Israeli officials concede.[30] Matters changed in June, when Fatah and Hamas forged a unity agreement, which established a new government of technocrats that had no Hamas participation and accepted all of the demands of the quartet. Israel was naturally furious, all the more so when even the Obama administration joined in signaling its approval. The unity agreement not only undercut Israel's claim that it cannot negotiate with a divided Palestine, but also threatened the long-term goal of dividing Gaza from the West Bank and pursuing its destructive policies in both regions.

Something had to be done, and an occasion arose shortly after, when the three Israeli boys were murdered in the West Bank. The Netanyahu government had strong evidence at once that they were dead, but pretended otherwise, which provided the opportunity to launch a rampage in the West Bank, targeting Hamas, undermining the feared unity government, and sharply increasing Israeli repression.

Netanhayu claimed to have certain knowledge that Hamas was responsible. That too was a lie, as was recognized early on. There has been no pretense of presenting evidence. One of Israel's leading authorities on Hamas, Shlomi Eldar, reported almost at once that the killers very likely came from a dissident clan in Hebron that has long been a thorn in the side of Hamas. Eldar added, "I'm sure they didn't get any green light from the leadership of Hamas, they just thought it was the right time to act."[31]

The eighteen-day rampage did succeed in undermining the feared unity government and sharply increasing Israeli repression. According to Israeli military sources, Israeli soldiers arrested 419 Palestinians, including 335 affiliated with Hamas, and killed 6, while searching thousands of locations and confiscating $350,000.[32] Israel also conducted dozens of attacks in Gaza, killing five Hamas members on July 7.[33]

Hamas finally reacted with its first rockets in nineteen months, Israeli officials reported, providing the pretext for Operation Protective Edge on July 8.[34]

There has been ample reporting on the exploits of the self-declared Most Moral Army in the World, which, according to Israel's ambassador to the United States, should receive the Nobel Peace Prize. By the end of July, some fifteen hundred Palestinians had been killed, exceeding the toll of the Operation Cast Lead crimes of 2008–9. Seventy percent of them were civilians, including hundreds of women and children.[35] Three civilians in Israel were also killed.[36] Large areas of Gaza were turned into rubble. During brief pauses in the bombing, relatives desperately sought shattered bodies or household items in the ruins of homes. Gaza's main power plant was attacked—not for the first time; this is an Israeli specialty—sharply curtailing the already limited electricity and, worse yet, reducing still further the minimal availability of fresh water—another war crime. Meanwhile, rescue teams and ambulances were repeatedly attacked. As atrocities mounted throughout Gaza, Israel claimed that its goal was to destroy tunnels at the border.

Four hospitals were attacked, each yet another war crime. The first was the Al-Wafa Rehabilitation Hospital in Gaza City, attacked on the day Israeli ground forces invaded the prison. A few lines in the *New York Times*, within a story about the ground invasion, reported that "most but not all of the 17 patients and 25 doctors and nurses were evacuated before the electricity was cut and heavy bombardments nearly destroyed the building, doctors said. 'We evacuated them under fire,' said Dr. Ali Abu Ryala, a hospital spokesman. 'Nurses and doctors had to carry the patients on their backs, some of them falling off the stairway. There is an unprecedented state of panic in the hospital.'"[37]

Three working hospitals were then attacked, while patients and staff were left to their own devices to survive. One Israeli crime did receive wide condemnation: the attack on a UN school that was harboring 3,300 terrified refugees who had fled the ruins of their neighborhoods on the orders of the Israeli army. The outraged UNRWA commissioner-general, Pierre Krähenbühl, said, "I condemn in the strongest possible terms this serious violation of international law by Israeli forces. . . . Today the world stands disgraced."[38] There were at least three Israeli strikes at the refugee shelter, a site well-known to the Israeli army. "The precise location of the Jabalia Elementary Girls School and the fact that it was housing thousands of internally displaced people was communicated to the Israeli army seventeen times, to ensure its protection," Krähenbühl said, "the last being at ten to nine last night, just hours before the fatal shelling."[39]

The attack was also condemned "in the strongest possible terms" by the normally reticent secretary-general of the United Nations, Ban Ki-moon. "Nothing is more shameful than attacking sleeping children," he said.[40] There is no record that the U.S. ambassador to the United Nations "choked up as she spoke of infants who perished" in the Israeli strike—or in the attack on Gaza altogether.

But White House spokesperson Bernadette Meehan did respond. She said that "we are extremely concerned that thousands of internally displaced Palestinians who have been called on by the Israeli military to evacuate their homes are not safe in UN designated shelters in Gaza. We also condemn those responsible for hiding weapons in United Nations facilities in Gaza." She omitted to mention that these facilities were empty and that the weapons were found by UNRWA, who had already condemned those who hid them.[41]

Later, the administration joined in stronger condemnations of this particular crime—while at the same time releasing more weapons to Israel. In doing so, however, Pentagon spokesman Steve Warren told reporters, "And it's become clear that the Israelis need to do more to live up to their very high standards . . . for protecting civilian life"—the high standards it had been exhibiting for many years while using U.S. arms.[42]

Attacks on UN compounds sheltering refugees is another Israeli specialty. One famous incident is the Israeli bombardment of the clearly identified UN refugee shelter in Qana during Shimon Peres's murderous

Grapes of Wrath campaign in 1996, killing 106 Lebanese civilians who had taken refuge there, including 52 children.[43] To be sure, Israel is not alone in this practice. Twenty years earlier, its ally South Africa launched an airborne strike deep into Angola against Cassinga, a refugee camp run by the Namibian resistance SWAPO.[44]

Israeli officials laud the humanity of their army, which even goes so far as to inform residents that their homes will be bombed. The practice is "sadism, sanctimoniously disguising itself as mercy," in the words of Israeli journalist Amira Hass: "A recorded message demanding hundreds of thousands of people leave their already targeted homes, for another place, equally dangerous, 10 kilometers away."[45] In fact, no place in the prison is safe from Israeli sadism.

Some find it difficult to profit from Israel's solicitude. An appeal to the world by the Gazan Catholic Church quoted a priest who explained the plight of residents of the House of Christ, a care home dedicated to looking after disabled children. They were removed to the Holy Family Church because Israel was targeting the area, but soon thereafter he wrote, "The church of Gaza has received an order to evacuate. They will bomb the Zeitun area and the people are already fleeing. The problem is that the priest Fr. George and the three nuns of Mother Teresa have 29 handicapped children and nine old ladies who can't move. How will they manage to leave? If anyone can intercede with someone in power, and pray, please do it."[46]

Actually, it shouldn't have been difficult. Israel already provided the instructions at the Al-Wafa Rehabilitation hospital. And fortunately, at least some states tried to intercede, as best they could. Five Latin American states—Brazil, Chile, Ecuador, El Salvador, and Peru—withdrew their ambassadors from Israel, following the course of Bolivia and Venezuela, which had broken relations in reaction to earlier Israeli crimes.[47] These principled acts were another sign of the remarkable change in world relations as much of Latin America begins to free itself from Western domination, sometimes providing a model of civilized behavior to those who controlled it for five hundred years.

The hideous revelations elicited a different reaction from the Most Moral President in the World, the usual one: great sympathy for Israelis, bitter condemnation of Hamas, and calls for moderation on both sides. In his August press conference, President Obama did express concern for Palestinians "caught in the crossfire" (where?) while again vigorously supporting the right of Israel to defend itself, like everyone. Not quite everyone—not, of course, Palestinians. They have no right to defend themselves, surely not when Israel is on good behavior, keeping to the norm of quiet for quiet: stealing their land, driving them out of their homes, subjecting them to a savage siege, and regularly attacking them with weapons provided by their protector.

Palestinians are like black Africans—the Namibian refugees in the Cassinga camp, for example—all terrorists for whom the right of defense does not exist.

A seventy-two-hour humanitarian truce was supposed to go into effect at 8:00 a.m. on August 1. It broke down almost at once. According to a press release of the Al Mezan Center for Human Rights in Gaza, which has a solid reputation for reliability, one of its field workers in Rafah, at the Egyptian border in the south, heard Israeli artillery firing at about 8:05 a.m. By about 9:30 a.m., after reports that an Israeli soldier had been captured, intensive air and artillery bombing of Rafah was underway, killing probably dozens of people and injuring hundreds who had returned to their homes after the cease-fire entered into effect, though numbers could not be verified.

The day before, on July 31, the Coastal Municipalities Water Utility, the sole provider of water in the Gaza Strip, had announced that it could no longer provide water or sanitation services because of lack of fuel and frequent attacks on its personnel. The Al Mezan Center for Human Rights reported that by then, "almost all primary health services [had] stopped in the Gaza Strip due to the lack of water, garbage collection and environment health services. UNRWA had also warned about the risk of imminent spreading of disease owing to the halt of water and sanitation services."[48] Meanwhile, on the eve of the cease-fire, Israeli missiles fired from aircraft continued to kill and wound victims throughout the region.

When the current episode of sadism is finally called off, whenever that will be, Israel hopes to be free to pursue its criminal policies in the Occupied Territories without interference. Gazans will be free to return to the norm in their Israeli-run prison, while in the West Bank they can watch in peace as Israel dismantles what remains of their possessions.

That is the likely outcome if the United States maintains its decisive and virtually unilateral support for Israeli crimes and its rejection of the long-standing international consensus on diplomatic settlement. But the future would be quite different if the United States withdraws that support. In that case it might be possible to move toward the "enduring solution" in Gaza that Secretary of State John Kerry called for, eliciting hysterical condemnation in Israel because the phrase could be interpreted as calling for an end to Israel's siege and regular attacks and—horror of horrors—the phrase might even be interpreted as calling for implementation of international law in the rest of the Occupied Territories.

It is not that Israel's security would be threatened by adherence to international law; it would likely be enhanced. But as explained forty years ago by Israeli general (and later president) Ezer Weizman, Israel could not then "exist according to the scale, spirit, and quality she now embodies."[49]

There are similar cases in recent history. Indonesian generals swore that they would never abandon what Australian foreign minister Gareth Evans called "the Indonesian province of East Timor" as he was making a deal to steal Timorese oil. As long as the ruling generals retained U.S. support, through decades of virtually genocidal slaughter, their goals were realistic. Finally, in September 1999, under considerable domestic and international pressure, President Clinton informed them quietly that the game was over and they instantly withdrew from East Timor, while Evans turned to a new career as the lauded apostle of "responsibility to protect"—in a version designed, of course, to permit a Western resort to violence at will.[50]

Another relevant case is South Africa. In 1958, South Africa's foreign minister informed the U.S. ambassador that although his country was becoming a pariah state, it would not matter as long as Washington's support continued. His assessment proved fairly accurate; thirty years later, Ronald Reagan was the last significant holdout in supporting the apartheid regime, which was still sustaining itself. Within a few years, Washington joined the world and the regime collapsed—not for that reason alone, of course; one crucial factor was the remarkable Cuban role in the liberation of Africa, generally ignored in the West, though not in Africa.[51]

Forty years ago, Israel made the fateful decision to choose expansion over security, rejecting a full peace treaty offered by Egypt in return for the evacuation of occupied Egyptian Sinai, where Israel was initiating extensive settlement and development projects. It has adhered to that policy ever since, making essentially the same judgment as South Africa did in 1958.

In the case of Israel, if the United States decided to join the world, the impact would be far greater. Relations of power allow nothing else, as has been demonstrated whenever Washington has seriously demanded that Israel abandon one of its cherished goals. By now, Israel has little recourse, having adopted policies that turned it from a greatly admired country to one feared and despised, a course it continues to pursue with blind determination in its resolute march toward moral deterioration and possible ultimate destruction.

Could U.S. policy change? It's not impossible. Public opinion has shifted considerably in recent years, particularly among the young, and it cannot be completely ignored. For some years, there has been a good basis for public demands that Washington observe its own laws and cut off military aid to Israel. U.S. law requires that "no security assistance may be provided to any country the government of which engages in a consistent pattern of gross violations of internationally recognized human rights." Israel most certainly is guilty of such a consistent pattern. That is why Amnesty International, in the course of Operation Cast Lead in Gaza, called for an arms embargo against Israel as well as

Hamas.[52] Senator Patrick Leahy, author of this provision of the law, has brought up its potential applicability to Israel in specific cases, and with a well-conducted educational, organizational, and activist effort such initiatives might be pursued successfully.[53] That could have a very significant impact in itself, while also providing a springboard for further actions not only to punish Israel for its criminal behavior, but also to compel Washington to become part of "the international community" and observe international law and decent moral principles.

Nothing could be more significant for the tragic Palestinian victims of many years of violence and repression.

15

How Many Minutes to Midnight?

If some extraterrestrial species were compiling a history of *Homo sapiens*, they might well break their calendar into two eras: BNW (before nuclear weapons) and NWE (the nuclear weapons era). The latter era, of course, opened on August 6, 1945, the first day of the countdown to what may be the inglorious end of this strange species, which attained the intelligence to discover the effective means to destroy itself, but—so the evidence suggests—not the moral and intellectual capacity to control its own worst instincts.

Day one of the NWE was marked by the "success" of Little Boy, a simple atomic bomb. On day four, Nagasaki experienced the technological triumph of Fat Man, a more sophisticated design. Five days later came what the official air force history calls the "grand finale," a one-thousand-plane raid—no mean logistical achievement—on Japan's cities, killing many thousands of people, with leaflets falling among the bombs reading "Japan has surrendered." President Truman announced that surrender before the last B-29 returned to its base.[1]

Those were the auspicious opening days of the NWE. As we now enter its seventieth year, we should be contemplating with wonder the fact that we have survived. We can only guess how many years remain.

Some reflections on these grim prospects were offered by General Lee Butler, former head of the U.S. Strategic Command (STRATCOM), which controls nuclear weapons and strategy. Twenty years ago, Butler wrote that we had so far survived the NWE "by some combination of skill, luck, and divine intervention, and I suspect the latter in greatest proportion."[2] Reflecting further on his long career in developing nuclear weapons strategies and organizing the forces to implement them efficiently, he described himself ruefully as having been "among the most avid of these keepers of the faith in nuclear weapons." But, he continued, he had come to realize that it was now his "burden to declare with all of the conviction I can muster that in my judgment they served us extremely ill." He asked, "By what authority do succeeding generations of leaders in the nuclear-weapons states usurp the power to dictate the odds of continued life on our planet? Most urgently, why does such breathtaking audacity persist at a moment when we should stand trembling in the face of our folly and united in our commitment to abolish its most deadly manifestations?"[3]

Butler termed the U.S. strategic plan of 1960 that called for an automated all-out strike on the Communist world "the single most absurd and irresponsible document I have ever reviewed in my life."[4] Its Soviet counterpart was probably even more insane. But it is important to bear in mind that there are competitors, not least among them the easy acceptance of extraordinary threats to survival.

SURVIVAL IN THE EARLY COLD WAR YEARS

According to received doctrine in scholarship and general intellectual discourse, the prime goal of state policy is "national security." There is ample evidence, however, that the doctrine of national security does not encompass the security of the population. The record reveals that, for instance, the threat of instant destruction by nuclear weapons has not ranked high among the concerns of planners. That much was demonstrated early on, and remains true to the present moment.

In the early days of the NWE, the United States was overwhelmingly powerful and enjoyed remarkable security: it controlled the hemisphere, the Atlantic and Pacific oceans, and the opposite sides of those oceans as well. Long before World War II, it had already become by far the richest country in the world, with incomparable advantages. Its economy boomed during the war, while other industrial societies were devastated or severely weakened. By the opening of the new era, the United States possessed about half of total world wealth and an even greater percentage of its manufacturing capacity.

There was, however, a potential threat: intercontinental ballistic missiles with nuclear warheads. That threat was discussed in the standard scholarly study of nuclear policies, carried out with access to high-level sources: *Danger and Survival: Choices About the Bomb in the First Fifty Years* by McGeorge Bundy, national security adviser during the Kennedy and Johnson presidencies.[5]

Bundy wrote that "the timely development of ballistic missiles during the Eisenhower administration is one of the best achievements of those eight years. Yet it is well to begin with a recognition that both the United States and the Soviet Union might be in much less nuclear danger today if [those] missiles had never been developed." He then added an instructive comment: "I am aware of no serious contemporary proposal, in or out of either government, that ballistic missiles should somehow be banned by agreement."[6] In short, there was apparently no thought of trying to prevent the sole serious threat to the United States, the threat of utter destruction in a nuclear war with the Soviet Union.

Could that threat have been taken off the table? We cannot, of course, be sure, but it was hardly inconceivable. The Russians, far behind in industrial development and technological sophistication, were in a far more threatening environment. Hence, they were significantly more vulnerable to such weapons systems than the United States. There might have been opportunities to explore the possibilities of disarmament, but in the extraordinary hysteria of the day they could hardly have even been perceived. And that hysteria was indeed extraordinary;

an examination of the rhetoric of central official documents of that moment like National Security Council Paper NSC-68 remains quite shocking.

One indication of possible opportunities to blunt the threat was a remarkable proposal by Soviet ruler Joseph Stalin in 1952 offering to allow Germany to be unified with free elections on the condition that it would not then join a hostile military alliance. That was hardly an extreme condition in light of the history of the past half century, during which Germany alone had practically destroyed Russia twice, exacting a terrible toll.

Stalin's proposal was taken seriously by the respected political commentator James Warburg, but otherwise mostly ignored or ridiculed at the time. Recent scholarship has begun to take a different view. The bitterly anti-Communist Soviet scholar Adam Ulam has taken the status of Stalin's proposal to be an "unresolved mystery." Washington "wasted little effort in flatly rejecting Moscow's initiative," he wrote, on grounds that "were embarrassingly unconvincing." The political, scholarly, and general intellectual failure left open "the basic question," Ulam added: "Was Stalin genuinely ready to sacrifice the newly created German Democratic Republic (GDR) on the altar of real democracy," with consequences for world peace and for American security that could have been enormous?[7]

Reviewing recent research in Soviet archives, one of the most respected Cold War scholars, Melvyn Leffler, observed that many scholars were surprised to discover "[Lavrenti] Beria—the sinister, brutal head of the [Russian] secret police—propos[ed] that the Kremlin offer the West a deal on the unification and neutralization of Germany," agreeing "to sacrifice the East German communist regime to reduce East-West tensions" and improve internal political and economic conditions in Russia—opportunities that were squandered in favor of securing German participation in NATO.[8]

Under the circumstances, it is not impossible that agreements might have been reached that would have protected the security of the American population from the gravest threat on the horizon. But that possibility apparently was not considered, a striking indication of how slight a role authentic security plays in state policy.

THE CUBAN MISSILE CRISIS AND BEYOND

That conclusion was underscored repeatedly in the years that followed. When Nikita Khrushchev took control in Russia in the years after Stalin's death, he recognized that the USSR could not compete militarily with the United States, the richest and most powerful country in history, with incomparable advantages. If it ever hoped to escape its economic backwardness and the devastating effects of the last world war, the Soviet Union would need to reverse the arms race.

Accordingly, Khrushchev proposed sharp mutual reductions in offensive weapons. The incoming Kennedy administration considered the offer and rejected it, instead turning to rapid military expansion, even though it was already far in the lead. The late Kenneth Waltz, supported by other strategic analysts with close connections to U.S. intelligence, wrote then that the Kennedy administration "undertook the largest strategic and conventional peace-time military build-up the world has yet seen . . . even as Khrushchev was trying at once to carry through a major reduction in the conventional forces and to follow a strategy of minimum deterrence, and we did so even though the balance of strategic weapons greatly favored the United States." Again, the government opted for harming national security while enhancing state power.

The Soviet reaction to the U.S. buildup of those years was to place nuclear missiles in Cuba in October 1962 to try to redress the balance at least slightly. The move was also motivated in part by Kennedy's terrorist campaign against Fidel Castro's Cuba, which was scheduled to lead to invasion that very month, as Russia and Cuba may have known. The ensuing "missile crisis" was "the most dangerous moment in history," in the words of historian Arthur M. Schlesinger Jr., Kennedy's adviser and confidant. Of no slight significance is the fact that Kennedy is highly praised for his cool courage and statesmanship in the decisions made at the peak of the crisis, even though he had needlessly placed the population at enormous risk for reasons of state and of personal image.

Ten years later, in the last days of the 1973 Israeli-Arab war, Henry Kissinger, then national security adviser to President Nixon, called a nuclear alert. The purpose was to warn the Russians not to interfere with his delicate diplomatic maneuvers designed to ensure an Israeli victory (of a limited sort, so that the United States would still be in control of the region unilaterally). And the maneuvers were indeed delicate: the United States and Russia had jointly imposed a cease-fire, but Kissinger secretly informed the Israelis that they could ignore it. Hence the need for the nuclear alert to frighten the Russians away. The security of Americans retained its usual status.[9]

Ten years after that, the Reagan administration launched operations to probe Russian air defenses by simulating air and naval attacks and a high-level nuclear alert that the Russians were intended to detect. These actions were undertaken at a very tense moment: Washington was deploying Pershing II strategic missiles in Europe with a ten-minute flight time to Moscow. President Reagan had also announced the Strategic Defense Initiative ("Star Wars") program, which the Russians understood to be effectively a first-strike weapon, a standard interpretation of missile defense on all sides. And other tensions were rising.

Naturally, these actions caused great alarm in Russia, which unlike the United States was quite vulnerable and had repeatedly been invaded and virtually destroyed. That led to a major war scare in 1983. Newly released archives reveal that the danger was even more severe than historians had previously assumed. A high-level U.S. intelligence study entitled "The War Scare Was for Real" concluded that U.S. intelligence may have underestimated Russian concerns and the threat of a Russian preventative nuclear strike. The exercises "almost became a prelude to a preventative nuclear strike," according to an account in the *Journal of Strategic Studies*.[10]

It was even more dangerous than that, as we learned in the fall of

2013, when the BBC reported that right in the midst of these world-threatening developments, Russia's early-warning systems detected an incoming missile strike from the United States, sending its nuclear system onto the highest-level alert. The protocol for the Soviet military was to retaliate with a nuclear attack of its own. Fortunately, the officer on duty, Stanislav Petrov, decided to disobey orders and not report the warnings to his superiors. He received an official reprimand. And thanks to his dereliction of duty, we're still alive to talk about it.[11]

The security of the population was no more a high priority for Reagan administration planners than for their predecessors. And so it continues to the present, even putting aside the numerous near-catastrophic nuclear accidents that have occurred over the years, many reviewed in Eric Schlosser's chilling study *Command and Control*.[12] In other words, it is hard to contest General Butler's conclusions.

SURVIVAL IN THE POST–COLD WAR ERA

The record of post–Cold War actions and doctrines is hardly reassuring either. Every self-respecting president has to have a doctrine. The Clinton doctrine was encapsulated in the slogan "multilateral when we can, unilateral when we must." In congressional testimony, the phrase "when we must" was explained more fully: the United States is entitled to resort to the "unilateral use of military power" to ensure "uninhibited access to key markets, energy supplies, and strategic resources."[13]

Meanwhile, STRATCOM in the Clinton era produced an important study entitled "Essentials of Post–Cold War Deterrence," issued well after the Soviet Union had collapsed and Clinton was extending President George H. W. Bush's program of expanding NATO to the east in violation of verbal promises to Soviet Premier Mikhail Gorbachev—with reverberations to the present.[14] That study was concerned with "the role of nuclear weapons in the post–Cold War era." A central conclusion: that the United States must maintain the right to launch a first strike, even against nonnuclear states. Furthermore, nuclear weapons must always be at the ready because they "cast a shadow over any crisis or conflict." They were, that is, constantly being used, just as you're using a gun if you aim but don't fire one while robbing a store (a point that Daniel Ellsberg has repeatedly stressed). STRATCOM went on to advise that "planners should not be too rational about determining . . . what the opponent values the most." Anything is a possible target. "It hurts to portray ourselves as too fully rational and cool-headed . . . That the US may become irrational and vindictive if its vital interests are attacked should be a part of the national persona we project." It is "beneficial [for our strategic posture] if some elements may appear to be potentially 'out of control,'" thus posing a constant threat of nuclear attack—a severe violation of the UN Charter, if anyone cares.

Not much here about the noble goals constantly proclaimed—or, for that matter, the obligation under the Non-Proliferation Treaty to make "good faith" efforts to eliminate this scourge of the earth. What resounds, rather, is an adaptation of Hilaire Belloc's famous couplet about the Maxim gun (to quote the great African historian Chinweizu):

> *Whatever happens, we have got*
> *The Atom Bomb, and they have not.*

After Clinton came, of course, George W. Bush, whose broad endorsement of preventive war easily encompasses Japan's attack in December 1941 on military bases in two U.S. overseas possessions, at a time when Japanese militarists were well aware that B-17 Flying Fortresses were being rushed off assembly lines and deployed to those bases with the intent "to burn out the industrial heart of the Empire with fire-bomb attacks on the teeming bamboo ant heaps of Honshu and Kyushu." That was how the prewar plans were described by their architect, Air Force General Claire Chennault, with the enthusiastic approval of President Franklin Roosevelt, Secretary of State Cordell Hull, and Army Chief of Staff General George Marshall.[15]

Then came Barack Obama, with pleasant words about working to abolish nuclear weapons—combined with plans to spend $1 trillion on the U.S. nuclear arsenal over the next thirty years, a percentage of the military budget "comparable to spending for procurement of new strategic systems in the 1980s under President Ronald Reagan," according to a study by the James Martin Center for Nonproliferation Studies at the Middlebury Institute of International Studies at Monterey.[16]

Obama has also not hesitated to play with fire for political gain. Take for example the capture and assassination of Osama bin Laden by Navy SEALs. Obama brought it up with pride in an important speech on national security in May 2013. The speech was widely covered, but one crucial paragraph was ignored.[17]

Obama hailed the operation but added that it could not be the norm. The reason, he said, was that the risks "were immense." The SEALs might have been "embroiled in an extended firefight." Even though, by luck, that didn't happen, "the cost to our relationship with Pakistan and the backlash among the Pakistani public over encroachment on their territory was . . . severe."

Let us now add a few details. The SEALs were ordered to fight their way out if apprehended. They would not have been left to their fate if "embroiled in an extended firefight"; the full force of the U.S. military would have been used to extricate them. Pakistan has a powerful, well-trained military, highly protective of state sovereignty. It also has nuclear weapons, and Pakistani specialists are concerned about the possible penetration of their nuclear security system by jihadi elements. It is also no secret that the population has been embittered and radicalized by Washington's drone terror campaign and other policies.

While the SEALs were still in the bin Laden compound, Pakistani Chief of Staff Ashfaq Parvez Kayani was informed of the raid and ordered the military "to confront any unidentified aircraft," which he assumed would be from India. Meanwhile, in Kabul, U.S. war commander General David Petraeus ordered "warplanes to respond" if the Pakistanis "scrambled their fighter jets."[18]

As Obama said, by luck the worst didn't happen, though it could have been quite ugly. But the risks were faced without noticeable concern. Or subsequent comment.

As General Butler observed, it is a near miracle that we have escaped destruction so far, and the longer we tempt fate, the less likely it is that we can hope for divine intervention to perpetuate the miracle.

16

Cease-fires in Which Violations Never Cease

On August 26, 2014, Israel and the Palestinian Authority (PA) both accepted a cease-fire agreement after a fifty-day Israeli assault on Gaza that left 2,100 Palestinians dead and vast landscapes of destruction behind. The agreement called for an end to military action by both Israel and Hamas as well as an easing of the Israeli siege that had strangled Gaza for many years.

This was, however, just the most recent in a series of cease-fire agreements reached after each of Israel's periodic escalations of its unremitting assault on Gaza. Throughout this period, the terms of these agreements remained essentially the same. The regular pattern has been for Israel to then disregard whatever agreement is in place, while Hamas observes it until a sharp increase in Israeli violence elicits a Hamas response, which is followed by even fiercer Israeli brutality. These escalations are often called "mowing the lawn" in Israeli parlance, though the 2014 Israeli operation was more accurately described by an appalled senior U.S. military officer as "removing the topsoil."

The first of this series of truces was the Agreement on Movement and Access between Israel and the Palestinian Authority in November 2005. It called for the opening of a crossing between Gaza and Egypt at Rafah for the export of goods and the transit of people, the continuous operation of crossings between Israel and Gaza for the import/export of goods and the transit of people, the reduction of obstacles to movement within the West Bank, bus and truck convoys between the West Bank and Gaza, the building of a seaport in Gaza, and the reopening of the airport in Gaza that Israeli bombing had demolished.

That agreement was reached shortly after Israel withdrew its settlers and military forces from Gaza. The motive for the withdrawal was explained with engaging cynicism by Dov Weisglass, a confidant of then prime minister Ariel Sharon, who was in charge of negotiating and implementing it. Summarizing the purpose of the operation, Weisglass explained that "the disengagement is actually formaldehyde. It supplies the amount of formaldehyde that is necessary so there will not be a political process with the Palestinians."[1]

In the background, Israeli hawks recognized that instead of investing substantial resources in maintaining a few thousand settlers in illegal subsidized communities in devastated Gaza, it made more sense to transfer them to illegal subsidized communities in areas of the West Bank that Israel intended to keep.

The disengagement was depicted as a noble effort to pursue peace, but the reality was quite different. Israel never relinquished control of Gaza and is accordingly recognized as the occupying power by the United Nations, the United States, and other states (apart from Israel itself, of course). In their comprehensive history of settlement in the Occupied Territories, Israeli scholars Idith Zertal and Akiva Eldar describe what actually happened when that country "disengaged": the ruined territory was not released "for even a single day from Israel's military grip or from the price of the occupation that the inhabitants pay every day." After the disengagement, "Israel left behind scorched earth, devastated services, and people with neither a present nor a future. The settlements were destroyed in an ungenerous move by an unenlightened occupier, which in fact continues to control the territory and kill and harass its inhabitants by means of its formidable military might."[2]

OPERATIONS CAST LEAD AND PILLAR OF DEFENSE

Israel soon had a pretext for violating the November Agreement more severely. In January 2006, the Palestinians committed a serious crime. They voted "the wrong way" in carefully monitored free elections, placing the parliament in the hands of Hamas. Israel and the United States immediately imposed harsh sanctions, telling the world very clearly what they mean by "democracy promotion," and soon began planning a military coup to overthrow the unacceptable elected government, a familiar procedure. When Hamas preempted the coup in 2007, the siege of Gaza grew far more severe, and regular Israeli military attacks commenced. Voting the wrong way in a free election was bad enough, but preempting a U.S.-planned military coup proved to be an unpardonable offense.

A new cease-fire agreement was reached in June 2008. It again called for opening the border crossings to "allow the transfer of all goods that were banned and restricted to go into Gaza." Israel formally agreed, but immediately announced that it would not abide by the agreement until Hamas released Gilad Shalit, an Israeli soldier it held.

Israel itself has a long history of kidnapping civilians in Lebanon and on the high seas and holding them for lengthy periods without credible charges, sometimes as hostages. Imprisoning civilians on dubious charges, or none at all, is also a regular practice in the territories Israel controls.

Israel not only maintained the siege in violation of the 2008 cease-fire agreement but did so with extreme rigor, even preventing the United Nations Relief and Works Agency, which cares for the huge number of official refugees in Gaza, from replenishing its stocks.[3] On November 4, while the media were focused on the U.S. presidential election, Israeli troops entered Gaza and killed half a dozen Hamas militants. That elicited a Hamas missile response and an exchange of fire. (All the deaths were Palestinian.) In late December, Hamas offered to renew the cease-fire. Israel considered the offer, but rejected it, preferring instead to launch Operation Cast Lead, a three-week incursion with the full power of the Israeli military into the Gaza Strip, resulting in atrocities well documented by international and Israeli human rights organizations.

On January 8, 2009, while Cast Lead was in full fury, the UN Security Council passed a unanimous resolution (with the United States abstaining) calling for "an immediate cease-fire leading to a full Israeli withdrawal, unimpeded provision through Gaza of food, fuel, and medical treatment, and intensified international arrangements to prevent arms and ammunition smuggling."[4]

A new cease-fire agreement was indeed reached, similar to the previous ones, but again was never really observed and broke down completely with the next major mowing-the-lawn episode, Operation Pillar of Defense, in November 2012. What happened in the interim can be illustrated by the casualty figures from January 2012 to the launching of that operation: one Israeli killed by fire from Gaza, seventy-eight Palestinians killed by Israeli fire.[5]

The first act of Operation Pillar of Defense was the murder of Ahmed Jabari, a high official of the military wing of Hamas. Aluf Benn, editor in chief of Israel's leading newspaper, *Ha'aretz*, described Jabari as Israel's "subcontractor" in Gaza, who enforced relative quiet there for more than five years. As always, there was a pretext for the assassination, but the likely reason was provided by Israeli peace activist Gershon Baskin. He had been involved in direct negotiations with Jabari for years and reported that, hours before he was assassinated, Jabari "received the draft of a permanent truce agreement with Israel, which included mechanisms for maintaining the cease-fire in the case of a flare-up between Israel and the factions in the Gaza Strip."[6]

There is a long record of Israeli actions designed to deter the threat of a diplomatic settlement.

After this exercise in mowing the lawn, a cease-fire agreement was reached yet again. Repeating the now-standard terms, it called for a cessation of military action by both sides and the effective ending of the siege of Gaza with Israel "opening the crossings and facilitating the movements of people and transfer of goods, and refraining from restricting residents' free movements and targeting residents in border areas."[7]

What happened next was reviewed by Nathan Thrall, senior Middle East analyst for the International Crisis Group. Israeli intelligence recognized that Hamas was observing the terms of the cease-fire. "Israel," Thrall wrote, "therefore saw little incentive in upholding its end of the deal. In the three months following the cease-fire, its forces made regular incursions into Gaza, strafed Palestinian farmers and those collecting scrap and rubble across the border, and fired at boats, preventing fishermen from accessing the majority of Gaza's waters." In other words, the siege never ended. "Crossings were repeatedly shut. So-called buffer zones inside Gaza [from which Palestinians are barred, and which include a third or more of the strip's limited arable land] were reinstated. Imports declined, exports were blocked, and fewer Gazans were given exit permits to Israel and the West Bank."[8]

OPERATION PROTECTIVE EDGE

So matters continued until April 2014, when an important event took place. The two major Palestinian groupings, Gaza-based Hamas and the Fatah-dominated Palestinian Authority in the West Bank, signed a unity agreement. Hamas made major concessions; the unity government contained none of its members or allies. In substantial measure, as Thrall observes, Hamas turned over governance of Gaza to the PA. Several thousand PA security forces were sent there, and the PA placed its guards at borders and crossings, with no reciprocal positions for Hamas in the West Bank security apparatus. Finally, the unity government accepted the three conditions that Washington and the European Union had long demanded: nonviolence, adherence to past agreements, and the recognition of Israel.

Israel was infuriated. Its government declared at once that it would refuse to deal with the unity government and cancelled negotiations. Its fury mounted when the United States, along with most of the world, signaled support for the unity government.

There are good reasons why Israel opposes the unification of Palestinians. One is that the Hamas-Fatah conflict has provided a useful pretext for refusing to engage in serious negotiations. How can one negotiate with a divided entity? More significantly, for more than twenty years, Israel has been committed to separating Gaza from the West Bank, in violation of the Oslo Accords, which declare Gaza and the West Bank to be an inseparable territorial unity. A look at a map explains the rationale: separated from Gaza, any West Bank enclaves left to Palestinians have no access to the outside world.

Furthermore, Israel has been systematically taking over the Jordan Valley, driving out Palestinians, establishing settlements, sinking wells, and otherwise ensuring that the region—about one-third of the West Bank, including much of its arable land—will ultimately be integrated into Israel along with the other regions that Israel is taking over. Hence remaining Palestinian cantons will be completely imprisoned. Unification with Gaza would interfere with these plans, which trace back to the early days of the occupation and have had steady support from the major political blocs, including from figures usually portrayed as doves, like former president Shimon Peres, one of the architects of settlement deep in the West Bank.

As usual, a pretext was needed to move on to the next escalation. Such an occasion arose with the brutal murder of three Israeli boys from the settler community in the West Bank. An eighteen-day rampage primarily targeting Hamas followed. On September 2, *Ha'aretz* reported that, after intensive interrogations, the Israeli security services concluded the abduction of the teenagers "was carried out by an independent cell" with no known direct links to Hamas.[9] By then, the eighteen-day rampage had succeeded in undermining the feared unity government."

Hamas finally reacted with its first rockets in eighteen months, providing Israel with the pretext to launch Operation Protective Edge on July 8. That fifty-day assault proved the most extreme exercise in mowing the lawn—so far.

OPERATION STILL TO BE NAMED

Israel is in a fine position today to reverse its decades-old policy of separating Gaza from the West Bank and observe a major cease-fire agreement for the first time. At least temporarily, the threat of democracy in neighboring Egypt has been diminished, and the brutal Egyptian military dictatorship of General Abdul Fattah al-Sisi is a welcome ally for Israel in maintaining control over Gaza.

With the Palestinian unity government placing U.S.-trained forces of the Palestinian Authority in control of Gaza's borders and governance possibly shifting into the hands of the PA, which depends on Israel for its survival as well as for its finances, Israel might feel that there is little to fear from some limited form of autonomy for the enclaves that remain to Palestinians.

There is also some truth to the observation of Prime Minister Benjamin Netanyahu: "Many elements in the region understand today that, in the struggle in which they are threatened, Israel is not an enemy but a partner."[10] Akiva Eldar, Israel's leading diplomatic correspondent, adds, however, that "all those 'many elements in the region' also understand that there is no brave and comprehensive diplomatic move on the horizon without an agreement on the establishment of a Palestinian state based on the 1967 borders and a just, agreed-upon solution to the refugee problem." That is not on Israel's agenda, he points out.[11]

Some knowledgeable Israeli commentators, notably columnist Danny Rubinstein, believe that Israel is poised to reverse course and relax its stranglehold on Gaza.

We'll see.

The record of these past years suggests otherwise, and the first signs are not auspicious. As Operation Protective Edge ended, Israel announced its largest appropriation of West Bank land in thirty years, almost a thousand acres. Israel Radio reported that the takeover was in response to the killing of the three Jewish teenagers by "Hamas militants." A Palestinian boy was burned to death in retaliation for the murders, but no Israeli land was handed over to the Palestinians, nor was there any reaction when an Israeli soldier murdered ten-year-old Khalil Anati on a quiet street in a refugee camp near Hebron and then drove away in his jeep as the child bled to death.[12]

Anati was one of the twenty-three Palestinians (including three children) killed by Israeli occupation forces in the West Bank during the Gaza onslaught, according to UN statistics, along with more than two thousand wounded, 38 percent by live fire. "None of those killed were endangering soldiers' lives," Israeli journalist Gideon Levy reported.[13] To none of this is there any reaction, just as there was no reaction while Israel killed, on average, more than two Palestinian children a week for the past fourteen years. They are unpeople, after all.

It is commonly claimed on all sides that, if the two-state settlement is dead as a result of Israel's takeover of Palestinian lands, then the outcome will be one state west of the Jordan River. Some Palestinians welcome this outcome, anticipating that they can then conduct a civil rights struggle for equal rights on the model of South Africa under apartheid. Many Israeli commentators warn that the resulting "demographic problem" of more Arab than Jewish births and diminishing Jewish immigration will undermine their hope for a "democratic Jewish state."

But these widespread beliefs are dubious. The realistic alternative to a two-state settlement is that Israel will continue to carry forward the plans it has been implementing for years, taking over whatever is of value to it in the West Bank, while avoiding Palestinian population concentrations and removing Palestinians from the areas it is integrating into Israel. That should preempt the dreaded "demographic problem."

These basic policies have been underway since the 1967 conquest, following a principle enunciated by then defense minister Moshe Dayan, one of the Israeli leaders most sympathetic to the Palestinians. He informed his party colleagues that they should tell Palestinian refugees in the West Bank, "We have no solution, you shall continue to live like dogs, and whoever wishes may leave, and we will see where this process leads."[14]

The suggestion was natural within the overriding conception articulated in 1972 by future president Chaim Herzog: "I do not deny the Palestinians a place or stand or opinion on every matter . . . But certainly I am not prepared to consider them as partners in any respect in a land that has been consecrated in the hands of our nation for thousands of years. For the Jews of this land there cannot be any partner." Dayan also called for Israel's "permanent rule" ("memshelet keva") over the Occupied Territories.[15] When Netanyahu expresses the same stand today, he is not breaking new ground.

For a century, the Zionist colonization of Palestine has proceeded primarily on the pragmatic principle of the quiet establishment of facts on the ground, which the world was to ultimately come to accept. It has been a highly successful policy. There is every reason to expect it to persist as long as the United States provides the necessary military, economic, diplomatic, and ideological support. For those concerned with the rights of the brutalized Palestinians, there can be no higher priority than working to change U.S. policies—not an idle dream by any means.

17

The U.S. Is a Leading Terrorist State

Imagine that the lead article in *Pravda* reported a study by the KGB reviewing major terrorist operations run by the Kremlin around the world in an effort to determine the factors that led to their success or failure. Its final conclusion: unfortunately, successes were rare, so some rethinking of policy is in order. Suppose that the article went on to quote Vladimir Putin as saying that he had asked the KGB to carry out such inquiries in order to find cases of "financing and supplying arms to an insurgency in a country that actually worked out well. And they couldn't come up with much." So he has some reluctance about continuing such efforts.

If, almost unimaginably, such an article were to appear, cries of outrage and indignation would rise to the heavens, and Russia would be bitterly condemned—or worse—not only for the vicious terrorist record it had openly acknowledged, but for the reaction among the leadership and the political class: no concern, except for how well Russian state terrorism works and whether the practices can be improved.

It is indeed hard to imagine that such an article might appear, except for the fact that it recently did—almost.

On October 14, 2014, the lead story in the *New York Times* reported a study by the CIA reviewing major terrorist operations run by the White House around the world in an effort to determine the factors that led to their success or failure, with the very conclusion mentioned above. The article went on to quote President Obama as saying that he had asked the CIA to carry out such an inquiry in order to find cases of "financing and supplying arms to an insurgency in a country that actually worked out well. And they couldn't come up with much." So he did indeed have some reluctance about continuing such efforts.[1]

There were no cries of outrage, no indignation, nothing.

The conclusion seems quite clear. In Western political culture, it is taken to be entirely natural and appropriate that the Leader of the Free World should be a terrorist rogue state and should openly proclaim its eminence in such crimes. And it is only natural and appropriate that the Nobel Peace Prize laureate and liberal constitutional lawyer who holds the reins of power should be concerned only with how to carry out such actions more efficaciously.

A closer look establishes these conclusions quite firmly.

The article opens by citing U.S. operations "from Angola to Nicaragua to Cuba." Let us add a little of what is omitted, drawing from the groundbreaking studies of Cuba's role in the liberation of Africa by Piero Gleijeses, notably in his recent book *Visions of Freedom*.[2]

In Angola, the United States joined South Africa in providing the crucial support for Jonas Savimbi's terrorist UNITA army. It continued to do so even after Savimbi had been roundly defeated in a carefully monitored free election and South Africa had withdrawn support from this "monster whose lust for power had brought appalling misery to his people," in the words of British ambassador to Angola Marrack Goulding, a statement seconded by the CIA station chief in neighboring Kinshasa. The CIA official warned that "it wasn't a good idea" to support the monster "because of the extent of Savimbi's crimes. He was terribly brutal."[3]

Despite extensive and murderous U.S.-backed terrorist operations in Angola, Cuban forces drove South African aggressors out of the country, compelled them to leave illegally occupied Namibia, and opened the way for the Angolan election in which, after his defeat, Savimbi "dismissed entirely the views of nearly 800 foreign elections observers here that the balloting . . . was generally free and fair," as the *New York Times* reported, and continued the terrorist war with U.S. support.[4]

Cuban achievements in the liberation of Africa and the ending of apartheid were hailed by Nelson Mandela when he was finally released from prison. Among his first acts was to declare that "during all my years in prison, Cuba was an inspiration and Fidel Castro a tower of strength . . . [Cuban victories] destroyed the myth of the invincibility of the white oppressor [and] inspired the fighting masses of South Africa . . . a turning point for the liberation of our continent—and of my people—from the scourge of apartheid. . . . What other country can point to a record of greater selflessness than Cuba has displayed in its relations to Africa?"[5]

The terrorist commander Henry Kissinger, in contrast, was "apoplectic" over the insubordination of the "pipsqueak" Castro, whom he felt should be "smash[ed]," as William LeoGrande and Peter Kornbluh reported in their book *Back Channel to Cuba*, relying on recently declassified documents.[6]

Turning to Nicaragua, we need not tarry on Ronald Reagan's terrorist war, which continued well after the International Court of Justice ordered Washington to cease its "illegal use of force"—that is, international terrorism—and pay substantial reparations, and after a resolution of the UN Security Council that called on all states (meaning the United States) to observe international law—vetoed by Washington.[7] It should be acknowledged, however, that Reagan's terrorist war against Nicaragua—extended by George H. W. Bush, the "statesman" Bush—was not as destructive as the state terrorism he enthusiastically backed in El Salvador and Guatemala. Nicaragua had the advantage of having an army to confront the U.S.-run terrorist forces, while in the neighboring states the terrorists assaulting the population were the security forces armed and trained by Washington.

In Cuba, Washington's terror operations were launched in full fury by President Kennedy and his brother, Attorney General Robert Kennedy, to punish Cubans for defeating the U.S.-run Bay of Pigs invasion. This terrorist war was no small affair. It involved four hundred Americans, two thousand Cubans, a private navy of fast boats, and a $50 million annual budget. It was run in part by a Miami CIA station functioning in violation of the Neutrality Act and, presumably, the law banning CIA operations in the United States. Operations included the bombing of hotels and industrial installations, the sinking of fishing boats, the poisoning of crops and livestock, the contamination of sugar exports, and so on. Some of these operations were not specifically authorized by the CIA but were carried out by the terrorist forces it funded and supported, a distinction without a difference in the case.

As has since been revealed, the terrorist war (Operation Mongoose) was a factor in Khrushchev's sending of missiles to Cuba and the "missile crisis," which came ominously close to a terminal nuclear war. U.S. "operations" in Cuba were no trivial matter.

Some attention has been paid to just one rather minor part of the terror war: the many attempts to assassinate Fidel Castro, generally dismissed as childish CIA shenanigans. Apart from that, none of what happened has elicited much interest or commentary. The first serious English-language inquiry into the impact of the terror war on Cubans was published in 2010 by Canadian researcher Keith Bolender, in his *Voices From the Other Side*, a valuable study that has largely been ignored.[8]

The three examples highlighted in the *New York Times* report on U.S. terrorism are only the tip of the iceberg. Nevertheless, it is useful to have this prominent acknowledgment of Washington's dedication to murderous and destructive terror operations and of the insignificance of all of this to the political class, which accepts it as normal and proper that the U.S. should be a terrorist superpower, immune to law and civilized norms.

Oddly, the world may not agree. Global polls show that the United States is regarded as the biggest threat to world peace by a very large margin.[9] Fortunately, Americans were spared this insignificant information.

18

Obama's Historic Move

The establishment of diplomatic ties between the United States and Cuba has been widely hailed as an event of historic importance. Correspondent Jon Lee Anderson, who has written perceptively about the region, sums up a general reaction among liberal intellectuals when he writes, in the *New Yorker*, that

> Barack Obama has shown that he can act as a statesman of historic heft. And so, at this moment, has Raúl Castro. For Cubans, this moment will be emotionally cathartic as well as historically transformational. Their relationship with their wealthy, powerful northern American neighbor has remained frozen in the nineteen-sixties for fifty years. To a surreal degree, their destinies have been frozen as well. For Americans, this is important, too. Peace with Cuba takes us momentarily back to that golden time when the United States was a beloved nation throughout the world, when a young and handsome J.F.K. was in office—before Vietnam, before Allende, before Iraq and all the other miseries—and allows us to feel proud about ourselves for finally doing the right thing.[1]

The past is not quite as idyllic as portrayed in the persistent Camelot image. JFK was not "before Vietnam"—or even before Allende and Iraq, but let us put that aside. In Vietnam, when JFK entered office, the brutality of the Ngo Dinh Diem regime that the United States had imposed had finally elicited domestic resistance that it could not control.

Kennedy therefore at once escalated the U.S. intervention to outright aggression, ordering the U.S. Air Force to bomb South Vietnam (under South Vietnamese markings, which deceived no one), authorizing napalm and chemical warfare to destroy crops and livestock, and launching programs to drive peasants into virtual concentration camps to "protect them" from the guerrillas whom Washington knew they were mostly supporting.

By 1963, reports from the ground seemed to indicate that Kennedy's war was succeeding, but a serious problem arose. In August, the administration learned that the Diem government was seeking negotiations with North Vietnam to end the conflict.

If JFK had had the slightest intention to withdraw, that would have been a perfect opportunity to do so gracefully, with no political cost. He could even have claimed, in the usual style, that it was American fortitude and its principled defense of freedom that had compelled the North Vietnamese to "surrender." Instead, Washington backed a military coup to install in power hawkish generals more attuned to JFK's actual commitments. President Diem and his brother were murdered in the process. With victory apparently within sight, Kennedy reluctantly accepted a proposal by Defense Secretary Robert McNamara to begin withdrawing troops (National Security Action Memo 263), but only with a crucial proviso: after victory had been attained. Kennedy maintained that demand insistently until his assassination a few weeks later. Many illusions have been concocted about these events, but they collapse quickly under the weight of the rich documentary record.[2]

The story elsewhere was also not quite as idyllic as in the Camelot legends. One of the most consequential of Kennedy's decisions, in 1962, was to shift the mission of Latin American militaries from "hemispheric defense" to "internal security," with horrendous consequences for the hemisphere. Those who do not prefer what international relations specialist Michael Glennon has called "intentional ignorance" can easily fill in the details.[3]

In Cuba, Kennedy inherited Eisenhower's policy of embargo and formal plans to overthrow the regime, and he quickly escalated them with the Bay of Pigs invasion. The failure of the invasion caused near hysteria in Washington. At the first cabinet meeting after the failed invasion, the atmosphere was "almost savage," Under Secretary of State Chester Bowles noted privately. "There was an almost frantic reaction for an action program."[4] Kennedy articulated the hysteria in his public pronouncements, though he was aware, as he said privately, that allies "think that we're slightly demented" on the subject of Cuba.[5] Not without reason.

Kennedy's actions were true to his words.

There is now much debate about whether Cuba should be removed from the list of states supporting terrorism. Such a question can only bring to mind the words of Tacitus that "crime once exposed had no refuge but in audacity."[6] Except that it is not exposed, thanks to the "treason of the intellectuals."

On taking office after Kennedy's assassination, President Lyndon Johnson relaxed the reign of terror, which nonetheless continued through the 1990s. But he was not about to allow Cuba to survive in peace. He explained to Senator William Fulbright that though "I'm not getting into any Bay of Pigs deal," he wanted advice about "what we ought to do to pinch their nuts more than we're doing."[7] Latin America historian Lars Schoultz observes that "Nut-pinching has been US policy ever since."[8]

Some, to be sure, have felt that such delicate means are not enough—take for example Richard Nixon's cabinet member Alexander Haig, who asked the president to "just give me the word and I'll turn that f——island into a parking lot."[9] His eloquence captured vividly the long-standing frustration in Washington about "that infernal little Cuban republic"—Theodore Roosevelt's phrase as he ranted in fury over Cuban unwillingness to accept graciously the invasion of 1898 that would block their liberation from Spain and turn them into a virtual colony. Surely his courageous ride up San Juan Hill had been in a noble cause. (Overlooked, commonly, is that African-American battalions were largely responsible for conquering the hill).[10]

Historian Louis Pérez writes that the intervention, hailed at home as a humanitarian act to "liberate" Cuba, achieved its actual objectives. "A Cuban war of liberation was transformed into a US war of conquest"— the "Spanish-American War," in imperial nomenclature—designed to obscure a Cuban victory that was quickly aborted by the invasion. The outcome relieved American anxieties about "what was anathema to all North American policymakers since Thomas Jefferson—Cuban independence."[11]

How things have changed in two centuries.

There have been tentative efforts to improve relations in the past fifty years, reviewed in detail by William LeoGrande and Peter Kornbluh in *Back Channel to Cuba*.[12] Whether we should feel "proud about ourselves" for the steps that Obama has taken may be debated, but they are "the right thing," even though the crushing embargo remains in place in defiance of the entire world (Israel excepted) and tourism is still barred. In his address to the nation announcing the new policy, the president made it clear that in other respects, too, the punishment of Cuba for refusing to bend to U.S. will and violence will continue, repeating pretexts that are too ludicrous for comment.

Worthy of attention, however, are these words of the president:

Proudly, the United States has supported democracy and human rights in Cuba through these five decades. We've done so primarily through policies that aim to isolate the island, preventing the most basic travel and commerce that Americans can enjoy anyplace else. And though this policy has been rooted in the best of intentions, no other nation joins us in imposing these sanctions and it has had little effect beyond providing the Cuban government with a rationale for restrictions on its people . . . Today, I'm being honest with you. We can never erase the history between us.[13]

ne has to admire the stunning audacity of this pronouncement, ich again recalls the words of Tacitus. Obama is surely not unaware f the actual history, which includes not only the murderous terrorist war and scandalous economic embargo, but also the military occupation of southeastern Cuba (Guantánamo Bay), including the country's major port, despite requests by the government since independence to return what was stolen at gunpoint—a policy justified only by a fanatic commitment to block Cuba's economic development. By comparison, Putin's illegal takeover of Crimea looks almost benign. Dedication to revenge against the impudent Cubans who resist U.S. domination has been so extreme that it has even overruled the wishes of powerful segments of the business community for normalization—pharmaceuticals, agribusiness, energy—an unusual development in U.S. foreign policy. Washington's cruel and vindictive policies have virtually isolated the country in the hemisphere and elicited contempt and ridicule throughout the world. Washington and its acolytes like to pretend that they have been "isolating" Cuba, as Obama intoned, but the record shows clearly that it is the United States that has been isolated, probably the primary reason for the partial change of course.

Domestic opinion no doubt is also a factor in Obama's "historic move"—though the public has been in favor of normalization for a long time. A CNN poll in 2014 showed that only a quarter of Americans now regard Cuba as a serious threat to the United States, as compared with over two-thirds thirty years earlier, when President Reagan was warning about the grave threat to our lives posed by the nutmeg capital of the world (Grenada) and by the Nicaraguan army, only two days' march from Texas.[14] With those fears now having somewhat abated, perhaps we can slightly relax our vigilance.

In the extensive commentary on Obama's decision, a leading theme has been that Washington's benign efforts to bring democracy and human rights to suffering Cubans, sullied only by childish CIA shenanigans, have been a failure. Our lofty goals were not achieved, so a reluctant change of course is finally in order.

Were the policies a failure? That depends on what the goal was. The answer is quite clear in the documentary record. The Cuban threat was the familiar one that runs through Cold War history. It was spelled out clearly by the incoming Kennedy administration; the primary concern was that Cuba might be a "virus" that would "spread contagion." As historian Thomas Paterson observes, "Cuba, as symbol and reality, challenged US hegemony in Latin America."[15]

The way to deal with a virus is to kill it and inoculate any potential victims. That sensible policy is just what Washington pursued, quite successfully. Cuba has survived, but without the ability to achieve its feared potential. And the region was "inoculated" with vicious military dictatorships, beginning with the Kennedy-inspired military coup that established a terror and torture regime in Brazil shortly after Kennedy's assassination. The generals had carried out a "democratic rebellion," Ambassador Lincoln Gordon cabled home. The revolution was "a great victory for free world," which prevented a "total loss to West of all South American Republics" and should "create a greatly improved climate for private investments." This democratic revolution was "the single most decisive victory of freedom in the mid-twentieth century," Gordon held, "one of the major turning points in world history" in this period, which removed what Washington saw as a Castro clone.[16]

Much the same was true of the Vietnam War, also considered a failure and a defeat. Vietnam itself was of no particular concern, but as the documentary record reveals, Washington was concerned that successful independent development there might spread contagion throughout the region. Vietnam was virtually destroyed; it would be a model for no one. And the region would be protected by installing murderous dictatorships, much as in Latin America in the same years. It is not unnatural that imperial policy should follow similar lines in different parts of the world.

The Vietnam War is described as a failure, an American defeat. In reality it was a partial victory. The United States did not achieve its maximal goal of turning Vietnam into the Philippines, but the major concerns were overcome, much as in the case of Cuba. Such outcomes therefore count as defeat, failure, terrible decisions.

The imperial mentality is wondrous to behold.

19

"Two Ways About It"

In the wake of the terrorist attack on *Charlie Hebdo*, which killed twelve people including the editor and four other cartoonists, and the murder of four Jews at a kosher supermarket shortly after, French prime minister Manuel Valls declared "a war against terrorism, against jihadism, against radical Islam, against everything that is aimed at breaking fraternity, freedom, solidarity."[1]

Millions of people demonstrated in condemnation of the atrocities, amplified by a chorus of horror under the banner "I Am Charlie." There were eloquent pronouncements of outrage, captured well by the head of Israel's Labor Party, Isaac Herzog, who declared that "terrorism is terrorism. There's no two ways about it," and that "all the nations that seek peace and freedom [face] an enormous challenge" from brutal violence.[2]

The crimes also elicited a flood of commentary, inquiring into the roots of these shocking assaults in Islamic culture and exploring ways to counter the murderous wave of Islamic terrorism without sacrificing our values. The *New York Times* described the assault as a "clash of civilizations," but was corrected by *Times* columnist Anand Giridharadas, who tweeted that it was "not & never a war of civilizations or between them. But a war FOR civilization against groups on the other side of that line."[3]

The scene in Paris was described vividly in the *New York Times* by veteran Europe correspondent Steven Erlanger: "a day of sirens, helicopters in the air, frantic news bulletins; of police cordons and anxious crowds; of young children led away from schools to safety. It was a day, like the previous two, of blood and horror in and around Paris."[4]

Erlanger also quoted a surviving journalist, who said: "Everything crashed. There was no way out. There was smoke everywhere. It was terrible. People were screaming. It was like a nightmare." Another reported a "huge detonation, and everything went completely dark." The scene, Erlanger reported, "was an increasingly familiar one of smashed glass, broken walls, twisted timbers, scorched paint and emotional devastation."

The quotes in the previous paragraph, however—as independent journalist David Peterson reminds us—are not from January 2015. Rather, they are from a report Erlanger wrote on April 24, 1999, which received far less attention. Erlanger was reporting on the NATO "missile attack on Serbian state television headquarters" that knocked Radio Television of Serbia (RTS) "off the air," killing sixteen journalists.

"NATO and American officials defended the attack," Erlanger reported, "as an effort to undermine the regime of President Slobodan Milosevic of Yugoslavia." Pentagon spokesman Kenneth Bacon told a briefing in Washington that "Serb TV is as much a part of Milosevic's murder machine as his military is," hence a legitimate target of attack.[5]

At the time, there were no demonstrations or cries of outrage, no chants of "We are RTS," no inquiries into the roots of the attack in Christian culture and history. On the contrary, the attack on the TV headquarters was lauded. The highly regarded diplomat Richard Holbrooke, then special envoy to Yugoslavia, described the successful attack on RTS as "an enormously important and, I think, positive development."[6]

There are many other events that call for no inquiry into Western culture and history: for example, the worst single terrorist atrocity in Europe in recent years, when Anders Breivik, a Christian ultra-Zionist extremist and Islamophobe, slaughtered seventy-seven people, mostly teenagers, in July 2011.

Also ignored in the "war against terrorism" is the most extreme terrorist campaign of modern times, Obama's global drone assassination campaign, targeting people suspected of perhaps intending to harm us someday and any unfortunates who happen to be nearby. Other unfortunates are also not lacking, such as the fifty civilians killed in a U.S.-led bombing raid in Syria in December, barely reported.[7]

One person was indeed punished in connection with the NATO attack on RTS: a Serbian court sentenced Dragoljub Milanović, general manager of Radio Television of Serbia, to ten years in prison for failing to evacuate the building. The International Criminal Tribunal for the former Yugoslavia considered the NATO attack, concluding that it was not a crime, and although civilian casualties were "unfortunately high, they do not appear to be clearly disproportionate."[8]

The comparison between these cases helps us understand the condemnation of the *New York Times* by civil rights lawyer Floyd Abrams, famous for his forceful defense of freedom of expression. "There are times for self-restraint," Abrams wrote, "but in the immediate wake of the most threatening assault on journalism in living memory, [the *Times* editors] would have served the cause of free expression best by engaging in it"—that is, by publishing the *Charlie Hebdo* cartoons ridiculing Mohammed that elicited the assault.[9]

Abrams is right in describing the *Charlie Hebdo* attack as "the most threatening assault on journalism in living memory." The reason has to do with the concept "living memory," a category carefully constructed to include *their* crimes against us while scrupulously excluding *our* crimes against them—the latter not crimes but a noble defense of the highest values, sometimes inadvertently flawed.

There are many other illustrations of the interesting category "living memory." One is provided by the Marine assault against Fallu-

jah in November 2004, one of the worst crimes of the U.S.-UK inva-
sion of Iraq. The assault opened with the occupation of Fallujah General
Hospital, a major war crime quite apart from how it was carried out.
The crime was reported prominently on the front page of the *New York
Times*, accompanied by a photograph depicting how "patients and hospital employees were rushed out of rooms by armed soldiers and ordered
to sit or lie on the floor while troops tied their hands behind their backs."
The occupation of the hospital was considered meritorious, and justified, since it "shut down what officers said was a propaganda weapon for
the militants: Falluja General Hospital, with its stream of reports of
civilian casualties."[10]

Evidently, shutting down this "propaganda weapon" was no assault
on free expression, and does not qualify for entry into "living memory."

There are other questions. One would naturally ask how France
upholds freedom of expression, for example, by the Gayssot Law, repeatedly implemented, which effectively grants the state the right to determine Historical Truth and punish deviation from its edicts. Or how it
upholds the sacred principles of "fraternity, freedom, solidarity" by
expelling miserable descendants of Holocaust survivors, the Roma, to
bitter persecution in Eastern Europe; or by its deplorable treatment of
North African immigrants in the banlieues of Paris, where the *Charlie
Hebdo* terrorists became jihadis.

Anyone with eyes open will quickly notice other rather striking
omissions from living memory. Ignored, for instance, is the assassination of three journalists in Latin America in December 2014, bringing
the number for the year to thirty-one. There have been dozens of journalists murdered in Honduras alone since the military coup of 2009 that
was effectively authorized by the United States, probably according
postcoup Honduras the per-capita championship when it comes to the
murder of journalists. But again, this was not an assault on freedom of
the press within living memory.

These few examples illustrate a very general principle observed with
impressive dedication and consistency: the more we can blame some

crimes on enemies, the greater the outrage; the greater our responsibility for crimes—and hence the more we can do to end them—the less the concern, tending to oblivion.

Contrary to the eloquent pronouncements, it is not the case that "terrorism is terrorism. There's no two ways about it." There definitely are two ways about it: theirs versus ours. And not just when it comes to terrorism.

20

One Day in the Life of a Reader of the
New York Times

The *New York Times* can plausibly be regarded as the world's leading newspaper. It is an indispensable source of news and commentary, but there is a lot more that one can learn by reading it carefully and critically. Let us keep to a single day, April 6, 2015—though almost any other day would have provided similar insights into prevailing ideology and intellectual culture.

A front-page article is devoted to a flawed story about a campus rape in *Rolling Stone* magazine, exposed in the *Columbia Journalism Review*. So severe is this departure from journalistic integrity that it is also the subject of the lead story in the business section, with a full inside page devoted to the continuation of the two reports. The shocked reports refer to several past crimes of the press: a few cases of fabrication, quickly exposed, and cases of plagiarism ("too numerous to list"). The specific crime of *Rolling Stone* is "lack of skepticism," which is "in many ways the most insidious" of the three categories.[1]

It is refreshing to see the commitment of the *Times* to the integrity of journalism.

On page seven of the same issue, there is an important story by Thomas Fuller headlined "One Woman's Mission to Free Laos from

Millions of Unexploded Bombs." It reports on the "single-minded effort" of a Lao-American woman, Channapha Khamvongsa, "to rid her native land of millions of bombs still buried there, the legacy of a nine-year American air campaign that made Laos one of the most heavily bombed places on earth." The story notes that as a result of Ms. Khamvongsa's lobbying, the United States increased its annual spending on the removal of unexploded bombs by a munificent $12 million. The most lethal are cluster bombs, which are designed to "cause maximum casualties to troops" by spraying "hundreds of bomblets onto the ground."[2] About 30 percent remain unexploded, so that they kill and maim children who pick up the pieces, farmers who strike them while working, and other unfortunates. An accompanying map features Xieng Khouang province in northern Laos, better known as the Plain of Jars, the primary target of the intensive bombing, which reached its peak of fury in 1969.

Fuller reports that Ms. Khamvongsa "was spurred into action when she came across a collection of drawings of the bombings made by refugees and collected by Fred Branfman, an antiwar activist who helped expose the Secret War."[3] The drawings appear in his remarkable book *Voices from the Plain of Jars*, published in 1972 and republished by the University of Wisconsin Press in 2013 with a new introduction. The drawings vividly display the torment of the victims, poor peasants in a remote area that had virtually nothing to do with the Vietnam War, as officially conceded. One typical report by a twenty-six-year-old nurse captures the nature of the air war: "There wasn't a night when we thought we'd live until morning, never a morning we thought we'd survive until night. Did our children cry? Oh, yes, and we did also. I just stayed in my cave. I didn't see the sunlight for two years. What did I think about? Oh, I used to repeat, 'please don't let the planes come, please don't let the planes come, please don't let the planes come.'"[4]

Branfman's valiant efforts did indeed bring some awareness of this hideous atrocity. His assiduous research also unearthed the reasons for the savage destruction of a helpless peasant society. He exposed them once again in the introduction to the new edition of *Voices*:

> One of the most shattering revelations about the bombing was discovering why it had so vastly increased in 1969, as described by the refugees. I learned that after President Lyndon Johnson had declared a bombing halt over North Vietnam in November 1968, he had simply diverted the planes into northern Laos. There was no military reason for doing so. It was simply because, as US Deputy Chief of Mission Monteagle Stearns testified to the US Senate Committee on Foreign Relations in October 1969, "Well, we had all those planes sitting around and couldn't just let them stay there with nothing to do."[5]

Therefore the unused planes were unleashed on poor peasants, devastating the peaceful Plain of Jars, far from the ravages of Washington's murderous wars of aggression in Indochina.

Let us now see how these revelations are transmuted into *New York Times* Newspeak. Writes Fuller, "The targets were North Vietnamese troops—especially along the Ho Chi Minh Trail, a large part of which passed through Laos—as well as North Vietnam's Laotian Communist allies."[6] Compare this to the words of the U.S. deputy chief of mission and the heartrending drawings and testimony in Fred Branfman's book.

True, the *Times* reporter has a source: U.S. propaganda. That surely suffices to overwhelm mere facts about one of the major crimes of the post–World War II era, as detailed in the very source he cites: Fred Branfman's crucial revelations.

We can be confident that this colossal lie in the service of the state will not merit lengthy exposure and denunciation of disgraceful misdeeds of the Free Press such as plagiarism and lack of skepticism.

The same issue of the *New York Times* treats us to a report by the inimitable Thomas Friedman, earnestly relaying the words of President Obama presenting what Friedman labels "the Obama Doctrine." (Every

President has to have a doctrine.) The profound doctrine is "'engagement,' combined with meeting core strategic needs."[7]

The president illustrated his doctrine with a crucial case: "You take a country like Cuba. For us to test the possibility that engagement leads to a better outcome for the Cuban people, there aren't that many risks for us. It's a tiny little country. It's not one that threatens our core security interests, and so [there's no reason not] to test the proposition. And if it turns out that it doesn't lead to better outcomes, we can adjust our policies."[8]

Here the Nobel Peace laureate expands on his reasons for undertaking what the leading left-liberal intellectual journal, the *New York Review of Books*, hails as the "brave" and "truly historic step" of reestablishing diplomatic relations with Cuba.[9] It is a move undertaken in order to "more effectively empower the Cuban people," the hero explained, our earlier efforts to bring them freedom and democracy having failed to achieve our noble goals.[10]

Searching further, we find other gems. There is, for example, a front-page think piece on the Iran nuclear deal by Peter Baker published a few days earlier, warning about the Iranian crimes regularly listed by Washington's propaganda system. All prove to be quite revealing on analysis, though none more so than the ultimate Iranian crime: "destabilizing" the region by supporting "Shiite militias that killed American soldiers in Iraq."[11] Here again is the standard picture. When the United States invades Iraq, virtually destroying it and inciting sectarian conflicts that are tearing the country and now the whole region apart, that counts as "stabilization" in official and hence media rhetoric. When Iran supports militias resisting the aggression, that is "destabilization." And there could hardly be a more heinous crime than killing American soldiers attacking one's home.

All of this, and far, far more, makes perfect sense if we show due obedience and uncritically accept approved doctrine: The United States owns the world, and it does so by right, for reasons also explained lucidly in the *New York Review of Books* in a March 2015 article by Jessica

Mathews, former president of the Carnegie Endowment for International Peace. "American contributions to international security, global economic growth, freedom, and human well-being have been so self-evidently unique and have been so clearly directed to others' benefit that Americans have long believed that the US amounts to a different kind of country. Where others push their national interests, the US tries to advance universal principles."[12]

The defense rests.

21

"The Iranian Threat": Who Is the Gravest Danger to World Peace?

Throughout the world there is great relief and optimism about the nuclear deal reached in Vienna between Iran and the P5 + 1 nations, the five veto-holding members of the UN Security Council and Germany. Most of the world apparently shares the assessment of the U.S. Arms Control Association that "the Joint Comprehensive Plan of Action establishes a strong and effective formula for blocking all of the pathways by which Iran could acquire material for nuclear weapons for more than a generation and a verification system to promptly detect and deter possible efforts by Iran to covertly pursue nuclear weapons that will last indefinitely."[1]

There are, however, striking exceptions to the general enthusiasm: the United States and its closest regional allies, Israel and Saudi Arabia. One consequence of this is that U.S. corporations, much to their chagrin, are prevented from flocking to Tehran along with their European counterparts. Prominent sectors of U.S. power and opinion share the stand of the two regional allies and so are in a state of virtual hysteria over "the Iranian threat." Sober commentary in the United States, pretty much across the spectrum, declares that country to be "the gravest threat to world peace." Even supporters of the agreement here are wary, given the exceptional gravity of that threat. After all, how can we trust the Iranians, with their terrible record of aggression, violence, disruption, and deceit?

Opposition within the political class is so strong that public opinion has shifted quickly from significant support for the deal to an even split.[2] Republicans are almost unanimously opposed to the agreement. The current Republican primaries illustrate the proclaimed reasons. Senator Ted Cruz, considered one of the intellectuals among the crowded field of presidential candidates, warns that Iran may still be able to produce nuclear weapons and could someday use one to set off an electromagnetic pulse that "would take down the electrical grid of the entire eastern seaboard" of the United States, killing "tens of millions of Americans."[3] Two other candidates, former Florida governor Jeb Bush and Wisconsin governor Scott Walker, battled over whether to bomb Iran immediately after being elected or after the first Cabinet meeting.[4] The one candidate with some foreign policy experience, Lindsey Graham, describes the deal as "a death sentence for the state of Israel," which will certainly come as a surprise to Israeli intelligence and strategic analysts—and which Graham knows to be utter nonsense, raising immediate questions about his actual motives for saying so.[5]

It is important to bear in mind that the Republicans long ago abandoned the pretense of functioning as a normal parliamentary party. They have, as respected conservative political commentator Norman Ornstein of the right-wing American Enterprise Institute observed, become a "radical insurgency" that scarcely seeks to participate in normal congressional politics.[6] Since the days of President Ronald Reagan, the party leadership has plunged so far into the pockets of the very rich and the corporate sector that they can attract votes only by mobilizing parts of the population that have not previously been an organized political force. Among them are extremist evangelical Christians, now probably a majority of Republican voters; remnants of the former slaveholding states; nativists who are terrified that "they" are taking our white, Christian, Anglo-Saxon country away from us; and others who turn the Republican primaries into spectacles remote from the mainstream of modern society—though not from the mainstream of the most powerful country in world history.

The departure from global standards, however, goes far beyond the bounds of the Republican radical insurgency. Across the spectrum there is general agreement with the "pragmatic" conclusion of General Martin Dempsey, chairman of the Joint Chiefs of Staff, that the Vienna deal does not "prevent the United States from striking Iranian facilities if officials decide that it is cheating on the agreement," even though a unilateral military strike is "far less likely" if Iran behaves.[7] Former Clinton and Obama Middle East negotiator Dennis Ross typically recommends that "Iran must have no doubts that if we see it moving towards a weapon, that would trigger the use of force" even after the termination of the deal, when Iran is free to do what it wants.[8] In fact, the existence of a termination point fifteen years hence is, he adds, "the greatest single problem with the agreement." He also suggests that the United States provide Israel with B 52 bombers and bunker busting bombs to protect itself before that terrifying date arrives.[9]

"THE GREATEST THREAT"

Opponents of the nuclear deal charge that it does not go far enough. Some supporters agree, holding that "if the Vienna deal is to mean anything, the whole of the Middle East must rid itself of weapons of mass destruction." The author of those words, Iran's Minister of Foreign Affairs Javad Zarif, added that "Iran, in its national capacity and as current chairman of the Non-Aligned Movement [the governments of the large majority of the world's population], is prepared to work with the international community to achieve these goals, knowing full well that, along the way, it will probably run into many hurdles raised by the skeptics of peace and diplomacy." Iran has signed "a historic nuclear deal," he continues, and now it is the turn of Israel, "the holdout."[10]

Israel, of course, is one of the three nuclear powers, along with India and Pakistan, whose nuclear weapons programs have been abetted by the United States and who refuse to sign the Non-Proliferation Treaty (NPT).

Zarif was referring to the regular five-year NPT review conference, which ended in failure in April when the United States (joined this time by Canada and Great Britain) once again blocked efforts to move toward a zone free of weapons of mass destruction in the Middle East. These efforts have been led by Egypt and other Arab states for twenty years. Two of the leading figures promoting them at the NPT and other UN agencies, and at the Pugwash Conferences, Jayantha Dhanapala and Sergio Duarte, observe that "the successful adoption in 1995 of the resolution on the establishment of a zone free of weapons of mass destruction (WMD) in the Middle East was the main element of a package that permitted the indefinite extension of the NPT." [11]

The NPT, in turn, is the most important arms control treaty of all. If it were adhered to, it could end the scourge of nuclear weapons. Repeatedly, implementation of the resolution has been blocked by the United States, most recently by President Obama in 2010 and again in 2015. Dhanapala and Duarte comment that the effort was again blocked "on behalf of a state that is not a party to the NPT and is widely believed to be the only one in the region possessing nuclear weapons"—a polite and understated reference to Israel. This failure, they hope, "will not be the coup de grâce to the two longstanding NPT objectives of accelerated progress on nuclear disarmament and establishing a Middle Eastern WMD-free zone." Their article, in the journal of the Arms Control Association, is entitled: "Is There a Future for the NPT?"

A nuclear weapons–free zone in the Middle East is a straightforward way to address whatever threat Iran allegedly poses, but a great deal more is at stake in Washington's continuing sabotage of the effort in order to protect its Israeli client. This is not the only case when opportunities to end the alleged Iranian threat have been undermined by Washington, raising further questions about just what is actually at stake.

In considering this matter, it is instructive to examine both the unspoken assumptions and the questions that are rarely asked. Let us consider a few of these assumptions, beginning with the most serious: that Iran is the gravest threat to world peace.

In the United States, it is a virtual cliché among high officials and commentators that Iran wins that grim prize. There is also a world outside the United States, and although its views are not reported in the mainstream here, perhaps they are of some interest. According to the leading Western polling agencies (WIN/Gallup International), the prize for "greatest threat" is won by the United States, which the world regards as the gravest threat to world peace by a large margin. In second place, far below, is Pakistan, its ranking probably inflated by the Indian vote. Iran is ranked below those two, along with China, Israel, North Korea, and Afghanistan.[12]

"THE WORLD'S LEADING SUPPORTER OF TERRORISM"

Turning to the next obvious question, what in fact is the Iranian threat? Why, for example, are Israel and Saudi Arabia trembling in fear over the threat of Iran? Whatever the threat is, it can hardly be military. Years ago, U.S. intelligence informed Congress that Iran has very low military expenditures by the standards of the region and that its strategic doctrines are defensive—designed, that is, to deter aggression.[13] This intelligence further reports that it has no evidence Iran is pursuing a nuclear weapons program and that "Iran's nuclear program and its willingness to keep open the possibility of developing nuclear weapons is a central part of its deterrent strategy."[14]

The authoritative Stockholm International Peace Research Institute (SIPRI) review of global armaments ranks the United States, as usual, far in the lead in military expenditures. China comes in second, with about one-third of U.S. expenditures. Far below are Russia and Saudi Arabia, which are nonetheless well above any western European state. Iran is scarcely mentioned.[15] Full details are provided in an April report from the Center for Strategic and International Studies (CSIS), which finds "a conclusive case that the Arab Gulf states have . . . an overwhelming advantage [over] Iran in both military spending and access to modern arms." Iran's military spending is a fraction of Saudi Arabia's and far below even the spending of the United Arab Emirates (UAE). Altogether, the Gulf Cooperation Council states—Bahrain, Kuwait, Oman, Qatar, Saudi Arabia, and the UAE—outspend Iran on arms by a factor of about eight, an imbalance that goes back decades.[16] The CSIS report adds that "the Arab Gulf states have acquired and are acquiring some of the most advanced and effective weapons in the world [while] Iran has essentially been forced to live in the past, often relying on systems originally delivered at the time of the Shah." In other words, they are virtually obsolete.[17] When it comes to Israel, of course, the imbalance is even greater. Possessing the most advanced U.S. weaponry and a virtual offshore military base for the global superpower, it also has a huge stock of nuclear weapons.

To be sure, Israel faces the "existential threat" of Iranian pronouncements: Supreme Leader Khamenei and former president Mahmoud Ahmadinejad famously threatened it with destruction. Except that they didn't—and if they had, it would have been of little moment.[18] They predicted that "under God's grace [the Zionist regime] will be wiped off the map" (according to another translation, Ahmadinejad says Israel "must vanish from the page of time," citing a statement by the Ayatollah Khomeini during the period when Israel and Iran were tacitly allied). In other words, they hope that regime change will someday take place. Even that falls far short of the direct calls in both Washington and Tel Aviv for regime change in Iran, not to speak of the actions taken to implement regime change. These, of course, go back to the actual "regime change" of 1953, when the United States and Britain organized a military coup to overthrow Iran's parliamentary government and install the dictatorship of the shah, who proceeded to amass one of the world's worst human rights records. These crimes were known to readers of the reports of Amnesty International and other human rights organizations, but not to readers of the U.S. press, which has devoted plenty of space to Iranian human rights violations—but only since 1979, when the shah's regime was overthrown. The instructive facts are documented carefully in a study by Mansour Farhang and William Dorman.[19]

None of this is a departure from the norm. The United States, as is well-known, holds the world championship title in regime change, and Israel is no laggard either. The most destructive of its invasions of Lebanon, in 1982, was explicitly aimed at regime change as well as at securing its hold on the occupied territories. The pretexts offered were thin and collapsed at once. That too is not unusual and pretty much independent of the nature of the society—from the laments in the Declaration of Independence about the "merciless Indian savages" to Hitler's defense of Germany from the "wild terror" of the Poles.

No serious analyst believes that Iran would ever use, or even threaten to use, a nuclear weapon if it had one, and thereby face instant destruction. There is, however, real concern that a nuclear weapon might fall into jihadi hands not from Iran, where the threat is minuscule, but from U.S. ally Pakistan, where it is very real. In the journal of the (British) Royal Institute of International Affairs (Chatham House), two leading Pakistani nuclear scientists, Pervez Hoodbhoy and Zia Mian, write that increasing fears of "militants seizing nuclear weapons or materials and unleashing nuclear terrorism [have led to] . . . the creation of a dedicated force of over 20,000 troops to guard nuclear facilities. There is no reason to assume, however, that this force would be immune to the problems associated with the units guarding regular military facilities," which have frequently suffered attacks with "insider help."[20] In brief, the problem is real, but is displaced to Iran thanks to fantasies concocted for other reasons.

Other concerns about the Iranian threat include its role as "the world's leading supporter of terrorism," which primarily refers to its support for Hizbollah and Hamas.[21] Both of those movements emerged in resistance to U.S.-backed Israeli violence and aggression, which vastly exceeds anything attributed to these organizations. Whatever one thinks about them, or other beneficiaries of Iranian support, Iran hardly ranks high in support of terror worldwide, even within the Muslim world. Among Islamic states, Saudi Arabia is far in the lead as a sponsor of Islamic terror, not only through direct funding by wealthy Saudis and others in the Gulf but even more by the missionary zeal with which the Saudis promulgate their extremist Wahhabi-Salafi version of Islam through Koranic schools, mosques, clerics, and other means available to a religious dictatorship with enormous oil wealth. ISIS is an extremist offshoot of Saudi religious extremism and its fanning of jihadi flames.

In generation of Islamic terror, however, nothing can compare with the U.S. war on terror, which has helped to spread the plague from a small tribal area in the Afghanistan-Pakistan borderlands to a vast region from West Africa to Southeast Asia. The invasion of Iraq alone escalated terror attacks by a factor of seven in the first year, well beyond even what had been predicted by intelligence agencies.[22] Drone warfare against marginalized and oppressed tribal societies also elicits demands for revenge, as ample evidence indicates.

Those two Iranian clients, Hizbollah and Hamas, also share the crime of winning the popular vote in the only free elections in the Arab world. Hizbollah is guilty of the even more heinous crime of compelling Israel to withdraw from its occupation of southern Lebanon in violation of Security Council orders dating back decades, an illegal regime of terror punctuated with episodes of extreme violence, murder, and destruction.

"FUELING INSTABILITY"

Another concern, voiced at the United Nations by U.S. Ambassador Samantha Power, is the "instability that Iran fuels beyond its nuclear program."[23] The United States will continue to scrutinize this misbehavior, she declared. In that, she echoed the assurance offered by Defense Secretary Ashton Carter while standing on Israel's northern border that "we will continue to help Israel counter Iran's malign influence" in supporting Hizbollah, and that the United States reserves the right to use military force against Iran as it deems appropriate.[24]

The way Iran "fuels instability" can be seen particularly dramatically in Iraq, where, among other crimes, it alone came at once to the aid of Kurds defending themselves from the ISIS invasion and where it is building a $2.5 billion power plant to try to bring electrical power back to its level before the U.S. invasion.[25] Ambassador Power's usage is standard: when the United States invades a country, resulting in hundreds of thousands killed and millions of refugees, along with barbarous torture and destruction that Iraqis compare to the Mongol invasions, leaving Iraq the unhappiest country in the world according to WIN/Gallup polls, meanwhile igniting sectarian conflict that is tearing the region to shreds and laying the basis for the ISIS monstrosity along with our Saudi ally—that is "stabilization."[26] Iran's shameful actions are "fueling instability." The farce of this standard usage sometimes reaches levels that are almost surreal, as when liberal commentator James Chace, former editor of *Foreign Affairs*, explained that the United States sought to "destabilize a freely elected Marxist government in Chile" because "we were determined to seek stability" under the Pinochet dictatorship.[27]

Others are outraged that Washington should negotiate at all with a "contemptible" regime like Iran's, with its horrifying human rights record, and urge instead that we pursue "an American-sponsored alliance between Israel and the Sunni states." So writes Leon Wieseltier, contributing editor to the venerable liberal journal the *Atlantic*, who can barely conceal his visceral hatred for all things Iranian. [28] With a straight face, this respected liberal intellectual recommends that Saudi Arabia, which makes Iran look like a virtual paradise, and Israel, with its vicious crimes in Gaza and elsewhere, should ally to teach that country good behavior. Perhaps the recommendation is not entirely unreasonable when we consider the human rights records of the regimes the United States has imposed and supported throughout the world.

Though the Iranian government is no doubt a threat to its own people, it regrettably breaks no records in this regard, and does not descend to the level of favored U.S. allies. That, however, cannot be the concern of Washington, and surely not Tel Aviv or Riyadh.

It might also be useful to recall—as surely Iranians do—that not a day has passed since 1953 when the United States was not harming Iranians. As soon as Iranians overthrew the hated U.S.-imposed regime of the shah in 1979, Washington at once turned to supporting Saddam Hussein's murderous attack on Iran. President Reagan went so far as to deny Saddam's major crime, his chemical warfare assault on Iraq's Kurdish population, which he blamed on Iran instead.[29] When Saddam was tried for crimes under U.S. auspices, that horrendous crime (as well as others in which the United States was complicit) was carefully excluded from the charges, which were restricted to one of his minor crimes, the murder of 148 Shiites in 1982, a footnote to his gruesome record.[30]

After the Iran-Iraq war ended, the United States continued to support Saddam Hussein, Iran's primary enemy. President George H. W. Bush even invited Iraqi nuclear engineers to the United States for advanced training in weapons production, an extremely serious threat to Iran.[31] Sanctions against Iran were intensified, including against foreign firms dealing with it, and actions were initiated to bar it from the international financial system.[32]

In recent years the hostility has extended to sabotage, the murder of nuclear scientists (presumably by Israel), and cyberwar, openly proclaimed with pride.[33] The Pentagon regards cyberwar as an act of war, justifying a military response, as does NATO, which affirmed in September 2014 that cyberattacks may trigger the collective defense obligations of the NATO powers—when we are the target, that is, not the perpetrators.[34]

"THE PRIME ROGUE STATE"

It is only fair to add that there have been breaks in this pattern. President George W. Bush provided several significant gifts to Iran by destroying its major enemies, Saddam Hussein and the Taliban. He even placed Iran's Iraqi enemy under its influence after the U.S. defeat, which was so severe that Washington had to abandon its officially declared goals of establishing permanent military bases ("enduring camps") and ensuring that U.S. corporations would have privileged access to Iraq's vast oil resources.[35]

Do Iranian leaders intend to develop nuclear weapons today? We can decide for ourselves how credible their denials are, but that they had such intentions in the past is beyond question, since it was asserted openly on the highest authority, which informed foreign journalists that Iran would develop nuclear weapons "certainly, and sooner than one thinks."[36] The father of Iran's nuclear energy program and former head of Iran's Atomic Energy Organization was confident that the leadership's plan "was to build a nuclear bomb."[37] The CIA also reported that it had "no doubt" Iran would develop nuclear weapons if neighboring countries did (as they have).[38]

All of this was under the shah, the "highest authority" just quoted— that is, during the period when high U.S. officials (Cheney, Rumsfeld, Kissinger and others) were urging the shah to proceed with nuclear programs and pressuring universities to accommodate these efforts.[39] As part of these efforts, my own university, MIT, made a deal with the shah to admit Iranian students to the nuclear engineering program in return for grants from the shah—over the very strong objections of the student body, but with comparably strong faculty support, in a meeting that older faculty will doubtless remember well.[40]

Asked later why he supported such programs under the shah but opposed them more recently, Kissinger responded honestly that Iran was an ally then.[41]

Putting aside absurdities, what is the real threat of Iran that inspires such fear and fury? A natural place to turn for an answer is, again, U.S. intelligence. Recall its analysis that Iran poses no military threat, that its strategic doctrines are defensive, and that its nuclear programs (with no effort to produce bombs, as far as intelligence can determine) are "a central part of its deterrent strategy."

Who, then, would be concerned by an Iranian deterrent? The answer is plain: the rogue states that rampage in the region and do not want to tolerate any impediment to their reliance on aggression and violence.

In the lead in this regard are the United States and Israel, with Saudi Arabia trying its best to join the club with its invasion of Bahrain (to support the crushing of a reform movement there) and now its murderous assault on Yemen, accelerating a growing humanitarian catastrophe in that country.

For the United States, the characterization is familiar. Fifteen years ago, the prominent political analyst Samuel Huntington warned in the establishment journal *Foreign Affairs* that for much of the world the United States was "becoming the rogue superpower . . . the single greatest external threat to their societies."[42] Shortly after, his words were echoed by Robert Jervis, the president of the American Political Science Association: "In the eyes of much of the world, in fact, the prime rogue state today is the United States."[43] As we have seen, global opinion supports this judgment by a substantial margin.

Furthermore, the mantle is worn with pride. That is the clear meaning of the insistence of the leadership and the political class that the United States reserves the right to resort to force if it determines, unilaterally, that Iran is violating some commitment. This policy is of long standing for liberal Democrats, and by no means restricted to Iran. The Clinton doctrine affirmed that the United States is entitled to resort to the "unilateral use of military power" even to ensure "uninhibited access to key markets, energy supplies, and strategic resources," let alone alleged "security" or "humanitarian" concerns.[44] Adherence to various versions of this doctrine has been well confirmed in practice, as need hardly be discussed among people willing to look at the facts of current history.

These are among the critical matters that should be the focus of attention in analyzing the nuclear deal at Vienna.

22

The Doomsday Clock

In January 2015, the *Bulletin of the Atomic Scientists* advanced its famous Doomsday Clock to three minutes before midnight, a threat level that had not been reached for thirty years. The *Bulletin*'s statement explaining this advance toward catastrophe invoked the two major threats to survival: nuclear weapons and "unchecked climate change." The call condemned world leaders, who "have failed to act with the speed or on the scale required to protect citizens from potential catastrophe," endangering "every person on Earth [by] failing to perform their most important duty—ensuring and preserving the health and vitality of human civilization."[1]

Since then, there has been good reason to consider moving the hands even closer to doomsday.

As the year ended, world leaders met in Paris to address the severe problem of "unchecked climate change." Hardly a day passes without new evidence of how severe the crisis is. To pick almost at random, shortly before the opening of the Paris conference, NASA's Jet Propulsion Lab released a study that both surprised and alarmed scientists who have been studying Arctic ice. The study showed that a huge Greenland glacier, Zachariae Isstrom, "broke loose from a glaciologically stable position in 2012 and entered a phase of accelerated retreat," an unexpected and ominous development. The glacier "holds enough water to raise global sea level by more than 18 inches (46 centimeters) if it were to melt completely. And now it's on a crash diet, losing 5 billion tons of mass every year. All that ice is crumbling into the North Atlantic Ocean."[2]

Yet there was little expectation that world leaders in Paris would "act with the speed or on the scale required to protect citizens from potential catastrophe." And even if by some miracle they had, it would have been of limited value, for reasons that should be deeply disturbing.

When the agreement was approved in Paris, French Foreign Minister Laurent Fabius, who hosted the talks, announced that it is "legally binding."[3] That may be the hope, but there are more than a few obstacles that are worthy of careful attention.

In all of the extensive media coverage of the Paris conference, perhaps the most important sentences are these, buried near the end of a long *New York Times* analysis: "Traditionally, negotiators have sought to forge a legally binding treaty that needed ratification by the governments of the participating countries to have force. There is no way to get that in this case, because of the United States. A treaty would be dead on arrival on Capitol Hill without the required two-thirds majority vote in the Republican-controlled Senate. So the voluntary plans are taking the place of mandatory, top-down targets." And voluntary plans are a guarantee of failure.[4]

"Because of the United States." More precisely, because of the Republican Party, which by now is becoming a real danger to decent human survival.

The conclusions are underscored in another *Times* piece on the Paris agreement. At the end of a long story lauding the achievement, the article notes that the system created at the conference "depends heavily on the views of the future world leaders who will carry out those policies. In the United States, every Republican candidate running for president in 2016 has publicly questioned or denied the science of climate change, and has voiced opposition to Mr. Obama's climate change policies. In the Senate, Mitch McConnell, the Republican leader, who has led the charge against Mr. Obama's climate change agenda, said, 'Before his international partners pop the champagne, they should remember that this is an unattainable deal based on a domestic energy plan that is likely illegal, that half the states have sued to halt, and that Congress has already voted to reject.'"[5]

Both parties have moved to the right during the neoliberal period of the past generation. Mainstream Democrats are now pretty much what used to be called "moderate Republicans." Meanwhile, the Republican Party has largely drifted off the spectrum, becoming what respected conservative political analyst Thomas Mann and Norman Ornstein call a "radical insurgency" that has virtually abandoned normal parliamentary politics. With the rightward drift, the Republican Party's dedication to wealth and privilege has become so extreme that its actual policies could not attract voters, so it has had to seek a new popular base, mobilized on other grounds: evangelical Christians who await the Second Coming,[6] nativists who fear that "they" are taking our country away from us, unreconstructed racists,[7] people with real grievances who gravely mistake their causes,[8] and others like them who are easy prey to demagogues and can readily become a radical insurgency.

In recent years, the Republican establishment had managed to suppress the voices of the base that it has mobilized. But no longer. By the end of 2015 the establishment was expressing considerable dismay and desperation over its inability to do so, as the Republican base and its choices fell out of control.

Republican elected officials and contenders for the next presidential election expressed open contempt for the Paris deliberations, refusing to even attend the proceedings. The three candidates who led in the polls at the time—Donald Trump, Ted Cruz, and Ben Carson—adopted the stand of the largely evangelical base: humans have no impact on global warming, if it is happening at all. The other candidates reject government action to deal with the matter. Immediately after Obama spoke in Paris, pledging that the United States would be in the vanguard seeking global action, the Republican-dominated Congress voted to scuttle his recent Environmental Protection Agency rules to cut carbon emissions. As the press reported, this was "a provocative message to more than 100 [world] leaders that the American president does not have the full support of his government on climate policy"—a bit of an understatement. Meanwhile Lamar Smith, Republican head of the House's Committee on Science, Space, and Technology, carried forward his jihad against government scientists who dare to report the facts.[9]

The message is clear. American citizens face an enormous responsibility right at home.

A companion story in the New York Times reports that "two-thirds of Americans support the United States joining a binding international agreement to curb growth of greenhouse gas emissions." And by a five-to-three margin, Americans regard the climate as more important than the economy. But it doesn't matter. Public opinion is dismissed. That fact, once again, sends a strong message to Americans. It is their task to cure the dysfunctional political system, in which popular opinion is a marginal factor. The disparity between public opinion and policy, in this case, has significant implications for the fate of the world.

We should, of course, have no illusions about a past "golden age." Nevertheless, the developments just reviewed constitute significant changes. The undermining of functioning democracy is one of the contributions of the neoliberal assault on the world's population in the past generation. And this is not happening just in the U.S.; in Europe the impact may be even worse.[10]

Let us turn to the other (and traditional) concern of the atomic scientists who adjust the Doomsday Clock: nuclear weapons. The current threat of nuclear war amply justifies their January 2015 decision to advance the clock two minutes toward midnight. What has happened since reveals the growing threat even more clearly, a matter that elicits insufficient concern, in my opinion.

The last time the Doomsday Clock reached three minutes before midnight was in 1983, at the time of the Able Archer exercises of the Reagan administration; these exercises simulated attacks on the Soviet Union to test their defense systems. Recently released Russian archives reveal that the Russians were deeply concerned by the operations and were preparing to respond, which would have meant, simply: The End.

We have learned more about these rash and reckless exercises, and about how close the world was to disaster, from U.S. military and intelligence analyst Melvin Goodman, who was CIA division chief and senior analyst at the Office of Soviet Affairs at the time. "In addition to the Able Archer mobilization exercise that alarmed the Kremlin," Goodman writes, "the Reagan administration authorized unusually aggressive military exercises near the Soviet border that, in some cases, violated Soviet territorial sovereignty. The Pentagon's risky measures included sending U.S. strategic bombers over the North Pole to test Soviet radar, and naval exercises in wartime approaches to the USSR where U.S. warships had previously not entered. Additional secret operations simulated surprise naval attacks on Soviet targets."[11]

We now know that the world was saved from likely nuclear destruction in those frightening days by the decision of a Russian officer, Stanislav Petrov, not to transmit to higher authorities the report of automated detection systems that the USSR was under missile attack. Accordingly, Petrov takes his place alongside Russian submarine commander Vasili Arkhipov, who, at a dangerous moment of the 1962 Cuban Missile Crisis, refused to authorize the launching of nuclear torpedoes when the subs were under attack by U.S. destroyers enforcing a quarantine.

Other recently revealed examples enrich the already frightening record. Nuclear security expert Bruce Blair reports that "the closest the US came to an inadvertent strategic launch decision by the President happened in 1979, when a NORAD early warning training tape depicting a full-scale Soviet strategic strike inadvertently coursed through the actual early warning network. National Security Adviser Zbigniew Brzezinski was called twice in the night and told the US was under attack, and he was just picking up the phone to persuade President Carter that a full-scale response needed to be authorized right away, when a third call told him it was a false alarm."[12]

This newly revealed example brings to mind a critical incident of 1995, when the trajectory of a U.S.-Norwegian rocket carrying scientific equipment resembled the path of a nuclear missile. This elicited Russian concerns that quickly reached President Boris Yeltsin, who had to decide whether to launch a nuclear strike.[13]

Blair adds other examples from his own experience. In one case, at the time of the 1967 Middle East war, "a carrier nuclear-aircraft crew was sent an actual attack order instead of an exercise/training nuclear order." A few years later, in the early 1970s, the Strategic Air Command, in Omaha, "retransmitted an exercise . . . launch order as an actual real-world launch order." In both cases code checks had failed; human intervention prevented the launch. "But you get the drift here," Blair adds. "It just wasn't that rare for these kinds of snafus to occur."

Blair made these comments in reaction to a report by airman John Bordne that has only recently been cleared by the U.S. Air Force. Bordne was serving on the U.S. military base in Okinawa in October 1962, at the time of the Cuban Missile Crisis and a moment of serious tensions in Asia as well. The U.S. nuclear alert system had been raised to DEFCON 2, one level below DEFCON 1, when nuclear missiles can be launched immediately. At the peak of the crisis, on October 28, a missile crew received authorization to launch its nuclear missiles, in error. They decided not to, averting likely nuclear war and joining Petrov and Arkhipov in the pantheon of men who decided to disobey protocol and thereby saved the world.

As Blair observed, such incidents are not uncommon. One recent expert study found dozens of false alarms every year during the period reviewed, 1977 to 1983; the study concluded that the range is 43 to 255 per year. The author of the study, Seth Baum, summarizes with appropriate words: "Nuclear war is the black swan we can never see, except in that brief moment when it is killing us. We delay eliminating the risk at our own peril. Now is the time to address the threat, because now we are still alive."[14]

These reports, like those of Eric Schlosser's extensive review *Command and Control*, keep mostly to U.S. systems.[15] The Russian ones are doubtless much more error-prone. That is not to mention the extreme danger posed by the systems of others, notably Pakistan.

Sometimes the threat has not been accident, but adventurism, as in the case of Able Archer. The most extreme case was the Cuban Missile Crisis in 1962, when the threat of disaster was all too real. The way it was handled is shocking; so is the manner in which it is commonly interpreted, as we have seen.

With this grim record in mind, it is useful to look at strategic debates and planning. One chilling case is the Clinton-era 1995 STRATCOM study "Essentials of Post–Cold War Deterrence." The study calls for retaining the right of first strike, even against nonnuclear states. It explains that nuclear weapons are constantly used, in the sense that they "cast a shadow over any crisis or conflict." It also urges a "national persona" of irrationality and vindictiveness to intimidate the world.

Current doctrine is explored in the lead article in the journal *International Security*, one of the most authoritative in the domain of strategic doctrine.[16] The authors explain that the United States is committed to "strategic primacy"—that is, insulation from retaliatory strike. This is the logic behind Obama's "new triad" (strengthening submarine and land-based missiles and the bomber force), along with missile defense to counter a retaliatory strike. The concern raised by the authors is that the U.S. demand for strategic primacy might induce China to react by abandoning its "no first use" policy and by expanding its limited deterrent. The authors think that they will not, but the prospect remains uncertain. Clearly the doctrine enhances the dangers in a tense and conflicted region.

The same is true of NATO expansion to the east in violation of verbal promises made to Mikhail Gorbachev when the USSR was collapsing and he agreed to allow a unified Germany to become part of NATO—quite a remarkable concession when one thinks about the history of the century. Expansion to East Germany took place at once. In the following years, NATO expanded to Russia's borders; there are now substantial threats even to incorporate Ukraine, in Russia's geostrategic heartland.[17] One can imagine how the United States would react if the Warsaw Pact were still alive, most of Latin America had joined, and now Mexico and Canada were applying for membership.

Aside from that, Russia understands as well as China (and U.S. strategists, for that matter) that the U.S. missile defense systems near Russia's borders are, in effect, a first strike weapon, aimed to establish strategic primacy—immunity from retaliation. Perhaps their mission is utterly unfeasible, as some specialists argue. But the targets can never be confident of that. And Russia's militant reactions are quite naturally interpreted by NATO as a threat to the West.

One prominent British Ukraine scholar poses what he calls a "fateful geographical paradox": that NATO "exists to manage the risks created by its existence."[18]

The threats are very real right now. Fortunately, the shooting down of a Russian plane by a Turkish F-16 in November 2015 did not lead to an international incident, but it might have, particularly given the circumstances. The plane was on a bombing mission in Syria. It passed for a mere seventeen seconds through a fringe of Turkish territory that protrudes into Syria, and evidently was heading for Syria, where it crashed. Shooting it down appears to have been a needlessly reckless and provocative act, and an act with consequences. In reaction, Russia announced that its bombers will henceforth be accompanied by jet fighters and that it is deploying sophisticated anti-aircraft missile systems in Syria. Russia also ordered its missile cruiser *Moskva*, with its long-range air defense system, to move closer to shore, so that it may be "ready to destroy any aerial target posing a potential danger to our aircraft," Defense Minister Sergei Shoigu announced. All of this sets the stage for confrontations that could be lethal.[19]

Tensions are also constant at NATO-Russian borders, including military maneuvers on both sides. Shortly after the Doomsday Clock was moved ominously close to midnight, the national press reported that "U.S. military combat vehicles paraded Wednesday through an Estonian city that juts into Russia, a symbolic act that highlighted the stakes for both sides amid the worst tensions between the West and Russia since the Cold War."[20] Shortly before, a Russian warplane came within seconds of colliding with a Danish civilian airliner. Both sides are practicing rapid mobilization and redeployment of forces to the Russia-NATO border, and "both believe a war is no longer unthinkable."[21]

If that is so, both sides are beyond insanity, since a war might well destroy everything. It has been recognized for decades that a first strike by a major power might destroy the attacker, even without retaliation, simply from the effects of nuclear winter.

But that is today's world. And not just today's—that is what we have been living with for seventy years. The reasoning throughout is remarkable. As we have seen, security for the population is typically not a leading concern of policymakers. That has been true from the earliest days of the nuclear age, when in the centers of policy formation there were no efforts—apparently not even expressed thoughts—to eliminate the one serious potential threat to the United States, as might have been possible. And so matters continue to the present, in ways just briefly sampled.

That is the world we have been living in, and live in today. Nuclear weapons pose a constant danger of instant destruction, but at least we know in principle how to alleviate the threat, even to eliminate it, an obligation undertaken (and disregarded) by the nuclear powers that have signed the Non-Proliferation Treaty. The threat of global warming is not instantaneous, though it is dire in the longer term and might escalate suddenly. That we have the capacity to deal with it is not entirely clear, but there can be no doubt that the longer the delay, the more extreme the calamity.

Prospects for decent long-term survival are not high unless there is a significant change of course. A large share of the responsibility is in our hands—the opportunities as well.

23

Masters of Mankind

When we ask "Who rules the world?" we commonly adopt the standard convention that the actors in world affairs are states, primarily the great powers, and we consider their decisions and the relations among them. That is not wrong. But we would do well to keep in mind that this level of abstraction can also be highly misleading.

States of course have complex internal structures, and the choices and decisions of the political leadership are heavily influenced by internal concentrations of power, while the general population is often marginalized. That is true even for the more democratic societies, and obviously for others. We cannot gain a realistic understanding of who rules the world while ignoring the "masters of mankind," as Adam Smith called them: in his day, the merchants and manufacturers of England; in ours, multinational conglomerates, huge financial institutions, retail empires, and the like. Still following Smith, it is also wise to attend to the "vile maxim" to which the "masters of mankind" are dedicated: "All for ourselves and nothing for other people"—a doctrine known otherwise as bitter and incessant class war, often one-sided, much to the detriment of the people of the home country and the world.

In the contemporary global order, the institutions of the masters hold enormous power, not only in the international arena but also within their home states, on which they rely to protect their power and to provide economic support by a wide variety of means. When we consider the role of the masters of mankind, we turn to such state policy priorities of the moment as the Trans-Pacific Partnership, one of the investor-rights agreements mislabeled "free-trade agreements" in propaganda and commentary. They are negotiated in secret, apart from the hundreds of corporate lawyers and lobbyists writing the crucial details. The intention is to have them adopted in good Stalinist style with "fast track" procedures designed to block discussion and allow only the choice of yes or no (hence yes). The designers regularly do quite well, not surprisingly. People are incidental, with the consequences one might anticipate.

THE SECOND SUPERPOWER

The neoliberal programs of the past generation have concentrated wealth and power in far fewer hands while undermining functioning democracy, but they have aroused opposition as well, most prominently in Latin America but also in the centers of global power.[1] The European Union (EU), one of the more promising developments of the post–World War II period, has been tottering because of the harsh effect of the policies of austerity during recession, condemned even by the economists of the International Monetary Fund (if not the IMF's political actors). Democracy has been undermined as decision making shifted to the Brussels bureaucracy, with the northern banks casting their shadow over their proceedings. Mainstream parties have been rapidly losing members to left and to right. The executive director of the Paris-based research group EuropaNova attributes the general disenchantment to "a mood of angry impotence as the real power to shape events largely shifted from national political leaders [who, in principle at least, are subject to democratic politics] to the market, the institutions of the European Union and corporations," quite in accord with neoliberal doctrine.[2]

Very similar processes are under way in the United States, for somewhat similar reasons, a matter of significance and concern not just for the country but, because of U.S. power, for the world.

The rising opposition to the neoliberal assault highlights another crucial aspect of the standard convention: it sets aside the public, which often fails to accept the approved role of "spectators" (rather than "participants") assigned to it in liberal democratic theory.[3] Such disobedience has always been of concern to the dominant classes. Just keeping to American history, George Washington regarded the common people who formed the militias that he was to command as "an exceedingly dirty and nasty people [evincing] an unaccountable kind of stupidity in the lower class of these people."[4] In *Violent Politics*, his masterful review of insurgencies from "the American insurgency" to contemporary Afghanistan and Iraq, William Polk concludes that General Washington "was so anxious to sideline [the fighters he despised] that he came close to losing the Revolution." Indeed, he "might have actually done so" had France not massively intervened and "saved the Revolution," which until then had been won by guerrillas—whom we would now call "terrorists"—while Washington's British-style army "was defeated time after time and almost lost the war."[5]

A common feature of successful insurgencies, Polk records, is that once popular support dissolves after victory, the leadership suppresses the "dirty and nasty people" who actually won the war with guerrilla tactics and terror, for fear that they might challenge class privilege. The elites' contempt for "the lower class of these people" has taken various forms throughout the years. In recent times one expression of this contempt is the call for passivity and obedience ("moderation in democracy") by liberal internationalists reacting to the dangerous democratizing effects of the popular movements of the 1960s.

Sometimes states do choose to follow public opinion, eliciting much fury in centers of power. One dramatic case was in 2003, when the Bush administration called on Turkey to join its invasion of Iraq. Ninety-five percent of Turks opposed that course of action and, to the amazement and horror of Washington, the Turkish government adhered to their views. Turkey was bitterly condemned for this departure from responsible behavior. Deputy Secretary of Defense Paul Wolfowitz, designated by the press as the "idealist-in-chief" of the administration, berated the Turkish military for permitting the malfeasance of the government and demanded an apology. Unperturbed by these and innumerable other illustrations of our fabled "yearning for democracy," respectable commentary continued to laud President George W. Bush for his dedication to "democracy promotion," or sometimes criticized him for his naïveté in thinking that an outside power could impose its democratic yearnings on others.

The Turkish public was not alone. Global opposition to U.S.-UK aggression was overwhelming. Support for Washington's war plans scarcely reached 10 percent almost anywhere, according to international polls. Opposition sparked huge worldwide protests, in the United States as well, probably the first time in history that imperial aggression was strongly protested even before it was officially launched. On the front page of the *New York Times*, journalist Patrick Tyler reported that "there may still be two superpowers on the planet: the United States and world public opinion."[6]

Unprecedented protest in the United States was a manifestation of the opposition to aggression that began decades earlier in the condemnation of the U.S. wars in Indochina, reaching a scale that was substantial and influential, even if far too late. By 1967, when the antiwar movement was becoming a significant force, military historian and Vietnam specialist Bernard Fall warned that "Vietnam as a cultural and historic entity . . . is threatened with extinction . . . [as] the countryside literally dies under the blows of the largest military machine ever unleashed on an area of this size."[7] But the antiwar movement did become a force that could not be ignored. Nor could it be ignored when Ronald Reagan came into office determined to launch an assault on Central America. His administration mimicked closely the steps John F. Kennedy had taken twenty years earlier in launching the war against South Vietnam, but had to back off because of the kind of vigorous public protest that had been lacking in the early 1960s. The assault was awful enough. The victims have yet to recover. But what happened to South Vietnam and later all of Indochina, where "the second superpower" imposed its impediments only much later in the conflict, was incomparably worse.

It is often argued that the enormous public opposition to the invasion of Iraq had no effect. That seems incorrect to me. Again, the invasion was horrifying enough, and its aftermath is utterly grotesque. Nevertheless, it could have been far worse. Vice President Dick Cheney, Secretary of Defense Donald Rumsfeld, and the rest of Bush's top officials could never even contemplate the sort of measures that President Kennedy and President Lyndon Johnson adopted forty years earlier largely without protest.

WESTERN POWER UNDER PRESSURE

There is far more to say, of course, about the factors in determining state policy that are put to the side when we adopt the standard convention that states are the actors in international affairs. But with such nontrivial caveats as these, let us nevertheless adopt the convention, at least as a first approximation to reality. Then the question of who rules the world leads at once to such concerns as China's rise to power and its challenge to the United States and "world order," the new cold war simmering in eastern Europe, the Global War on Terror, American hegemony and American decline, and a range of similar considerations.

The challenges faced by Western power at the outset of 2016 are usefully summarized within the conventional framework by Gideon Rachman, chief foreign-affairs columnist for the London *Financial Times*.[8] He begins by reviewing the Western picture of world order: "Ever since the end of the Cold War, the overwhelming power of the U.S. military has been the central fact of international politics." This is particularly crucial in three regions: East Asia, where "the U.S. Navy has become used to treating the Pacific as an 'American lake'"; Europe, where NATO—meaning the United States, which "accounts for a staggering three-quarters of NATO's military spending"—"guarantees the territorial integrity of its member states"; and the Middle East, where giant U.S. naval and air bases "exist to reassure friends and to intimidate rivals."

The problem of world order today, Rachman continues, is that "these security orders are now under challenge in all three regions" because of Russian intervention in Ukraine and Syria, and because of China turning its nearby seas from an American lake to "clearly contested water." The fundamental question of international relations, then, is whether the United States should "accept that other major powers should have some kind of zone of influence in their neighborhoods." Rachman thinks it should, for reasons of "diffusion of economic power around the world—combined with simple common sense."

There are, to be sure, ways of looking at the world from different standpoints. But let us keep to these three regions, surely critically important ones.

THE CHALLENGES TODAY: EAST ASIA

Beginning with the "American lake," some eyebrows might be raised over the report in mid-December 2015 that "an American B-52 bomber on a routine mission over the South China Sea unintentionally flew within two nautical miles of an artificial island built by China, senior defense officials said, exacerbating a hotly divisive issue for Washington and Beijing."[9] Those familiar with the grim record of the seventy years of the nuclear weapons era will be all too aware that this is the kind of incident that has often come perilously close to igniting terminal nuclear war. One need not be a supporter of China's provocative and aggressive actions in the South China Sea to notice that the incident did not involve a Chinese nuclear-capable bomber in the Caribbean, or off the coast of California, where China has no pretensions of establishing a "Chinese lake." Luckily for the world.

Chinese leaders understand very well that their country's maritime trade routes are ringed with hostile powers from Japan through the

Malacca Straits and beyond, backed by overwhelming U.S. military force. Accordingly, China is proceeding to expand westward with extensive investments and careful moves toward integration. In part, these developments are within the framework of the Shanghai Cooperation Organization (SCO), which includes the Central Asian states and Russia, and soon India and Pakistan with Iran as one of the observers— a status that was denied to the United States, which was also called on to close all military bases in the region. China is constructing a modernized version of the old silk roads, with the intent not only of integrating the region under Chinese influence, but also of reaching Europe and the Middle Eastern oil-producing regions. It is pouring huge sums into creating an integrated Asian energy and commercial system, with extensive high-speed rail lines and pipelines.

One element of the program is a highway through some of the world's tallest mountains to the new Chinese-developed port of Gwadar in Pakistan, which will protect oil shipments from potential U.S. interference. The program may also, China and Pakistan hope, spur industrial development in Pakistan, which the United States has not undertaken despite massive military aid, and might also provide an incentive for Pakistan to clamp down on domestic terrorism, a serious issue for China in western Xinjiang Province. Gwadar will be part of China's "string of pearls," bases being constructed in the Indian Ocean for commercial purposes but potentially also for military use, with the expectation that China might someday be able to project power as far as the Persian Gulf for the first time in the modern era.[10]

All of these moves remain immune to Washington's overwhelming military power, short of annihilation by nuclear war, which would destroy the United States as well.

In 2015, China also established the Asian Infrastructure Investment Bank (AIIB), with itself as the main shareholder. Fifty-six nations participated in the opening in Beijing in June, including U.S. allies Australia, Britain, and others which joined in defiance of Washington's wishes. The United States and Japan were absent. Some analysts believe that the new bank might turn out to be a competitor to the Bretton Woods institutions (the IMF and the World Bank), in which the United States holds veto power. There are also some expectations that the SCO might eventually become a counterpart to NATO.[11]

THE CHALLENGES TODAY: EASTERN EUROPE

Turning to the second region, eastern Europe, there is a crisis brewing at the NATO-Russian border. It is no small matter. In his illuminating and judicious scholarly study of the region, Richard Sakwa writes—all too plausibly—that the "Russo-Georgian war of August 2008 was in effect the first of the 'wars to stop NATO enlargement'; the Ukraine crisis of 2014 is the second. It is not clear whether humanity would survive a third."[12]

The West sees NATO enlargement as benign. Not surprisingly, Russia, along with much of the Global South, has a different opinion, as do some prominent Western voices. George Kennan warned early on that NATO enlargement is a "tragic mistake," and he was joined by senior American statesmen in an open letter to the White House describing it as a "policy error of historic proportions."[13]

The present crisis has its origins in 1991, with the end of the Cold War and the collapse of the Soviet Union. There were then two contrasting visions of a new security system and political economy in Eurasia. In Sakwa's words, one vision was of a " 'Wider Europe,' with the EU at its heart but increasingly coterminous with the Euro-Atlantic security and political community; and on the other side there [was] the idea of 'Greater Europe,' a vision of a continental Europe, stretching from Lisbon to Vladivostok, that has multiple centers, including Brussels, Moscow and Ankara, but with a common purpose in overcoming the divisions that have traditionally plagued the continent."

Soviet leader Mikhail Gorbachev was the major proponent of Greater Europe, a concept that also had European roots in Gaullism and other initiatives. However, as Russia collapsed under the devastating market reforms of the 1990s, the vision faded, only to be renewed as Russia began to recover and seek a place on the world stage under Vladimir Putin who, along with his associate Dmitry Medvedev, has repeatedly "called for the geopolitical unification of all of 'Greater Europe' from Lisbon to Vladivostok, to create a genuine 'strategic partnership.'"[14]

These initiatives were "greeted with polite contempt," Sakwa writes, regarded as "little more than a cover for the establishment of a 'Greater Russia' by stealth" and an effort to "drive a wedge" between North America and western Europe. Such concerns trace back to earlier Cold War fears that Europe might become a "third force" independent of both the great and minor superpowers and moving toward closer links to the latter (as can be seen in Willy Brandt's Ostpolitik and other initiatives).

The Western response to Russia's collapse was triumphalist. It was hailed as signaling "the end of history," the final victory of Western capitalist democracy, almost as if Russia were being instructed to revert to its pre–World War I status as a virtual economic colony of the West. NATO enlargement began at once, in violation of verbal assurances to Gorbachev that NATO forces would not move "one inch to the east" after he agreed that a unified Germany could become a NATO member—a remarkable concession, in the light of history. That discussion kept to East Germany. The possibility that NATO might expand *beyond* Germany was not discussed with Gorbachev, even if privately considered.[15]

Soon, NATO did begin to move beyond, right to the borders of Russia. The general mission of NATO was officially changed to a mandate to protect "crucial infrastructure" of the global energy system, sea lanes and pipelines, giving it a global area of operations. Furthermore, under a crucial Western revision of the now widely heralded doctrine of "responsibility to protect," sharply different from the official UN version, NATO may now also serve as an intervention force under U.S. command.[16]

Of particular concern to Russia are plans to expand NATO to Ukraine. These plans were articulated explicitly at the Bucharest NATO summit of April 2008, when Georgia and Ukraine were promised eventual membership in NATO. The wording was unambiguous: "NATO welcomes Ukraine's and Georgia's Euro-Atlantic aspirations for membership in NATO. We agreed today that these countries will become members of NATO." With the "Orange Revolution" victory of pro-Western candidates in Ukraine in 2004, State Department representative Daniel Fried rushed there and "emphasized U.S. support for Ukraine's NATO and Euro-Atlantic aspirations," as a WikiLeaks report revealed.[17]

Russia's concerns are easily understandable. They are outlined by international relations scholar John Mearsheimer in the leading U.S. establishment journal, *Foreign Affairs*. He writes that "the taproot of the current crisis [over Ukaine] is NATO expansion and Washington's commitment to move Ukraine out of Moscow's orbit and integrate it into the West," which Putin viewed as "a direct threat to Russia's core interests."

"Who can blame him?" Mearsheimer asks, pointing out that "Washington may not like Moscow's position, but it should understand the logic behind it." That should not be too difficult. After all, as everyone knows, "The United States does not tolerate distant great powers deploying military forces anywhere in the Western hemisphere, much less on its borders." In fact, the U.S. stand is far stronger. It does not tolerate what is officially called "successful defiance" of the Monroe Doctrine of 1823, which declared (but could not yet implement) U.S. control of the hemisphere. And a small country that carries out such successful defiance may be subjected to "the terrors of the earth" and a crushing embargo—as happened to Cuba. We need not ask how the United States would have reacted had the countries of Latin America joined the Warsaw Pact, with plans for Mexico and Canada to join as well. The merest hint of the first tentative steps in that direction would have been "terminated with extreme prejudice," to adopt CIA lingo.[18]

As in the case of China, one does not have to regard Putin's moves and motives favorably to understand the logic behind them, nor to grasp the importance of understanding that logic instead of issuing imprecations against it. As in the case of China, a great deal is at stake, reaching as far—literally—as questions of survival.

THE CHALLENGES TODAY: THE ISLAMIC WORLD

Let us turn to the third region of major concern, the (largely) Islamic world, also the scene of the Global War on Terror (GWOT) that George W. Bush declared in 2001 after the 9/11 terrorist attack. To be more accurate, *re*-declared. The GWOT was declared by the Reagan administration when it took office, with fevered rhetoric about a "plague spread by depraved opponents of civilization itself" (as Reagan put it) and a "return to barbarism in the modern age" (the words of George Shultz, his secretary of state). The original GWOT has been quietly removed from history. It very quickly turned into a murderous and destructive terrorist war afflicting Central America, southern Africa, and the Middle East, with grim repercussions to the present, even leading to condemnation of the United States by the World Court (which Washington dismissed). In any event, it is not the right story for history, so it is gone.

The success of the Bush-Obama version of GWOT can readily be evaluated on direct inspection. When the war was declared, the terrorist targets were confined to a small corner of tribal Afghanistan. They were protected by Afghans, who mostly disliked or despised them, under the tribal code of hospitality—which baffled Americans when poor peasants refused "to turn over Osama bin Ladin for the, to them, astronomical sum of $25 million."[19]

There are good reasons to believe that a well-constructed police action, or even serious diplomatic negotiations with the Taliban, might have placed those suspected of the 9/11 crimes in American hands for trial and sentencing. But such options were off the table. Instead, the reflexive choice was large-scale violence—not with the goal of overthrowing the Taliban (that came later) but to make clear U.S. contempt for tentative Taliban offers of the possible extradition of bin Laden. How serious these offers were we do not know, since the possibility of exploring them was never entertained. Or perhaps the United States was just intent on "trying to show its muscle, score a victory and scare everyone in the world. They don't care about the suffering of the Afghans or how many people we will lose."

That was the judgment of the highly respected anti-Taliban leader Abdul Haq, one of the many oppositionists who condemned the American bombing campaign launched in October 2001 as "a big setback" for their efforts to overthrow the Taliban from within, a goal they considered within their reach. His judgment is confirmed by Richard A. Clarke, who was chairman of the Counterterrorism Security Group at the White House under President George W. Bush when the plans to attack Afghanistan were made. As Clarke describes the meeting, when informed that the attack would violate international law, "the President yelled in the narrow conference room, 'I don't care what the international lawyers say, we are going to kick some ass.'" The attack was also bitterly opposed by the major aid organizations working in Afghanistan, who warned that millions were on the verge of starvation and that the consequences might be horrendous.[20]

The consequences for poor Afghanistan years later need hardly be reviewed.

The next target of the sledgehammer was Iraq. The U.S.-UK invasion, utterly without credible pretext, is the major crime of the twenty-first century. The invasion led to the death of hundreds of thousands of people in a country where the civilian society had already been devastated by American and British sanctions that were regarded as "genocidal" by the two distinguished international diplomats who administered them, and resigned in protest for this reason.[21] The invasion also generated millions of refugees, largely destroyed the country, and instigated a sectarian conflict that is now tearing apart Iraq and the entire region. It is an astonishing fact about our intellectual and moral culture that in informed and enlightened circles it can be called, blandly, "the liberation of Iraq."[22]

Pentagon and British Ministry of Defense polls found that only 3 percent of Iraqis regarded the U.S. security role in their neighborhood as legitimate, less than 1 percent believed that "coalition" (U.S.-UK) forces were good for their security, 80 percent opposed the presence of coalition forces in the country, and a majority supported attacks on coalition troops. Afghanistan has been destroyed beyond the possibility of reliable polling, but there are indications that something similar may be true there as well. Particularly in Iraq the United States suffered a severe defeat, abandoning its official war aims, and leaving the country under the influence of the sole victor, Iran.[23]

The sledgehammer was also wielded elsewhere, notably in Libya, where the three traditional imperial powers (Britain, France, and the United States) procured Security Council resolution 1973 and instantly violated it, becoming the air force of the rebels. The effect was to undercut the possibility of a peaceful, negotiated settlement; sharply increase casualties (by at least a factor of ten, according to political scientist Alan Kuperman); leave Libya in ruins, in the hands of warring militias; and, more recently, to provide the Islamic State with a base that it can use to spread terror beyond. Quite sensible diplomatic proposals by the African Union, accepted in principle by Libya's Muammar Qaddafi, were ignored by the imperial triumvirate, as Africa specialist Alex de Waal reviews. A huge flow of weapons and jihadis has spread terror and violence from West Africa (now the champion for terrorist murders) to the Levant, while the NATO attack also sent a flood of refugees from Africa to Europe.[24]

Yet another triumph of "humanitarian intervention," and, as the long and often ghastly record reveals, not an unusual one, going back to its modern origins four centuries ago.

THE COSTS OF VIOLENCE

In brief, the GWOT sledgehammer strategy has spread jihadi terror from a tiny corner of Afghanistan to much of the world, from Africa through the Levant and South Asia to Southeast Asia. It has also incited attacks in Europe and the United States. The invasion of Iraq made a substantial contribution to this process, much as intelligence agencies had predicted. Terrorism specialists Peter Bergen and Paul Cruickshank estimate that the Iraq war "generated a stunning sevenfold increase in the yearly rate of fatal jihadist attacks, amounting to literally hundreds of additional terrorist attacks and thousands of civilian lives lost; even when terrorism in Iraq and Afghanistan is excluded, fatal attacks in the rest of the world have increased by more than one-third." Other exercises have been similarly productive.[25]

A group of major human rights organizations—Physicians for Social Responsibility (U.S.), Physicians for Global Survival (Canada), and International Physicians for the Prevention of Nuclear War (Germany)— conducted a study that sought "to provide as realistic an estimate as possible of the total body count in the three main war zones [Iraq, Afghanistan, and Pakistan] during 12 years of 'war on terrorism,'" including an extensive review "of the major studies and data published on the numbers of victims in these countries," along with additional information on military actions. Their "conservative estimate" is that these wars killed about 1.3 million people, a toll that "could also be in excess of 2 million."[26] A database search by independent researcher David Peterson in the days following the publication of the report found virtually no mention of it. Who cares?

More generally, studies carried out by the Oslo Peace Research Institute show that two-thirds of the region's conflict fatalities were produced in originally internal disputes where outsiders imposed their solutions. In such conflicts, 98 percent of fatalities were produced only after outsiders had entered the domestic dispute with their military might. In Syria, the number of direct conflict fatalities more than tripled after the West initiated air strikes against the self-declared Islamic State and the CIA started its indirect military interference in the war[27]—interference which appears to have drawn the Russians in as advanced US antitank missiles were decimating the forces of their ally Bashar al-Assad. Early indications are that Russian bombing is having the usual consequences.

The evidence reviewed by political scientist Timo Kivimäki indicates that the "protection wars [fought by 'coalitions of the willing'] have become the main source of violence in the world, occasionally contributing over 50 percent of total conflict fatalities." Furthermore, in many of these cases, including Syria, as he reviews, there were opportunities for diplomatic settlement that were ignored. As discussed elsewhere, that has also been true in other horrific situations, including the Balkans in the early 1990s, the first Gulf war, and of course the Indochina wars, the worst crime since World War II. In the case of Iraq the question does not even arise. There surely are some lessons here.

The general consequences of resorting to the sledgehammer against vulnerable societies comes as little surprise. William Polk's careful study of insurgencies, cited above, should be essential reading for those who want to understand today's conflicts, and surely for planners, assuming that they care about human consequences and not merely power and domination. Polk reveals a pattern that has been replicated over and over. The invaders—perhaps professing the most benign motives—are naturally disliked by the population, who disobey them, at first in small ways, eliciting a forceful response, which increases opposition and support for resistance. The cycle of violence escalates until the invaders withdraw—or gain their ends by something that may approach genocide.

Obama's global drone assassination campaign, a remarkable innovation in global terrorism, exhibits the same patterns. By most accounts, it is generating terrorists more rapidly than it is murdering those suspected of someday intending to harm us—an impressive contribution by a constitutional lawyer on the eight hundredth anniversary of Magna Carta, which established the basis for the principle of presumption of innocence that is the foundation of civilized law.

Another characteristic feature of such interventions is the belief that the insurgency will be overcome by eliminating its leaders. But when such an effort succeeds, the reviled leader is regularly replaced by someone younger, more determined, more brutal and more effective. Polk gives many examples. Military historian Andrew Cockburn has reviewed

American campaigns to kill drug and then terror "kingpins" over a long period in his important study *Kill Chain* and found the same results. And one can expect with fair confidence that the pattern will continue. No doubt right now U.S. strategists are seeking ways to murder the "Caliph of the Islamic State" Abu Bakr al-Baghdadi, who is a bitter rival of al-Qaeda leader Ayman al-Zawahiri. The likely result of this achievement is forecast by the prominent terrorism scholar Bruce Hoffman, senior fellow at the U.S. Military Academy's Combating Terrorism Center. He predicts that "al-Baghdadi's death would likely pave the way for a rapprochement [with al-Qaeda] producing a combined terrorist force unprecedented in scope, size, ambition and resources."[28]

Polk cites a treatise on warfare by Henry Jomini, influenced by Napoleon's defeat at the hands of Spanish guerrillas, that became a textbook for generations of cadets at the West Point military academy. Jomini observed that such interventions by major powers typically result in "wars of opinion," and nearly always "national wars," if not at first then becoming so in the course of the struggle, by the dynamics that Polk describes. Jomini concludes that "commanders of regular armies are ill-advised to engage in such wars because they will lose them," and even apparent successes will prove short-lived.[29]

Careful studies of al-Qaeda and ISIS have shown that the United States and its allies are following their game plan with some precision. Their goal is to "draw the West as deeply and actively as possible into the quagmire" and "to perpetually engage and enervate the United States and the West in a series of prolonged overseas ventures" in which they will undermine their own societies, expend their resources, and increase the level of violence, setting off the dynamic that Polk reviews.[30]

Scott Atran, one of the most insightful researchers on jihadi movements, calculates that "the 9/11 attacks cost between $400,000 and $500,000 to execute, whereas the military and security response by the US and its allies is in the order of 10 million times that figure. On a strictly cost-benefit basis, this violent movement has been wildly successful, beyond even Bin Laden's original imagination, and is increasingly so.

Herein lies the full measure of jujitsu-style asymmetric warfare. After all, who could claim that we are better off than before, or that the overall danger is declining?" And if we continue to wield the sledgehammer, tacitly following the jihadi script, the likely effect is even more violent jihadism with broader appeal. The record, Atran advises, "should inspire a radical change in our counter-strategies."

Al-Qaeda/ISIS are assisted by Americans who follow their directives; for example, Ted "carpet-bomb 'em" Cruz, a top Republican presidential candidate. Or, at the other end of the mainstream spectrum, the leading Middle East and international affairs columnist of the *New York Times*, Thomas Friedman, who in 2003 offered Washington advice on how to fight in Iraq on the *Charlie Rose* show: "There was what I would call the terrorism bubble. . . . And what we needed to do was to go over to that part of the world and burst that bubble. We needed to go over there basically, and, uh, take out a very big stick, right in the heart of that world, and burst that bubble. And there was only one way to do it. . . . What they needed to see was American boys and girls going house to house from Basra to Baghdad, and basically saying, which part of this sentence don't you understand? You don't think we care about our open society, you think this bubble fantasy we're going to just let it go? Well, suck on this. Ok. That, Charlie, was what this war was about."[31]

That'll show the ragheads.

LOOKING FORWARD

Atran and other close observers generally agree on the prescriptions. We should begin by recognizing what careful research has convincingly shown: those drawn to jihad "are longing for something in their history, in their traditions, with their heroes and their morals; and the Islamic State, however brutal and repugnant to us and even to most in the Arab-Muslim world, is speaking directly to that. . . . What inspires the most lethal assailants today is not so much the Quran but a thrilling cause and a call to action that promises glory and esteem in the eyes of friends." In fact, few of the jihadis have much of a background in Islamic texts or theology, if any.[32]

The best strategy, Polk advises, would be "a multinational, welfare-oriented and psychologically satisfying program . . . that would make the hatred ISIS relies upon less virulent. The elements have been identified for us: communal needs, compensation for previous transgressions, and calls for a new beginning."[33] He adds, "A carefully phrased apology for past transgressions would cost little and do much." Such a project could be carried out in refugee camps or in the "hovels and grim housing projects of the Paris banlieues," where, Atran writes, his research team "found fairly wide tolerance or support for ISIS's values." And even more could be done by true dedication to diplomacy and negotiations instead of reflexive resort to violence.

Not least in significance would be an honorable response to the "refugee crisis" that was a long time in coming but surged to prominence in Europe in 2015. That would mean, at the very least, sharply increasing humanitarian relief to the camps in Lebanon, Jordan, and Turkey where miserable refugees from Syria barely survive. But the issues go well beyond, and provide a picture of the self-described "enlightened states" that is far from attractive and should be an incentive to action.

There are countries that generate refugees through massive violence, like the United States, secondarily Britain and France. Then there are countries that admit huge numbers of refugees, including those fleeing from Western violence, like Lebanon (easily the champion, per capita), Jordan, and Syria before it imploded, among others in the region. And partially overlapping, there are countries that both generate refugees and refuse to take them in, not only from the Middle East but also from the U.S. "backyard" south of the border. A strange picture, painful to contemplate.

An honest picture would trace the generation of refugees much further back into history. Veteran Middle East correspondent Robert Fisk reports that one of the first videos produced by ISIS "showed a bulldozer pushing down a rampart of sand that had marked the border between

Iraq and Syria. As the machine destroyed the dirt revetment, the camera panned down to a handwritten poster lying in the sand. 'End of Sykes-Picot,' it said."

For the people of the region, the Sykes-Picot agreement is the very symbol of the cynicism and brutality of Western imperialism. Conspiring in secret during World War I, Britain's Mark Sykes and France's François Georges-Picot carved up the region into artificial states to satisfy their own imperial goals, with utter disdain for the interests of the people living there and in violation of the wartime promises issued to induce Arabs to join the Allied war effort. The agreement mirrored the practices of the European states that devastated Africa in a similar manner. It "transformed what had been relatively quiet provinces of the Ottoman Empire into some of the least stable and most internationally explosive states in the world."[34]

Repeated Western interventions since then in the Middle East and Africa have exacerbated the tensions, conflicts, and disruptions that have shattered the societies. The end result is a "refugee crisis" that the innocent West can scarcely endure. Germany has emerged as the conscience of Europe, at first (but no longer) admitting almost one million refugees—in one of the richest countries in the world with a population of 80 million. In contrast, the poor country of Lebanon has absorbed an estimated 1.5 million Syrian refugees, now a quarter of its population, on top of half a million Palestinian refugees registered with the UN refugee agency UNRWA, mostly victims of Israeli policies.

Europe is also groaning under the burden of refugees from the countries it has devastated in Africa—not without U.S. aid, as Congolese and Angolans, among others, can testify. Europe is now seeking to bribe Turkey (with over 2 million Syrian refugees) to distance those fleeing the horrors of Syria from Europe's borders, just as Obama is pressuring Mexico to keep U.S. borders free from miserable people seeking to escape the aftermath of Reagan's GWOT along with those seeking to escape more recent disasters, including a military coup in Honduras that Obama almost alone legitimized, which created one of the worst horror chambers in the region.[35]

Words can hardly capture the U.S. response to the Syrian refugee crisis, at least any words I can think of.

Returning to the opening question, "Who rules the world?" we might also want to pose another question: "What principles and values rule the world?" That question should be foremost in the minds of the citizens of the rich and powerful states, who enjoy an unusual legacy of freedom, privilege, and opportunity thanks to the struggles of those who came before them, and who now face fateful choices as to how to respond to challenges of great human import.

NOTES

INTRODUCTION

1. James Morgan, BBC economics correspondent, *Financial Times* (London), 25–26 April 1992.
2. Martin Gilens and Benjamin Page, "Testing Theories of American Politics: Elites, Interest Groups, and Average Citizens," *Perspectives on Politics* 12, no. 3 (September 2014), http://www.princeton.edu/~mgilens/Gilens%20home page%20materials/Gilens%20and%20Page/Gilens%20and%20Page%202014 -Testing%20Theories%203-7-14.pdf; Martin Gilens, *Affluence and Influence: Economic Inequality and Political Power in America* (Princeton, NJ: Princeton University Press, 2010); Larry Bartels, *Unequal Democracy: The Political Economy of the New Gilded Age* (Princeton, NJ: Princeton University Press, 2008); Thomas Ferguson, *Golden Rule: The Investment Theory of Party Competition and the Logic of Money-Driven Political Systems* (Chicago: University of Chicago Press, 1995).
3. Burnham, in Thomas Ferguson and Joel Rogers, eds., *Hidden Election* (New York: Random House, 1981). Burnham and Ferguson, "Americans Are Sick to Death of Both Parties: Why Our Politics Is in Worse Shape Than We Thought," 17 December 2014, http://www.alternet.org/americans-are-sick-death-both -parties-why-our-politics-worse-shape-we-thought?paging=off&current_page =1#bookmark.
4. Ken Caldeira, "Stop Emissions," *MIT Technology Review* 119, no. 1 (January/February 2016); "Current Pace of Environmental Change Is Unprecedented in Earth's History," press release, University of Bristol, 4 January 2016, published the same day online in *Nature Geoscience*, http://www.bristol.ac.uk/news/2016 /january/pace-environment-change.html.

5. Julian Borger, "Nuclear Weapons Risk Greater Than in Cold War, Says Ex-Pentagon Chief," *Guardian* (London), 7 January 2016, http://www.theguardian.com/world/2016/jan/07/nuclear-weapons-risk-greater-than-in-cold-war-says-ex-pentagon-chief; William Broad and David Sanger, "As U.S. Modernizes Nuclear Weapons, 'Smaller' Leaves Some Uneasy," *New York Times*, 12 January 2016, http://www.nytimes.com/2016/01/12/science/as-us-modernizes-nuclear-weapons-smaller-leaves-some-uneasy.html?_r=0.

1. THE RESPONSIBILITY OF INTELLECTUALS, REDUX

1. Steven Lukes, *Emile Durkheim: His Life and Work* (Palo Alto, CA: Stanford University Press, 1973), 335.
2. "Manifesto of the Ninety-Three German Intellectuals to the Civilized World," 1914, World War I Document Archive, http://www.gwpda.org/1914/93intell.html.
3. "Who Willed American Participation," *New Republic*, 14 April 1917, 308–10.
4. John Dewey, *The Middle Works of John Dewey, Volume 11, 1899–1924: Journal Articles, Essays, and Miscellany Published in the 1918–1919 Period*, ed. Jo Ann Boydston (Carbondale: Southern Illinois University Press, 1982), 81–82.
5. John Dewey, "Our Un-Free Press," in *The Later Works of John Dewey, Volume 11, 1925–1953: Essays, Reviews, Trotsky Inquiry, Miscellany, and Liberalism and Social Action*, ed. Jo Ann Boydston (Carbondale: Southern Illinois University Press, 1987), 270.
6. Randolph Bourne, "Twilight of Idols," *Seven Arts*, October 1917, 688–702.
7. Michael Crozier, Samuel P. Huntington, and Joji Watanuke, *The Crisis of Democracy: Report on the Governability of Democracies to the Trilateral Commission* (New York: New York University Press, 1975), http://www.trilateral.org/download/doc/crisis_of_democracy.pdf.
8. Adam Smith, *The Wealth of Nations* (New York: Bantam Classics, 2003), 96.
9. Gordon S. Wood, *The Creation of the American Republic, 1776–1787* (New York: W. W. Norton, 1969), 513–14. Lance Banning, in *The Sacred Fire of Liberty: James Madison and the Founding of the Federal Republic* (Ithaca: Cornell University Press, 1995), strongly affirms Madison's dedication to popular rule but nevertheless concurs with Wood's assessment of the Constitutional design (245).
10. James Madison to Thomas Jefferson, 9 December 1787, http://founders.archives.gov/documents/Madison/01-10-02-0197. See also Ralph Louis Ketcham, *James Madison: A Biography* (Charlottesville: University of Virginia Press, 1990), 236, 247, 298.
11. Edward Thorndike, "How May We Improve the Selection, Training, and Life Work of Leaders?" *Teachers College Record*, April 1939, 593–605.
12. "Terrorist Group Profiles," Department of State, January 1989. See also Robert Pear, "US Report Stirs Furor in South Africa," *New York Times*, 14 January 1989.
13. United Nations Inter-Agency Task Force, Africa Recovery Programme/Eco-

nomic Commission for Africa, *South African Destabilization: The Economic Cost of Frontline Resistance to Apartheid*, 1989, 13.

14. Noam Chomsky, "The Evil Scourge of Terrorism," (speech to the International Erich Fromm Society, Stuttgart, Germany, 23 March 2010).

15. Remarks made about Reagan by Martin Anderson and Annelise Anderson of the Hoover Institution at Stanford University, cited by Paul Boyer, "Burnishing Reagan's Disarmament Credentials," *Army Control Today*, September 2009.

16. John Coatsworth, "The Cold War in Central America, 1975–1991," in *The Cambridge History of the Cold War: Volume 3: Endings*, Melvyn P. Leffler and Odd Arne Westad, eds., (Cambridge: Cambridge University Press, 2010).

17. Noam Chomsky, *Hopes and Prospects* (Chicago: Haymarket Books, 2010), 272.

18. Papers of John F. Kennedy, Presidential Papers, National Security Files, Meetings and Memoranda, National Security Action Memoranda [NSAM]: NSAM 134, Report on Internal Security Situation in South America, JFKNSF-335-013, John F. Kennedy Presidential Library and Museum, Boston, Massachusetts.

19. Lars Schoultz, *Human Rights and United States Policy Toward Latin America* (Princeton, NJ: Princeton University Press, 1981); Charles Maechling Jr., "The Murderous Mind of the Latin American Military," *Los Angeles Times*, 18 March 1982.

20. As found in Adam Isacson and Joy Olson, *Just the Facts* (Washington, DC: Latin America Working Group and Center for International Policy, 1999), ix.

21. Noam Chomsky, "Humanitarian Imperialism: The New Doctrine of Imperial Right," *Monthly Review*, 1 September 2008.

22. Noam Chomsky, *Rogue States* (Chicago: Haymarket Books, 2015), 88.

23. Noam Chomsky, *Deterring Democracy* (New York: Hill and Wang, 1991), 131.

24. Chomsky, *Hopes and Prospects*, 261.

25. Daniel Wilkinson, "Death and Drugs in Colombia," *New York Review of Books*, 23 June 2011.

26. Anthony Lewis, "Abroad at Home," *New York Times*, 2 March 1990.

27. Mary McGrory, "Havel's Gentle Rebuke," *Washington Post*, 25 February 1990.

28. Mark Mazzetti, Helene Cooper, and Peter Baker, "Behind the Hunt for Bin Laden," *New York Times*, 2 May 2011.

29. Eric Alterman, "Bin Gotten," *Nation*, 4 May 2011.

30. Elaine Scarry, "Rules of Engagement," *Boston Review*, 8 November 2006.

31. Russell Baker, "A Heroic Historian on Heroes," *New York Review of Books*, 11 June 2009.

32. Mark Mazower, "Short Cuts," *London Review of Books*, 8 April 2010.

33. Eric S. Margolis, "Osama's Ghost," *American Conservative*, 20 May 2011.

34. Daniel Trotta, "Cost of War at Least $3.7 Trillion and Counting," Reuters, 29 June 2011.

35. Michael Scheuer, *Imperial Hubris: Why the West Is Losing the War on Terror* (Washington, DC: Potomac Books, 2004).

36. Accusation of Dreyfusards as quoted in Geoffrey Hawthorn, *Enlightenment and Despair: A History of Social Theory* (Cambridge: Cambridge University Press, 1976), 117.

2. TERRORISTS WANTED THE WORLD OVER

1. Nada Bakri and Graham Bowley, "Top Hezbollah Commander Killed in Syria," *New York Times*, 13 February 2008.
2. Associated Press, "Intelligence Chief: Hezbollah Leader May Have Been Killed by Insiders or Syria," 17 February 2008.
3. Cynthia O'Murchu and Farrid Shamsuddin, "Seven Days," *Financial Times* (London), 16 February 2008.
4. Ferry Biedermann, "A Militant Wanted the World Over," *Financial Times* (London), 14 February 2008.
5. A media review by Jeff Nygaard found one reference to the Gallup poll, a brief notice in the *Omaha World-Herald* that "completely misrepresented the findings." *Nygaard Notes Independent Weekly News and Analysis*, 16 November 2001, reprinted in *Counterpoise* 5, nos. 3/4 (2002).
6. Biedermann, "A Militant Wanted the World Over."
7. Noam Chomsky, *Middle East Illusions* (London: Rowman & Littlefield, 2004), 235.
8. Amnon Kapeliouk, *Yediot Ahronot*, 15 November 1985.
9. Bernard Gwertzman, "U.S. Defends Action in U.N. on Raid," *New York Times*, 7 October 1985.
10. *Yearbook of the United Nations*, Vol. 39, 1985, 291.
11. Bernard Weinraub, "Israeli Extends 'Hand of Peace' to Jordanians," *New York Times*, 18 October 1985.
12. See Noam Chomsky, *Necessary Illusions* (Toronto: House of Anansi, 1995), chapter 5.
13. See, for example, Aviv Lavie, "Inside Israel's Secret Prison," *Ha'aretz*, 23 August 2003.
14. Yoav Biran, Minister Plenipotentiary, Embassy of Israel, letter, *Manchester Guardian Weekly*, 25 July 1982; Gad Becker, *Yediot Ahronot*, 13 April 1983; Reuters, "Shamir Promises to Crush Rioters," *New York Times*, 1 April 1988.
15. Yoram Peri, *Davar*, 10 December 1982.
16. Justin Huggler and Phil Reeves, "Once Upon a Time in Jenin," *Independent* (London), 25 April 2002.
17. Amira Hass, *Ha'aretz*, April 19, 2002, reprinted in Hass, *Reporting from Ramallah: An Israeli Journalist in an Occupied Land* (Los Angeles: Semiotext(e), distributed by MIT Press, 2003).
18. Biedermann, "A Militant Wanted the World Over."
19. Bob Woodward and Charles Babcock, "Anti-Terrorist Unit Blamed in Beirut Bombing," *Washington Post*, 12 May 1985.
20. Nora Boustany, "Beirut Bomb's Legacy Suspicion and Tears," *Washington Post*, 6 March 1988.
21. Ethan Bronner, "Israel Lets Reporters See Devastated Gaza Site and Image of a Confident Military," *New York Times*, 16 January 2009.
22. Julie Flint, "Israeli Soldiers in New Terror Raid on Shi'ite Village," *Guardian* (London), 6 March 1985.

23. Adam Goldman and Ellen Nakashima, "CIA and Mossad Killed Senior Hezbollah Figure in Car Bomb," *Washington Post*, 30 January 2008.
24. "Three Decades of Terror," *Financial Times*, 2 July 2007.
25. Fawaz A. Gerges, *Journey of the Jihadist: Inside Muslim Militancy* (New York: Mariner Books, 2007).
26. "Text of Reagan's Letter to Congress on Marines in Lebanon," *New York Times*, 30 September 1982. See also Micah Zenko, "When Reagan Cut and Run," *Foreign Policy*, 7 February 2014.
27. Jimmy Carter, *Palestine: Peace Not Apartheid* (New York: Simon & Schuster, 2006).
28. Tobias Buck, "Israel Denies Killing Hizbollah Commander," *Financial Times* (London), 13 February 2008.
29. Noam Chomsky, *Fateful Triangle: The United States, Israel, and the Palestinians* (Chicago: Haymarket Books, 2015), 591.
30. Ibid.
31. Ibid., 589.
32. Henry Kamm, "Ruins of War Litter Hills and Valleys of Lebanon," *New York Times*, 20 June 1982.
33. Chomsky, *Fateful Triangle*, 590.
34. Ibid.
35. Isabel Kershner, "Israel Reduces Electricity Flow to Gaza," *New York Times*, 9 February 2008.
36. James Astill, "Strike One," *Guardian* (London), 2 October 2001.

3. THE TORTURE MEMOS AND HISTORICAL AMNESIA

1. Inquiry into the Detainees in U.S. Custody, Report of the Committee on Armed Services, U.S. Senate, 20 November 2008, http://documents.nytimes.com/report-by-the-senate-armed-services-committee-on-detainee-treatment#p=72. Jonathan Landay, "Abusive Tactics Used to Seek Iraq–al Qaida Link," McClatchyDC, 21 April 2009.
2. Paul Krugman, "Reclaiming America's Soul," *New York Times*, 23 April 2009.
3. Hans Morgenthau, *The Purpose of American Politics* (New York: Knopf, 1964).
4. Ibid.
5. Roger Cohen, "America Unmasked," *New York Times*, 24 April 2009.
6. See Richard Drinnon, *Facing West: The Metaphysics of Indian-Hating and Empire-Building* (Norman: University of Oklahoma Press, 1997). Knox cited by Reginald Horsman in *Expansion and American Indian Policy 1783–1812* (Norman: University of Oklahoma Press, 1992), 64.
7. Krugman, "Reclaiming America's Soul."
8. See discussion in Horsman, *Expansion and American Indian Policy 1783–1812*; William Earl Weeks, *John Quincy Adams and American Global Empire* (Lexington: University Press of Kentucky, 1992).
9. On the record of Providentialist justifications for the most shocking crimes and its more general role in forging "the American idea," see Nicholas Guyatt,

Providence and the Invention of the United States, 1607–1876 (Cambridge: Cambridge University Press, 2007).

10. Cited by Lars Schoultz in *That Infernal Little Cuban Republic: The United States and the Cuban Revolution* (Chapel Hill: University of North Carolina Press, 2009), 4.

11. Arthur M. Schlesinger Jr., *Robert Kennedy and His Times* (Boston: Mariner Books, 2002), 480.

12. Republican Party Platforms: "Republican Party Platform of 1900," June 19, 1900. Online by Gerhard Peters and John T. Woolley, *The American Presidency Project*, http://www.presidency.ucsb.edu/ws/?pid=29630.

13. Alfred McCoy, *Policing America's Empire: The United States, the Philippines, and the Rise of the Surveillance State* (Madison: University of Wisconsin Press, 2009).

14. Jennifer Harbury, *Truth, Torture, and the American Way: The History and Consequences of U.S. Involvement in Torture* (Boston: Beacon Press, 2005).

15. Alfred McCoy, *A Question of Torture: CIA Interrogation, from the Cold War to the War on Terror* (New York: Metropolitan Books, 2006). See also McCoy, "The U.S. Has a History of Using Torture," History News Network, 6 December 2006.

16. Noam Chomsky, *Hopes and Prospects* (Chicago: Haymarket Books, 2010), 261.

17. Allan Nairn, "The Torture Ban That Doesn't Ban Torture: Obama's Rules Keep It Intact, and Could Even Accord with an Increase in US-Sponsored Torture Worldwide," www.allannairn.org, 24 January 2009.

18. Chomsky, *Hopes and Prospects*, 261.

19. Lars Schoultz, "U.S. Foreign Policy and Human Rights Violations in Latin America: A Comparative Analysis of Foreign Aid Distributions," *Comparative Politics* 13, no. 2 (January 1981): 149–70; Herman in Noam Chomsky and Edward S. Herman, *The Washington Connection and Third World Fascism: The Political Economy of Human Rights: Volume I* (Boston: South End Press, 1999); Noam Chomsky and Edward S. Herman, *After the Cataclysm: Postwar Indochina and the Reconstruction of Imperial Ideology: The Political Economy of Human Rights—Volume II* (Chicago: Haymarket Books, 2014); Edward S. Herman, *The Real Terror Network: Terrorism in Fact and Propaganda* (Boston: South End Press, 1982).

20. McCoy, "The U.S. Has a History of Using Torture"; Danford Levinson, "Torture in Iraq and the Rule of Law in America," *Daedalus* 133, no. 3 (Summer 2004).

21. Linda Greenhouse, "Justices, 5-4, Back Detainee Appeals for Guantánamo," *New York Times*, 13 June 2008.

22. Glenn Greenwald, "Obama and Habeas Corpus—Then and Now," *Salon*, 11 April 2009.

23. Ibid.

24. Daphne Eviatar, "Obama Justice Department Urges Dismissal of Another Torture Case," *Washington Independent*, 12 March 2009.

25. William Glaberson, "U.S. May Revive Guantánamo Military Courts," *New York Times*, 1 May 2009.

26. Michael Kinsley, "Down the Memory Hole with the Contras," *Wall Street Journal*, 26 March 1987.

27. Patrick Cockburn, "Torture? It Probably Killed More Americans than 9/11," *Independent* (London), 6 April 2009.

28. Rajiv Chandrasekaran, "From Captive to Suicide Bomber," *Washington Post*, 22 February 2009.

29. Chomsky, *Hopes and Prospects*, 266.

30. Ibid., 267.

31. Ibid., 268.

4. THE INVISIBLE HAND OF POWER

1. Tareq Y. Ismael and Glenn E. Perry, *The International Relations of the Contemporary Middle East: Subordination and Beyond* (London: Routledge, 2014), 73; Noam Chomsky, *Hegemony or Survival: America's Quest for Global Dominance* (New York: Metropolitan Books, 2003), 150; Daniel Yergin, *The Prize: The Epic Quest for Oil, Money and Power* (New York: Free Press, 1991).

2. Noam Chomsky, *Hopes and Prospects* (Chicago: Haymarket Books, 2010), 55.

3. Laurence H. Shoup and William Minter, *Imperial Brain Trust: The Council on Foreign Relations and United States Foreign Policy* (New York: Monthly Review Press, 1977), 130.

4. Chomsky, *Hopes and Prospects*, 238.

5. Gerard Van Bilzen, *The Development of Aid* (Newcastle upon Tyne, UK: Cambridge Scholars Publishing, 2015), 497.

6. White House, "Declaration of Principles for a Long-Term Relationship of Cooperation and Friendship Between the Republic of Iraq and the United States of America," press release, 26 November 2007, http://georgewbush-whitehouse.archives.gov/news/releases/2007/11/20071126-11.html.

7. Charlie Savage, "Bush Declares Exceptions to Sections of Two Bills He Signed into Law," *New York Times*, 15 October 2008.

8. Marina Ottoway and David Ottoway, "Of Revolutions, Regime Change, and State Collapse in the Arab World," Carnegie Endowment for International Peace, 28 February 2011, http://carnegieendowment.org/2011/02/28/of-revolutions-regime-change-and-state-collapse-in-arab-world.

9. Pew Research Center, "Egyptians Embrace Revolt Leaders, Religious Party and Military, As Well," 25 April 2011, http://pewglobal.org/files/2011/04/Pew-Global-Attitudes-Egypt-Report-FINAL-April-25-2011.pdf.

10. Marwan Muasher, "Tunisia's Crisis and the Arab World," Carnegie Endowment for International Peace, 24 January 2011, http://carnegieendowment.org/2011/01/24/tunisia-s-crisis-and-arab-world.

11. Thom Shanker, "U.S. Fails to Explain Policies to Muslim World, Panel Says," *New York Times*, 24 November 2004.

12. Afaf Lutfi Al-Sayyid Marsot, *Egypt in the Reign of Muhammad Ali* (Cambridge: Cambridge University Press, 1984). For more extensive discussion on post–World War II Egypt, see Noam Chomsky, *World Orders Old and New* (New York: Columbia University Press, 1994), chapter 2.

13. Adam Smith, *The Wealth of Nations* (New York: Bantam Classics, 2003), 309.

14. Noam Chomsky, *Year 501: The Conquest Continues* (Chicago: Haymarket Books, 2014), 150.

15. Chomsky, *Hopes and Prospects*, 80.

16. David Ricardo, *The Works of David Ricardo: With a Notice of the Life and Writings of the Author by J. R. McCulloch*, (London: John Murray, 1846), 77.

17. Tony Magliano, "The Courageous Witness of Blessed Oscar Romero," *National Catholic Reporter*, 11 May 2015.

18. Martin van Creveld, "Sharon on the Warpath: Is Israel Planning to Attack Iran?," *New York Times*, 21 August 2004.

19. Clayton Jones, "China Is a Barometer on Whether Israel Will Attack Nuclear Plants in Iran," *Christian Science Monitor*, 6 August 2010.

20. Kim Ghattas, "US Gets Serious on Iran Sanctions," BBC News, 3 August 2010.

21. Thom Shanker, "Pentagon Cites Concerns in China Military Growth," *New York Times*, 16 August 2010.

22. Joshua Kurlantzick, "The Belligerents," *New Republic*, 17 February 2011.

23. Stephen Braun and Jack Gillum, "2012 Presidential Election Cost Hits $2 Billion Mark," Associated Press, 6 December 2012; Amie Parnes and Kevin Cirilli, "The $5 Billion Presidential Campaign?," *The Hill*, 21 January 2015.

24. Editors, "The Secret Behind Big Bank Profits," *Bloomberg News*, 21 February 2013.

25. Christine Harper and Michael J. Moore, "Goldman Sachs CEO Blankfein Is Awarded $12.6 Million in Stock," Bloomberg Business, 29 January 2011.

26. Eszter Zalan, "Hungary's Orban Wins Another Term, Jobbik Support Jumps," *EU Observer*, 7 April 2014.

27. See Wikipedia, "Austrian Legislative Election, 2008," https://en.wikipedia.org /wiki/Austrian_legislative_election,_2008#Results.

28. Donny Gluckstein, *Nazis, Capitalism, and the Working Class* (Chicago: Haymarket Books, 1999), 37.

29. Matthew Weaver, "Angela Merkel: German Multiculturalism Has 'Utterly Failed,'" *Guardian* (London), 17 October 2010.

30. Darren Samuelsohn, "John Shimkus Cites Genesis on Climate Change," *Politico*, 10 December 2010.

31. Joseph Stiglitz, "Some Lessons from the East Asian Miracle," *World Bank Research Observer*, August 1996, https://feb.kuleuven.be/public/ndaag37/1996 _Some_Lessons_from_the_East_Asian_Miracle.pdf.

5. AMERICAN DECLINE: CAUSES AND CONSEQUENCES

1. Giacomo Chiozza, review of *America's Global Advantage: US Hegemony and International Cooperation*, by Carla Norrlof, *Political Science Quarterly* (Summer 2011): 336–37.

2. Geoffrey Warner, "The Cold War in Retrospect," *International Affairs* 87, no. 1 (January 2011): 173–84.

3. Noam Chomsky, *On Power and Ideology* (Chicago: Haymarket Books, 2015), 15.

4. "The Chinese Revolution of 1949," U.S. Department of State, Office of the Historian, https://history.state.gov/milestones/1945-1952/chinese-rev.

5. Robert Kagan, "Not Fade Away," *New Republic*, 2 February 2012.

6. Noam Chomsky, *Powers and Prospects: Reflections on Human Nature and the Social Order* (Chicago: Haymarket Books, 2015), 185.

7. For these and other pronouncements, see Noam Chomsky, *New Military Humanism: Lessons from Kosovo* (Monroe, ME: Common Courage, 2002) and Noam Chomsky, *A New Generation Draws the Line: Kosovo, East Timor, and the Responsibility to Protect Today, Updated and Expanded Edition* (Boulder, CO: Paradigm, 2011).

8. Noam Chomsky, *Hopes and Prospects* (Chicago: Haymarket Books, 2010), 277.

9. Samuel P. Huntington, "The Lonely Superpower," *Foreign Affairs* 78, no. 2 (March/April 1999); Robert Jervis, "Weapons Without Purpose? Nuclear Strategy in the Post–Cold War Era," review of *The Price of Dominance: The New Weapons of Mass Destruction and Their Challenge to American Leadership*, by Jan Lodal, *Foreign Affairs* 80, no. 4 (July/August 2001).

10. Jeremy White, "Obama Approval Rating in Arab World Now Worse Than Bush," *International Business Times*, 13 July 2011.

11. Department of State Bulletin, 8 December 1969, 506–07, as cited in David F. Schmitz, *The United States and Right-Wing Dictatorships, 1965–1989* (Cambridge: Cambridge University Press, 2006), 89.

12. Bill Keller, "The Return of America's Missionary Impulse," *New York Times Magazine*, 17 April 2011.

13. Yochi Dreazen, Aamer Madhani, and Marc Ambinder, "The Goal Was Never to Capture bin Laden," *Atlantic*, 4 May 2011.

14. Nick Turse, "Iraq, Afghanistan, and Other Special Ops 'Successes,'" *TomDispatch*, 25 October 2015, http://www.tomdispatch.com/blog/176060/.

15. See also Nick Turse, *The Changing Face of Empire: Special Ops, Drones, Spies, Proxy Fighters, Secret Bases, and Cyberwarfare* (Chicago: Haymarket Books/ Dispatch Books, 2012) and Nick Turse, *Tomorrow's Battlefield: U.S. Proxy Wars and Secret Ops in Africa* (Chicago: Haymarket Books/Dispatch Books, 2015).

16. Robert Westbrook, *John Dewey and American Democracy* (Ithaca, NY: Cornell University Press, 1991), 440.

17. Jennifer Epstein, "Poll: Tax Hike Before Medicare Cuts," *Politico*, 20 April 2011.

18. Jon Cohen, "Poll Shows Americans Oppose Entitlement Cuts to Deal with Debt Problem," *Washington Post*, 20 April 2011.

19. University of Maryland–College Park, "Public's Budget Priorities Differ Dramatically from House and Obama," press release, Newswise.com, 2 March 2011, http://www.newswise.com/articles/publics-budget-priorities-differ-dramatically-from-house-and-obama.

20. Catherine Lutz, Neta Crawford, and Andrea Mazzarino, "Costs of War," Brown University Watson Institute for International and Public Affairs, http://watson.brown.edu/costsofwar/.

21. Martin Wolf, "From Italy to the US, Utopia vs. Reality," *Financial Times* (London), 12 July 2011.

22. Lawrence Summers, "Relief at an Agreement Will Give Way to Alarm," *Financial Times* (London), 2 August 2011.
23. "Health Care Budget Deficit Calculator," Center for Economic and Policy Research, http://www.cepr.net/calculators/hc/hc-calculator.html.
24. Matthew L. Wald and John M. Broder, "Utility Shelves Ambitious Plan to Limit Carbon," *New York Times*, 13 July 2011.
25. Thomas Ferguson, "Best Buy Targets are Stopping a Debt Deal," *Financial Times* (London), 26 July 2011.
26. Robert Pear, "New Jockeying in Congress for Next Phase in Budget Fight," *New York Times*, 3 August 2011.
27. Stephanie Clifford, "Even Marked Up, Luxury Goods Fly Off Shelves," *New York Times*, 3 August 2011.
28. Louis Uchitelle, "Job Insecurity of Workers Is a Big Factor in Fed Policy," *New York Times*, 27 February 1997.
29. Ajay Kapur, "Plutonomy: Buying Luxury, Explaining Global Imbalances," 16 October 2005, as found at http://delong.typepad.com/plutonomy-1.pdf.
30. Noam Chomsky, *Making the Future: Occupations, Interventions, Empire and Resistance* (San Francisco: City Lights, 2012), 289.

6 IS AMERICA OVER?

1. Elizabeth Becker, "Kissinger Tapes Describe Crises, War and Stark Photos of Abuse," *New York Times*, 27 May 2004.
2. John F. Kennedy, "The President and the Press," (address before the American Newspaper Publishers Society, Waldorf-Astoria Hotel, New York, NY, 27 April 1961) http://www.jfklibrary.org/Research/Research-Aids/JFK-Speeches/American-Newspaper-Publishers-Association_19610427.aspx.
3. John F. Kennedy as quoted in Thomas G. Paterson, "Fixation with Cuba: The Bay of Pigs, Missile Crisis, and Covert War Against Castro," in *Kennedy's Quest for Victory: American Foreign Policy, 1961–1963*, ed. Thomas G. Paterson (Oxford: Oxford University Press, 1989), 136.
4. Edward S. Herman and Noam Chomsky, *Manufacturing Consent: The Political Economy of the Mass Media* (New York: Pantheon, 1988), 183.
5. Jimmy Carter: "The President's News Conference," March 24, 1977. Online by Gerhard Peters and John T. Woolley, *The American Presidency Project*, http://www.presidency.ucsb.edu/ws/?pid=7229.
6. Suzanne Goldenberg, "Bush Commits Troops to Iraq for the Long Term," *Guardian* (London), 26 November 2007. See also Guy Raz, "Long-Term Pact with Iraq Raises Questions," *Morning Edition*, National Public Radio, 24 January 2008. For further analysis, see Noam Chomsky, *Making the Future: Occupations, Interventions, Empire and Resistance* (San Francisco: City Lights Books, 2012), 64–66; Charlie Savage, "Bush Asserts Authority to Bypass Defense Act," *Boston Globe*, 30 January 2008.
7. Joseph M. Parent and Paul K. MacDonald, "The Wisdom of Retrenchment," *Foreign Affairs* 90, no. 6 (November/December 2011).

8. Yosef Kuperwasser and Shalom Lipner, "The Problem Is Palestinian Rejectionism," *Foreign Affairs* 90, no. 6 (November/December 2011).

9. Ronald R. Krebs, "Israel's Bunker Mentality," *Foreign Affairs* 90, no. 6 (November/December 2011).

10. Matthew Kroenig, "Time to Attack Iran," *Foreign Affairs* 90, no. 1 (January/February 2012).

11. Xizhe Peng, "China's Demographic History and Future Challenges," *Science* 333, no. 6042, 29 July 2011, 581–87.

12. Daniel Yergin, "US Energy Is Changing the World Again," *Financial Times* (London), 16 November 2012.

13. Fiona Harvey, "World Headed for Irreversible Climate Change in Five Years, IEA Warns," *Guardian* (London), 9 November 2011.

14. "'Monster' Greenhouse Gas Levels Seen," Associated Press, 3 November 2011.

15. Noam Chomsky, *Powers and Prospects* (Chicago: Haymarket Books, 2015), 220.

16. John W. Dower, "The Superdomino In and Out of the Pentagon Papers," in *The Pentagon Papers: The Senator Gravel Edition, Volume 5*, eds. Noam Chomsky and Howard Zinn (Boston: Beacon Press, 1972), 101–42.

17. Seymour Topping, "Slaughter of Reds Gives Indonesia a Grim Legacy," *New York Times*, 24 August 1966.

18. James Reston, "A Gleam of Light in Asia," *New York Times*, 19 June 1966.

19. David Sanger, "Why Suharto Is In and Castro Is Out," *New York Times*, 31 October 1995.

20. Noam Chomsky, *Hegemony or Survival* (New York: Henry Holt, 2003), 150.

21. Alan J. Kuperman, "Obama's Libya Debacle," *Foreign Affairs* 94, no. 2 (March/April 2015).

22. Barbara Ferguson, "Israel Defies US on Illegal Settlements," *Arab News*, 6 September 2006.

23. Herb Keinon, "EU Condemns Building in Har Homa, Neveh Ya'akov, Pisgat Ze'ev," *Jerusalem Post*, 6 February 2014.

24. "U.S. Daily Warns of Threat of 'Nasserite Virus' to Moroccan, Algerian Jews," Jewish Telegraphic Agency, 21 February 1961, http://www.jta.org/1961/02/21/archive/u-s-daily-warns-of-threat-of-nasserite-virus-to-moroccan-algerian-jews.

25. Debbie Buchwald, "Israel's High-Tech Boom," *inFocus Quarterly* II, no.2 (Summer 2008).

26. Noam Chomsky, *Making the Future: Occupations, Interventions, Empire and Resistance* (San Francisco: City Lights, 2012), 251.

27. Peter Beaumont, "Israel Outraged as EU Poll Names It a Threat to Peace," *Guardian* (London), 19 November 2003. The poll, conducted by Taylor Nelson Sofres/ EOS Gallup Europe, was conducted 8–16 October 2003.

28. 2010 Arab Public Opinion Survey, Zogby International/Brookings Institution, 2010, http://www.brookings.edu/~/media/research/files/reports/2010/8/05-arab-opinion-poll-telhami/0805_arabic_opinion_poll_telhami.pdf.

29. Ibid. In response to the question, "Name the two countries that you think pose the biggest threat to you," Israel was named by 88 percent of respondents, the

United States by 77 percent, and Iran by 9 percent among those aged thirty-six and over and 11 percent among those aged thirty-six and under.

30. Scott Clement, "Iranian Threat: Public Prefers Sanctions over Bombs," *Washington Post*, 14 March 2012; Steven Kull et al., "Public Opinion in Iran and America on Key International Issues, January 24, 2007: A WorldPublicOpinion.org Poll," http://www.worldpublicopinion.org/pipa/pdf/jan07/Iran_Jan07_rpt.pdf.

31. Department of Defense, "Unclassified Report on Military Power of Iran, April 2010," http://www.politico.com/static/PPM145_link_042010.html.

32. Gavan McCormack, "'All Japan' versus 'All Okinawa'—Abe Shinzo's Military-Firstism," *Asia-Pacific Journal* 13, issue 10, no. 4 (March 15, 2015).

33. Paul Godwin, "Asia's Dangerous Security Dilemma," *Current History* 109, no. 728 (September 2010): 264–66.

7. MAGNA CARTA, ITS FATE, AND OURS

1. William Blackstone, *The Great Charter and the Charter of the Forest* (Oxford, 1759), held by the British Library.

2. Winston S. Churchill, *A History of the English Speaking Peoples, Volume 2: The New World* (London: Bloomsbury, 2015).

3. James Kendall Hosmer, *The Life of Young Sir Henry Vane, Governor of Massachusetts Bay, and Leader of the Long Parliament: With a Consideration of the English Commonwealth as a Forecast of America* (Boston: Houghton Mifflin, 1888), held by Cornell University Library, 462.

4. *The Famous Old Charter of Rhode Island, Granted by King Charles II, in 1663* (Providence, RI: I. H. Cady, 1842). See also Wikipedia, "Rhode Island Royal Charter," https://en.wikipedia.org/wiki/Rhode_Island_Royal_Charter.

5. Peter Linebaugh, *The Magna Carta Manifesto: Liberties and Commons for All* (Berkeley: University of California Press, 2009).

6. Dudley Jones and Tony Watkins, eds., *A Necessary Fantasy?: The Heroic Figure in Children's Popular Culture*, (New York: Taylor and Francis, 2000).

7. Emily Achtenberg, "From Water Wars to Water Scarcity: Bolivia's Cautionary Tale," *NACLA Report on the Americas*, 6 June 2013, https://nacla.org/blog/2013/6/5/water-wars-water-scarcity-bolivia%E2%80%99s-cautionary-tale.

8. Randal C. Archibold, "El Salvador: Canadian Lawsuit over Mine Allowed to Proceed," *New York Times*, 5 June 2012.

9. Erin Banco, "Is Your Cell Phone Fueling Civil War in Congo?," *Atlantic*, July 11, 2011.

10. Garrett Hardin, "The Tragedy of the Commons," *Science* 162, no. 3859 13 December 1968, 1243–48.

11. See Paul Corcoran, "John Locke on the Possession of Land: Native Title vs. the 'Principle' of *Vacuum domicilium*." Paper presented at the Australian Political Studies Association Annual Conference, September 2007, https://digital.library.adelaide.edu.au/dspace/bitstream/2440/44958/1/hdl_44958.pdf.

12. Norman Ware, *The Industrial Worker 1840–1860: The Reaction of American*

Industrial Society to the Advance of the Industrial Revolution (Chicago: Ivan Dee, 1990). This is a reprint of the first edition from 1924.

13. Michael J. Sandel, *Democracy's Discontent: America in Search of a Public Philosophy* (Cambridge, MA: Belknap Press, 1996).

14. Thorstein Veblen, *The Theory of the Leisure Class: An Economic Study of Institutions* (London: Macmillan, 1899).

15. Clinton Rossiter and James Lare, eds., *The Essential Lippmann: A Political Philosophy for Liberal Democracy* (Cambridge, MA: Harvard University Press, 1982), 91–92; Edward Bernays, *Propaganda* (Brooklyn, NY: Ig Publishing, 2005).

16. Scott Bowman, *The Modern Corporation and American Political Thought: Law, Power, and Ideology* (University Park: Penn State University Press, 1996), 133.

17. Desmond King, "America's Hidden Government: The Costs of a Submerged State," review of *The Submerged State: How Invisible Government Policies Undermine American Democracy*, by Suzanne Mettler, in *Foreign Affairs* 91, no. 3 (May/June 2012).

18. Robert W. McChesney, "Public Scholarship and the Communications Policy Agenda," in . . . *And Communications for All: A Policy Agenda for a New Administration*, ed. Amit M. Schejter (New York: Lexington Books, 2009), 50.

19. Ralph Waldo Emerson, *The Prose Works of Ralph Waldo Emerson: In Two Volumes* (Boston: Fields, Osgood, and Company, 1870).

20. Michael Crozier, Samuel P. Huntington, and Joji Watanuke, *The Crisis of Democracy: Report on the Governability of Democracies to the Trilateral Commission* (New York: New York University Press, 1975), http://www.trilateral.org/down load/doc/crisis_of_democracy.pdf.

21. Margaret E. McGuinness, "Peace v. Justice: The Universal Declaration of Human Rights and the Modern Origins of the Debate," *Diplomatic History* 35, no. 5 (November 2011), 749.

22. William Blackstone, *Commentaries on the Laws of England, Vol. 1* (University of Chicago Press, 1979).

23. *Somerset v. Stewart*, 1772, English Court of King's Bench, http://www.commonlii .org/int/cases/EngR/1772/57.pdf.

24. Samuel Johnson, *Taxation No Tyranny; An Answer to the Resolutions and Address of the American Congress* (London, 1775).

25. Douglas Blackmon, *Slavery by Another Name: The Re-Enslavement of Black Americans from the Civil War to World War II* (New York: Anchor Books, 2009).

26. Ian Cobain, "Revealed: How Blair Colluded with Gaddafi Regime in Secret," *Guardian* (London), 23 January 2015; Benjamin Wieser, "Appeals Court Rejects Suit by Canadian Man over Detention and Torture Claim," *New York Times*, 3 November 2009.

27. Department of Justice, "Lawfulness of a Lethal Operation Directed Against a US Citizen Who Is a Senior Operational Leader of Al-Qa'ida or an Associated Force," undated white paper released by NBC, 4 February 2013.

28. Anthony Shadid and David D. Kirkpatrick, "As the West Celebrates a Cleric's Death, the Mideast Shrugs," *New York Times*, 1 October 2011.

29. Jo Becker and Scott Shane, "Secret 'Kill List' Proves a Test of Obama's Principles and Will," *New York Times*, 29 May 2012.

30. *Convention (IV) Relative to the Protection of Civilian Persons in Time of War*, Article 3, Geneva, 12 August 1949, https://www.icrc.org/applic/ihl/ihl.nsf /Article.xsp?action=openDocument&documentId=A4E145A2A7A68875C125 63CD0051B9AE.

31. Matthew Yglesias, "International Law Is Made by Powerful States," *ThinkProgress*, 13 May 2011.

32. Holder v. Humanitarian Law Project, 561 U.S. 1 (2010), http://www.supreme court.gov/opinions/09pdf/08-1498.pdf.

33. Paul Beckett, "Shutdown of Al Barakaat Severs Lifeline for Many Somalia Residents," *Wall Street Journal*, 4 December 2001.

34. Ibrahim Warde, *The Price of Fear: The Truth Behind the Financial War on Terror* (Berkeley: University of California Press, 2007), 101–02.

35. Ibid., 102.

36. Nnimmo Bassey, *To Cook a Continent: Destructive Extraction and Climate Crisis in Africa* (Oxford: Pambazuka Press, 2012), 25.

37. Melvyn P. Leffler, *A Preponderance of Power: National Security, the Truman Administration, and the Cold War* (Palo Alto, CA: Stanford University Press, 1993), 144.

38. John M. Broder, "Bashing E.P.A. Is New Theme in G.O.P. Race," *New York Times*, 17 August 2011.

39. "57% Favor Use of 'Fracking' to Find More US Oil and Gas," Rasmussen Reports, 26 March 2012, http://www.rasmussenreports.com/public_content/business /gas_oil/march_2012/57_favor_use_of_fracking_to_find_more_u_s_oil_and _gas; "Who's Holding Us Back: How Carbon-Intensive Industry Is Preventing Effective Climate Change Legislation," report by Greenpeace, November 2011, http://www.greenpeace.org/international/Global/international/publications /climate/2011/391%20-%20WhosHoldingUsBack.pdf.

40. "Remarks by the President in State of the Union Address," White House Office of the Press Secretary, 24 January 2012, https://www.whitehouse.gov/the-press -office/2012/01/24/remarks-president-state-union-address.

41. Guy Chazan, "US on Path to Energy Self-Sufficiency," *Financial Times* (London), 18 January 2012.

42. Full texts of the People's Agreement and Universal Declaration can be found at https://pwccc.wordpress.com/programa/.

8. THE WEEK THE WORLD STOOD STILL

1. Sheldon Stern, *The Week the World Stood Still: Inside the Secret Cuban Missile Crisis* (Palo Alto, CA: Stanford University Press, 2005), 5.

2. Noam Chomsky, *Hegemony or Survival* (New York: Henry Holt, 2003), 74.

3. Michael Dobbs, *One Minute to Midnight: Kennedy, Khrushchev, and Castro on the Brink of Nuclear War* (New York: Vintage, 2008), 251.

4. Ibid., 310.

5. Ibid., 311.
6. Ibid., xiii.
7. Chauncey G. Parker III, "Missile Crisis: Cooked Up for Camelot?" *Orlando Sentinel*, 18 October 1992; Robert McNamara, interview by Richard Roth, CNN, aired 28 November 2003. Transcript published by CNN.com, http://www.cnn.com/TRANSCRIPTS/0311/28/i_dl.00.html.
8. "The Submarines of October," in *National Security Archive Electronic Briefing Book No. 75*, William Burr and Thomas S. Blanton, eds., 21 October 2002, http://nsarchive.gwu.edu/NSAEBB/NSAEBB75/.
9. Edward Wilson, "Thank You Vasili Arkhipov, the Man Who Stopped Nuclear War," *Guardian* (London), 27 October 2012.
10. Graham Allison, "The Cuban Missile Crisis at 50: Lessons for U.S. Foreign Policy Today," *Foreign Affairs* 91, no. 4, (July/August 2012).
11. Don Clawson, *Is That Something the Crew Should Know?: Irreverent Anecdotes of an Air Force Pilot* (Twickenham, UK: Athena Press, 2003), 80–81.
12. Office of Air Force History, Oral History Interview of General David A. Burchinal, USAF, by Col. John B. Schmidt and Lt. Col. Jack Straser, 11 April 1975, Iris No. 01011174, in USAF Collection, AFHRA.
13. Stern, *The Week the World Stood Still*, 146.
14. Ibid., 147.
15. Ibid., 148.
16. Ibid., 149. Italics in the original.
17. Ibid., 154.
18. Summary Record of the Seventh Meeting of the Executive Committee of the National Security Council, 27 October 1962, John F. Kennedy Presidential Library and Museum, http://microsites.jfklibrary.org/cmc/oct27/doc1.html.
19. Jorge I. Domínguez, "The @#$%& Missile Crisis (Or, What Was 'Cuban' About U.S. Decisions During the Cuban Missile Crisis," *Diplomatic History* 24, no. 5 (Spring 2000): 305–15.
20. Ernest R. May and Philip D. Zelikow, *The Kennedy Tapes: Inside the White House During the Cuban Missile Crisis*, concise edition (New York: W. W. Norton, 2002), 47.
21. Jon Mitchell, "Okinawa's First Nuclear Missile Men Break Silence," *Japan Times*, 8 July 2012.
22. Dobbs, *One Minute to Midnight*, 309.
23. Sheldon M. Stern, *Averting "The Final Failure": John F. Kennedy and the Secret Cuban Missile Crisis Meetings* (Palo Alto, CA: Stanford University Press, 2003), 273.
24. Piero Gleijeses, *Conflicting Missions: Havana, Washington, and Africa, 1959–1976* (Chapel Hill: University of North Carolina Press, 2003), 26.
25. Ervand Abrahamian, *The Coup: 1953, the CIA, and the Roots of Modern U.S.-Iranian Relations* (New York: New Press, 2013).
26. "Most Americans Willing to Re-Establish Ties with Cuba," Angus Reid Public Opinion Poll, February 2012, https://www.american.edu/clals/upload/2012-02-06_Polling-on-Cuba_USA-1.pdf.

27. Dobbs, *One Minute to Midnight*, 337.
28. Ibid., 333.
29. Stern, *Averting "The Final Failure."*
30. Ibid., 406.
31. Raymond L. Garthoff, "Documenting the Cuban Missile Crisis," *Diplomatic History* 24, no. 2 (Spring 2000): 297–303.
32. Papers of John F. Kennedy, Presidential Papers, National Security Files, Meetings and Memoranda, National Security Action Memoranda [NSAM]: NSAM 181, Re: Action to be taken in response to new Bloc activity in Cuba (B), September 1962, JFKNSF-338-009, John F. Kennedy Presidential Library and Museum, Boston, Massachusetts.
33. Garthoff, "Documenting the Cuban Missile Crisis."
34. Keith Bolender, *Voices From the Other Side: An Oral History of Terrorism Against Cuba* (London: Pluto Press, 2010).
35. Montague Kern, review of *Selling Fear: Counterterrorism, the Media, and Public Opinion* by Brigitte L. Nacos, Yaeli Bloch-Elkon, and Robert Y. Shapiro, *Political Science Quarterly* 127, no. 3 (Fall 2012): 489–92.
36. Stern, *The Week the World Stood Still*, 2.
37. Dobbs, *One Minute to Midnight*, 344.
38. Gleijeses, *Conflicting Missions*, 16.
39. Arthur M. Schlesinger Jr., *Robert Kennedy and His Times* (Boston: Mariner Books, 2002), 480; Noam Chomsky, *Hegemony or Survival: America's Quest for Global Dominance* (New York: Henry Holt, 2003), p. 83.
40. Chomsky, *Hegemony or Survival*, 78–83.
41. Stern, *The Week the World Stood Still*, 2.
42. Desmond Ball, *Politics and Force Levels: The Strategic Missile Program of the Kennedy Administration* (Berkeley: University of California Press, 1980), 97.
43. Garthoff, "Documenting the Cuban Missile Crisis."
44. Dobbs, *One Minute to Midnight*, 342.
45. Allison, "The Cuban Missile Crisis at 50."
46. Sean M. Lynn-Jones, Steven E. Miller, and Stephen Van Evera, *Nuclear Diplomacy and Crisis Management: An International Security Reader* (Cambridge, MA: The MIT Press 1990), 304.
47. William Burr, ed., "The October War and U.S. Policy," National Security Archive, published 7 October 2003, http://nsarchive.gwu.edu/NSAEBB/NSAEBB98/.
48. The phrase "super-sudden first strike" was coined by McGeorge Bundy and cited in John Newhouse, *War and Peace in the Nuclear Age* (New York: Knopf, 1989), 328.
49. Noam Chomsky, *Failed States: The Abuse of Power and the Assault on Democracy* (New York: Henry Holt, 2006), 3.

9. THE OSLO ACCORDS: THEIR CONTEXT, THEIR CONSEQUENCES

1. See for example David M. Shribman, "At White House, Symbols of a Day of Awe," *Boston Globe*, 29 September 1995; Maureen Dowd, "Mideast Accord: The

Scene; President's Tie Tells It All: Trumpets for a Day of Glory," *New York Times*, 14 September 1993 ("the jaded were awed").

2. George H. W. Bush, interview on *NBC Nightly News*, 2 February 1991.

3. Deputy Permanent Observer of the Palestine Liberation Organization to the United Nations secretary general, 16 November 1988, http://domino.un.org/UNISPAL.NSF/0/6EB54A389E2DA6C6852560DE0070E392.

4. R. C. Longworth, "Shultz Helps Arafat Get Right Words," *Chicago Tribune*, 15 December 1988.

5. George P. Shultz, *Turmoil and Triumph: My Years as Secretary of State* (New York: Scribner, 1993), 1043.

6. "Israel's Peace Initiative," U.S. Embassy in Israel Archive, 14 May 1989.

7. Elaine Sciolino, "Mideast Accord: The Ceremony; Old Enemies Arafat and Rabin to Meet," *New York Times*, 12 September 1993.

8. Anthony Lewis, "Abroad at Home; A Chance to Live," *New York Times*, 13 September 1993.

9. Edward W. Said, "Intifada and Independence," in *Intifada: The Palestinian Uprising Against Israeli Occupation*, eds. Zachary Lockman and Joel Beinin (Boston: South End Press, 1989), 5–22.

10. Dan Fisher, "Israeli Settlers Kill Arab Girl, 17, at Gaza Protest," *Los Angeles Times*, 11 November 1987.

11. Avi Raz, *The Bride and the Dowry: Israel, Jordan, and the Palestinians in the Aftermath of the June 1967 War* (New Haven, CT: Yale University Press, 2012).

12. Noam Chomsky, *Fateful Triangle: The United States, Israel, and the Palestinians* (Chicago: Haymarket Books, 2015), 542–87.

13. UN Security Council Resolution 446, 22 March 1979, http://domino.un.org/UNISPAL.NSF/0/ba123cded3ea84a5852560e50077c2dc.

14. "Legal Consequences of the Construction of a Wall in the Occupied Palestinian Territory," International Court of Justice, 30 January 2004, http://www.icj-cij.org/docket/files/131/1591.pdf; Gershom Gorenberg, *The Accidental Empire: Israel and the Birth of the Settlements, 1967-1977* (New York: Times Books, 2006).

15. Danny Rubinstein, *Ha'aretz*, 23 October 1991. On sources here and below, where not cited, see Noam Chomsky, *World Orders Old and New* (New York: Columbia University Press, 1994).

16. Chomsky, *Fateful Triangle*, 612.

17. Chomsky, *World Orders Old and New*, 261–64.

18. Dean Andromidas, "Israeli 'Peace Now' Reveals Settlements Grew Since Oslo," *EIR International* 27, no. 49 (15 December 2000); Chomsky, *World Orders Old and New*, 282.

19. Chomsky, *World Orders Old and New*, 282.

20. *The Other Front*, October 1995; *News from Within*, November 1995. See also Noam Chomsky, *World Orders Old and New* and *Powers and Prospects* (Chicago: Haymarket Books, 2015).

21. Unless otherwise cited, the preceding material is quoted from Lamis Andoni, "Arafat and the PLO in Crisis," *Middle East International* 457 (28 August 1993)

and Lamis Andoni, "Arafat Signs Pact Despite Misgivings All Around Him," *Christian Science Monitor*, 5 May 1994.

22. Chomsky, *World Orders Old and New*, 269.

23. Youssef M. Ibrahim, "Mideast Accord: Jericho; Where P.L.O Is to Rule, It Is Nowhere to Be Seen," *New York Times*, 6 May 1994.

24. Chomsky, *World Orders Old and New*, p. 269.

25. For a detailed analysis of Ross's positions see Norman Finkelstein, *Dennis Ross and the Peace Process: Subordinating Palestinian Rights to Israeli "Needs"* (Washington, DC: Institute of Palestine Studies, 2007).

26. UN Security Council Resolution 242, 22 November 1967, http://domino.un.org /unispal.nsf/0/7D35E1F729DF491C85256EE700686136; UN Security Council Resolution 338, 22 October 1973, https://unispal.un.org/DPA/DPR/unispal.nsf /181c4bf00c44e5fd85256cef0073c426/7fb7c26fcbe80a31852560c50065f878 ?OpenDocument.

27. Israeli-Palestinian Interim Agreement on the West Bank and the Gaza Strip, Article XI, 28 September 1995, http://www.unsco.org/Documents/Key/Israeli -Palestinian%20Interim%20Agreement%20on%20the%20West%20Bank%20 and%20the%20Gaza%20Strip.pdf.

28. Chomsky, *World Orders Old and New*, 248.

29. Israeli-Palestinian Interim Agreement on the West Bank and the Gaza Strip, Article XI, 28 September 1995.

30. Chomsky, *World Orders Old and New*, 278.

31. Hilde Henriksen Waage, "Postscript to Oslo: The Mystery of Norway's Missing Files," *Journal of Palestine Studies* 38 (Autumn 2008).

32. See, for example, Edward Said, "Arafat's Deal," *Nation*, 20 September 1993, and "The Israel-Arafat Agreement," *Z Magazine*, October 1993.

33. Waage, "Postscript to Oslo."

10. THE EVE OF DESTRUCTION

1. Statement by Hugo Chavez at 61st United Nations General Assembly, 20 September 2006, http://www.un.org/webcast/ga/61/pdfs/venezuela-e.pdf.

2. National Security Archive, "Kissinger Gave Green Light for Israeli Offensive Violating 1973 Cease-Fire," press release, 7 October 2003, http://nsarchive.gwu .edu/NSAEBB/NSAEBB98/press.htm.

3. Nate Jones, "The Able Archer 83 Sourcebook," National Security Archive, 7 November 2013, http://nsarchive.gwu.edu/nukevault/ablearcher/.

4. Jillian Kestler-D'Amours, "Opportunity Missed for Nuclear-Free Middle East," Inter Press Service, 2 December 2012.

5. On bombing of dikes as a war crime, see for example Gabriel Kolko, "Report on the Destruction of Dikes: Holland, 1944–45 and Korea, 1953," in *Against the Crime of Silence: Proceedings of the Russell International War Crimes Tribunal, Stockholm and Copenhagen, 1967*, ed. John Duffett (New York: O'Hare Books, 1968), 224–26; see also Jon Halliday and Bruce Cumings, *Korea: The Unknown War* (New York: Viking, 1988), 195–96; Noam Chomsky, *Towards a New Cold*

War: Essays on the Current Crisis and How We Got There (New York: Pantheon, 1982), 121–22.

6. Oded Granot, "Background on North Korea–Iran Missile Deal," *Ma'ariv*, 14 April 1995.

7. Fred Kaplan, "Rolling Blunder: How the Bush Administration Let North Korea Get Nukes," *Washington Monthly*, May 2004.

8. Shreeya Sinha and Susan C. Beachy, "Timeline on North Korea's Nuclear Program," *New York Times*, 19 November 2014; Leon Sigal, "The Lessons of North Korea's Test," *Current History* 105, no. 694 (November 2006).

9. Bill Gertz, "U.S. B-52 Bombers Simulated Raids over North Korea During Military Exercises," *Washington Times*, 19 March 2013.

11. ISRAEL-PALESTINE: THE REAL OPTIONS

1. Yuval Diskin, "Israel Nears Point of No Return on Two-State Solution," *Jerusalem Post*, 13 July 2013.

2. Clive Jones and Beverly Milton-Edwards, "Missing the 'Devils' We Knew? Israel and Political Islam Amid the Arab Awakening," *International Affairs* 89, no.2 (March 2013): 399–415.

3. Yonatan Mendel, "New Jerusalem," *New Left Review* 81 (May/June 2013).

4. Amos Harel, "West Bank Fence Not Done and Never Will Be, It Seems," *Ha'aretz*, 14 July 2009.

5. See United Nations Office for the Coordination of Humanitarian Affairs, "How Dispossession Happens: The Humanitarian Impact of the Takeover of Palestinian Water Springs by Israeli Settlers," March 2012; United Nations Office for the Coordination of Humanitarian Affairs, "10 Years Since the International Court of Justice Advisory Opinion," 9 July 2014; United Nations Office for the Coordination of Humanitarian Affairs, "Case Study: The Impact of Israeli Settler Violence on Palestinian Olive Harvest," October 2013; United Nations Office for the Coordination of Humanitarian Affairs, Humanitarian Monitor Monthly Report, December 2012.

6. UN Office for the Coordination of Humanitarian Affairs, "The Humanitarian Impact of the Barrier," July 2013.

7. "A Dry Bone of Contention," *The Economist*, 25 November 2010.

8. David Bar-Illan, "Palestinian Self-Rule, Israeli Security," *Palestine-Israel Journal* 3, nos. 3–4 (1996).

9. "Obama Calls Israeli Settlement Building in East Jerusalem 'Dangerous,'" *Fox News*, 18 November 2009.

10. "United States Vetoes Security Council Resolution on Israeli Settlement," United Nations News Service, 18 February 2011, http://www.un.org/apps/news/story.asp?NewsID=37572#.VoLKpxUrKhc.

11. United Nations Security Council Official Records, 1879th Meeting Notes, 26 January 1976.

12. Noam Chomsky, *Hegemony or Survival: America's Quest for Global Dominance* (New York: Henry Holt, 2003), 168.

13. Marwan Bishara, "Gauging Arab Public Opinion," *Al Jazeera*, 8 March 2012.
14. Joyce Battle, "Shaking Hands with Saddam Hussein, The US Tilts Toward Iraq 1980–1984," National Security Archive Briefing Book No. 82, 25 February 2003, http://nsarchive.gwu.edu/NSAEBB/NSAEBB82/.
15. Gary Milhollin, "Building Saddam Hussein's Bomb," *New York Times Magazine*, 8 March 1992, 30.
16. United Nations Security Council Resolution 687, 1991, http://www.un.org /Depts/unmovic/documents/687.pdf.

12. "NOTHING FOR OTHER PEOPLE": CLASS WAR IN THE UNITED STATES

1. Norman Ware, *The Industrial Worker 1840–1860* (Chicago: Ivan Dee, 1990).
2. David Montgomery, *The Fall of the House of Labor: The Workplace, the State, and American Labor Activism, 1865–1925* (Cambridge: Cambridge University Press, 1989).
3. Charles Lindholm and John A. Hall, "Is the United States Falling Apart?" *Daedalus* 26, no. 2 (Spring 1997), 183–209.
4. Montgomery, *The Fall of the House of Labor.*
5. Alex Carey, *Taking the Risk out of Democracy: Corporate Propaganda Versus Freedom and Liberty* (Champaign: University of Illinois Press, 1997), 26.
6. Adam Smith, *The Wealth of Nations* (New York: Bantam Classics, 2003).
7. Kate Bronfenbrenner, "We'll Close! Plant Closings, Plant-Closing Threats, Union Organizing and NAFTA," *Multinational Monitor* 18, no. 3 (March 1997): 8–14.
8. Richard B. Freeman, "Do Workers Still Want Unions? More than Ever," Economic Policy Institute, 22 February 2007, http://www.sharedprosperity.org /bp182.html; Gallup Poll, "In U.S. Majority Approves of Unions, but Say They'll Weaken," 30 August 2013, http://www.gallup.com/poll/164186/majority -approves-unions-say-weaken.aspx.
9. Richard Fry and Rakesh Kochhar, "America's Wealth Gap Between Middle-Income and Upper-Income Families Is Widest on Record," Pew Research Center, 17 December 2014, http://www.pewresearch.org/fact-tank /2014/12/17/wealth-gap-upper-middle-income/.
10. "Income and Poverty in the United States: 2013, Current Population Report," U.S. Census Bureau Publication, September 2014.
11. John Bellamy Foster and Robert W. McChesney, *The Endless Crisis: How Monopoly-Finance Capital Produces Stagnation and Upheaval from the USA to China* (New York: Monthly Review Press, 2012), 21.
12. Unless otherwise cited, the preceding material is quoted from Ware, *The Industrial Worker 1840–1860.*
13. Abraham Lincoln, "First Annual Message," December 3, 1861. Online by Gerhard Peters and John T. Woolley, *The American Presidency Project*, http://www .presidency.ucsb.edu/ws/?pid=29502.
14. John Stuart Mill, *Principles of Political Economy with Some of Their Applications to Social Philosophy*, 3rd ed. (London: John W. Parker, 1852).

15. G. D. H. Cole, *Guild Socialism: A Plan for Economic Democracy* (New York: Frederick A. Stokes Company, 1921).
16. Lawrence Goodwyn, *The Populist Moment: A Short History of the Agrarian Revolt in America* (New York: Oxford University Press, 1978).
17. Ware, *The Industrial Worker 1840–1860.*

13. WHOSE SECURITY? HOW WASHINGTON PROTECTS ITSELF AND THE CORPORATE SECTOR

1. Don Shannon, "U.N. Assembly Condemns U.S. Invasion," *Los Angeles Times*, 30 December 1989.
2. "National Security Strategy of the United States," White House, March 1990, https://bush41library.tamu.edu/files/select-documents/national_security _strategy_90.pdf.
3. Ibid.
4. See Noam Chomsky, *Hopes and Prospects* (Chicago: Haymarket Books, 2010), ch. 12.
5. Ibid.
6. "U.S. Economic and Industrial Proposals Made at Inter-American Conference," *New York Times*, 26 February 1945.
7. David Green, *The Containment of Latin America: A History of the Myths and Realities of the Good Neighbor Policy* (New York: Quadrangle Books, 1971), 175.
8. Ibid., vii.
9. "United States Objectives and Courses of Action with Respect to Latin America," *Foreign Relations of the United States, 1952–1954, Vol. IV*, Document 3, 18 March 1953.
10. Luis Paiz to Noam Chomsky, 13 June 2014, in author's possesion.
11. Dwight Eisenhower, as quoted by Richard Immerman in "Confession of an Eisenhower Revisionist: An Agonizing Reappraisal," *Diplomatic History* 14, no. 3 (Summer 1990); John Foster Dulles in a telephone call to Alan Dulles, "Minutes of Telephone Conversations of John Foster Dulles and Christian Herter," 19 June 1958, Dwight D. Eisenhower Presidential Library.
12. Noam Chomsky, *Rogue States* (Chicago: Haymarket Books, 2015), 114.
13. Piero Gleijeses, *Conflicting Missions: Havana, Washington, and Africa, 1959–1976* (Chapel Hill: University of North Carolina Press, 2003), 22.
14. Noam Chomsky, *Hegemony or Survival: America's Quest for Global Dominance.* (New York: Henry Holt, 2003), 90.
15. Ibid.
16. Walter LaFeber, *The New Empire: An Interpretation of American Expansion, 1860–1898* (Ithaca, NY: Cornell University Press, 1963), 4.
17. Ernest R. May and Philip D. Zelikow, eds., *The Kennedy Tapes: Inside the White House During the Cuban Missile Crisis* (Cambridge, MA: Harvard University Press, 1997), xi.
18. Chomsky, *Hopes and Prospects*, 116.

19. Somini Sengupta, "U.N. Will Weigh Asking Court to Investigate War Crimes in Syria," *New York Times*, 22 May 2014.
20. H. R. 4775, 2002 Supplemental Appropriations Act for Further Recovery from and Response to Terrorist Attacks on the United States, 107th Congress (2001–02), https://www.congress.gov/bill/107th-congress/house-bill/4775.
21. Samuel P. Huntington, *American Politics: The Promise of Disharmony* (Cambridge, MA: Harvard University Press, 1981), 75.
22. Stanley Hoffmann, Samuel P. Huntington, Ernest R. May, Richard N. Neustadt, and Thomas C. Schelling, "Vietnam Reappraised," *International Security* 6, no. 1 (Summer 1981): 3–26.
23. Justin Elliott and Theodoric Meyer, "Claim on 'Attacks Thwarted' by NSA Spreads Despite Lack of Evidence", *ProPublica*, 23 October 2013, http://www.propublica.org/article/claim-on-attacks-thwarted-by-nsa-spreads-despite-lack-of-evidence.
24. James Ball, "US and UK Struck Secret Deal to Allow NSA to 'Unmask' Britons' Personal Data," *Guardian* (London), 20 November 2013.
25. Gallup Poll, "Americans Show Low Levels of Concern on Global Warming," 4 April 2014, http://www.gallup.com/poll/168236/americans-show-low-levels-concern-global-warming.aspx.
26. Robert S. Eshelman, "The Danger of Fair and Balanced," *Columbia Journalism Review*, 1 May 2014.

14. OUTRAGE

1. Katie Zezima, "Obama: Plane Crash in Ukraine an 'Outrage of Unspeakable Proportions,'" *Washington Post*, 18 July 2014.
2. "Explanation of Vote by Ambassador Samantha Power, US Permanent Representative to the United Nations, After a Vote on Security Council Resolution 2166 on the Downing of Malaysian Airlines Flight 17 in Ukraine," United States Mission to the United Nations, 21 July 2014, http://usun.state.gov/remarks/6109.
3. Timothy Garton Ash, "Putin's Deadly Doctrine," Opinion, *New York Times*, 18 July 2014.
4. William Taylor, interview by Anderson Cooper, CNN, 18 July 2014, transcript published at http://www.cnn.com/TRANSCRIPTS/1407/18/acd.01.html.
5. United Press International, "Vincennes Too Aggressive in Downing Jet, Officer Writes," *Los Angeles Times*, 2 September 1989.
6. David Evans, "Vincennes Medals Cheapen Awards for Heroism," *Daily Press*, 15 April 1990.
7. Ronald Reagan, "Statement on the Destruction of an Iranian Jetliner by the United States Navy over the Persian Gulf," 3 July 1988. Online by Gerhard Peters and John T. Woolley, *The American Presidency Project*, http://www.presidency.ucsb.edu/ws/?pid=36080.
8. Michael Kinsley, "Rally Round the Flag, Boys," *Time*, 12 September 1988.
9. Philip Shenon, "Iran's Chief Links Aid to Better Ties," *New York Times*, 6 July 1990.

10. Dominic Lawson, "Conspiracy Theories and the Useful Idiots Who Are Happy to Believe Putin's Lies," *Daily Mail* (London), 20 July 2014.

11. Dilip Hiro, *The Longest War: The Iran-Iraq Military Conflict* (New York: Psychology Press, 1989).

12. John Crewdson, "New Revelations in Attack on American Spy Ship," *Chicago Tribune*, 2 October 2007.

13. Miron Rezun, *Saddam Hussein's Gulf Wars: Ambivalent Stakes in the Middle East* (Westport, CT: Praeger, 1992), 58f.

14. Michael Omer-Man, "This Week in History: IAF Shoots Down Libyan Flight 114," *Jerusalem Post*, 25 February 2011.

15. Edward W. Said and Christopher Hitchens, *Blaming the Victims: Spurious Scholarship and the Palestinian Question* (New York: Verso, 2001), 133.

16. Somini Sengupta, "Why the U.N. Can't Solve the World's Problems" *New York Times*, 26 July 2014.

17. Ibid.

18. Laura Barron-Lopez, "Obama Pushes for 'Immediate' Cease-Fire Between Israel, Hamas," *The Hill*, 27 July 2014.

19. "A resolution expressing the sense of the Senate regarding United States support for the State of Israel as it defends itself against unprovoked rocket attacks from the Hamas terrorist organization," Senate Resolution 498, 113th Congress (2013–14), https://www.congress.gov/bill/113th-congress/senate-resolution/498.

20. Gallup Poll, "Congress Approval Sits at 14% Two Months Before Elections," 8 September 2014, http://www.gallup.com/poll/175676/congress-approval-sits -two-months-elections.aspx.

21. Mouin Rabbani, "Institutionalised Disregard for Palestinian Life," LRB Blog, 9 July 2014.

22. Mads Gilbert, "Brief Report to UNRWA: The Gaza Health Sector as of June 2014," University Hospital of North Norway, 3 July 2014.

23. Ibid.

24. Roma Rajpal Weiss, "Interview with Raji Sourani," *Qantara*, 16 July 2014.

25. Ari Shavit, "The Big Freeze," *Ha'aretz*, 7 October 2004.

26. Conal Urquhart, "Gaza on Brink of Implosion as Aid Cut-Off Starts to Bite," *Guardian* (London), 15 April 2006.

27. Jimmy Carter, *Palestine: Peace Not Apartheid* (New York: Simon & Schuster, 2006).

28. Archived Copy of Knesset website, "Likud—Platform," http://web.archive.org /web/20070930181442/http://www.knesset.gov.il/elections/knesset15/elikud _m.htm.

29. "Israel: Gaza Beach Investigation Ignores Evidence," Human Rights Watch report, 19 June 2006, https://www.hrw.org/news/2006/06/19/israel-gaza-beach -investigation-ignores-evidence.

30. Nathan Thrall, "Hamas's Chances," *London Review of Books* 36, no. 16 (21 August 2014): 10–12.

31. Jodi Rudoren and Said Ghazali, "A Trail of Clues Leading to Victims and Heartbreak," *New York Times*, 1 July 2014.

32. Ibid.

33. "Live Updates: July 7, 2014: Rockets Bombard South, Hamas Claims Responsibility," *Ha'aretz*, 8 July 2014.

34. Ibid.

35. Jason Burke, "Gaza 'Faces Precipice' as Death Toll Passes 1,400," *Guardian* (London), 31 July 2014.

36. "Live Updates: Operation Protective Edge, Day 21," *Ha'aretz*, 29 July 2014.

37. Jodi Rudoren and Anne Barnard, "Israeli Military Invades Gaza, with Sights Set on Hamas Operations," *New York Times*, 17 July 2014.

38. "UNRWA Strongly Condemns Israeli Shelling of Its School in Gaza as a Serious Violation of International Law," United Nations Relief and Works Agency for Palestine Refugees, 30 July 2014, http://www.unrwa.org/newsroom/official -statements/unrwa-strongly-condemns-israeli-shelling-its-school-gaza -serious.

39. Ibid.

40. "Secretary-General's Remarks to Media on Arrival in San Jose, Costa Rica," United Nations, 30 July 2014, http://www.un.org/sg/offthecuff/index.asp?nid =3503.

41. Barak Ravid, "UN Chief Condemns 'Shameful' Shelling of School in Gaza," *Ha'aretz*, 30 July 2014.

42. Sudarsan Raghavan, William Booth, and Ruth Eglash, "Israel, Hamas Agree to 72-Hour Humanitarian Cease-Fire," *Washington Post*, 1 August 2014.

43. United Nations Security Council Document 337, S/1996/337, 7 May 1996, http:// www.un.org/ga/search/view_doc.asp?symbol=S/1996/337.

44. Annemarie Heywood, *The Cassinga Event: An Investigation of the Records* (National Archives of Namibia, 1996).

45. Amira Hass, "Reaping What We Have Sown in Gaza," *Ha'aretz*, 21 July 2014.

46. "Gaza: Catholic Church Told to Evacuate Ahead of Israeli Bombing," *Independent Catholic News*, 29 July 2014.

47. "Five Latin American Countries Withdraw Envoys from Israel," *Middle East Monitor*, 30 July 2014.

48. Al Mezan Center for Human Rights, "Humanitarian Truce Fails and IOF Employ Carpet Bombardment in Rafah Killing Dozens of People," press release, 1 August 2014, http://www.mezan.org/en/post/19290/Humanitarian+Truce +Fails+and+IOF+Employ+Carpet+Bombardment+in+Rafah+Killing+Dozens +of+people%3Cbr%3EAl+Mezan%3A+Death+Toll+Reaches+1,497%3B+81 .8%25+Civilians%3B+358+Children+and+196+Women%3B+Excluding +Rafah.

49. Ezer Weizman, lecture recorded in *Ha'aretz*, 20 March 1972.

50. See Lou Pingeot and Wolfgang Obenland, "In Whose Name? A Critical View on the Responsibility to Protect," Global Policy Institute, May 2014, https:// www.globalpolicy.org/images/pdfs/images/pdfs/In_whose_name_web.pdf.

51. See Piero Gleijesus, *Visions of Freedom: Havana, Washington, Pretoria, and the Struggle for Southern Africa, 1976–1991* (University of North Carolina Press, 2013).

52. "Fuelling Conflict: Foreign Arms Supplies to Israel/Gaza," Amnesty International, 23 February 2009, https://www.amnesty.ie/sites/default/files/report/2010/04/Fuelling%20conflict_Final.pdf.

53. Barak Ravid, "US Senator Seeks to Cut Aid to Elite IDF Units Operating in West Bank and Gaza," Ha'aretz, 16 August 2011.

15. HOW MANY MINUTES TO MIDNIGHT?

1. Wesley F. Craven and James L. Cate, eds., *The Army Air Forces in World War II, Volume 5* (Chicago: University of Chicago Press, 1953), 732–33; Makoto Oda, "The Meaning of 'Meaningless Death,'" *Tenbo*, January 1965, translated in the *Journal of Social and Political Ideas in Japan*, August 1966, 75–84. See also Noam Chomsky, "On the Backgrounds of the Pacific War," *Liberation*, September/October 1967, reprinted in Noam Chomsky, *American Power and the New Mandarins: Historical and Political Essays* (New York: New Press, 2002).

2. General Lee Butler, address to the Canadian Network Against Nuclear Weapons, Montreal, Canada, 11 March 1999.

3. General Lee Butler, "At the End of the Journey: The Risks of Cold War Thinking in a New Era," *International Affairs* 82, no. 4 (July 2006): 763–769.

4. General Lee Butler, address to the Canadian Network Against Nuclear Weapons, 11 March 1999.

5. McGeorge Bundy, *Danger and Survival: Choices About the Bomb in the First Fifty Years* (New York: Random House, 1988), 326.

6. Ibid.

7. James Warburg, *Germany: Key to Peace* (Cambridge, MA: Harvard University Press, 1953), 189; Adam Ulam, "A Few Unresolved Mysteries About Stalin and the Cold War in Europe," *Journal of Cold War Studies* 1, no. 1 (Winter 1999): 110–116.

8. Melvyn P. Leffler, "Inside Enemy Archives: The Cold War Reopened," *Foreign Affairs* 75, no. 4 (July/August 1996).

9. Noam Chomsky and Irene Gendzier, "Exposing Israel's Foreign Policy Myths: The Work of Amnon Kapeliuk," *Jerusalem Quarterly* 54, Summer 2013.

10. Benjamin B. Fischer, "A Cold War Conundrum: The 1983 Soviet War Scare," Center for the Study of Intelligence, 7 July 2008, https://www.cia.gov/library/center-for-the-study-of-intelligence/csi-publications/books-and-monographs/a-cold-war-conundrum/source.htm; Dmitry Dima Adamsky, "The 1983 Nuclear Crisis—Lessons for Deterrence Theory and Practice," *Journal of Strategic Studies* 36, no.1 (2013): 4–41.

11. Pavel Aksenov, "Stanislav Petrov: The Man Who May Have Saved the World," BBC News Europe, 26 September 2013, http://www.bbc.com/news/world-europe-24280831.

12. Eric Schlosser, *Command and Control: Nuclear Weapons, the Damascus Accident, and the Illusion of Safety* (New York: Penguin, 2013).

13. President Bill Clinton, Speech before the UN General Assembly, 27 September 1993, http://www.state.gov/p/io/potusunga/207375.htm; Secretary of Defense

William Cohen, Annual Report to the President and Congress: 1999 (Washington, DC: Department of Defense, 1999) http://history.defense.gov/Portals/70/Documents/annual_reports/1999_DoD_AR.pdf.

14. "Essentials of Post–Cold War Deterrence," declassified portions reprinted in Hans Kristensen, *Nuclear Futures: Proliferation of Weapons of Mass Destruction and US Nuclear Strategy*, British American Security Information Council, Appendix 2, Basic Research Report 98.2, March 1998.

15. Michael Sherry, *The Rise of American Airpower: The Creation of Armageddon* (New Haven, CT: Yale University Press, 1987).

16. Jon B. Wolfstahl, Jeffrey Lewis, and Marc Quint, *The Trillion Dollar Nuclear Triad: US Strategic Nuclear Modernization over the Next Thirty Years*, James Martin Center for Nonproliferation Studies, January 2014, http://cns.miis.edu/opapers/pdfs/140107_trillion_dollar_nuclear_triad.pdf. See also Tom Z. Collina, "Nuclear Costs Undercounted, GAO Says," *Arms Control Today*, July/August 2014.

17. White House, Office of the Press Secretary "Remarks by the President at the National Defense University," press release, 23 March 2013, https://www.whitehouse.gov/the-press-office/2013/05/23/remarks-president-national-defense-university.

18. Jeremy Scahill, *Dirty Wars: The World Is a Battlefield* (New York: Nation Books, 2013), 450, 443.

16. CEASE-FIRES IN WHICH VIOLATIONS NEVER CEASE

1. Ari Shavit, "The Big Freeze," *Ha'aretz*, 7 October 2004.

2. Idith Zertal and Akiva Eldar, *Lords of the Land: The War for Israel's Settlements in the Occupied Territories, 1967–2007* (New York: Nation Books, 2007), xii.

3. United Nations, "United Nations Relief, Works Agency for Palestine Refugees Copes with Major Crises in Three Fields of Operations, Commissioner-General Tells Fourth Committee," press release, 29 October 2008, http://www.un.org/press/en/2008/gaspd413.doc.htm.

4. United Nations Security Council, "Security Council Calls for Immediate, Durable, Fully Respected Ceasefire in Gaza Leading to Full Withdrawal of Israeli Forces," press release, 8 January 2009, http://www.un.org/press/en/2009/sc9567.doc.htm.

5. Isabel Kershner, "Gaza Deaths Spike in 3rd Day of Air Assaults While Rockets Hit Israel," *New York Times*, 10 July 2014.

6. Amos Harel, Avi Issacharoff, Gili Cohen, Allison Kaplan Sommer, and news agencies, "Hamas Military Chief Ahmed Jabari Killed by Israeli Strike," *Ha'aretz*, 14 November 2012.

7. Reuters, "Text: Cease-Fire Agreement Between Israel and Hamas," *Ha'aretz*, 21 November 2012.

8. Nathan Thrall, "Hamas's Chances," *London Review of Books* 36, no. 16 (21 August 2014): 10–12.

9. Amos Harel, "Notes from an Interrogation: How the Shin Bet Gets the Low-Down on Terror," *Ha'aretz*, 2 September 2014.

10. Akiva Eldar, "Bibi Uses Gaza as Wedge Between Abbas, Hamas," *Al-Monitor*, 1 September 2014.

11. Ibid.

12. Gideon Levy and Ariel Levac, "Behind the IDF Shooting of a 10-Year-Old Boy," *Ha'aretz*, 21 August 2014.

13. Gideon Levy, "The IDF's Real Face," *Ha'aretz*, 30 August 2014.

14. Zertal and Eldar, *Lords of the Land*, 13.

15. Noam Chomsky, *Deterring Democracy* (New York: Hill and Wang, 1991), 435.

17. THE U.S. IS A LEADING TERRORIST STATE

1. Mark Mazzetti, "C.I.A. Study of Covert Aid Fueled Skepticism About Helping Syrian Rebels," *New York Times*, 14 October 2014.

2. Piero Gleijeses, *Visions of Freedom: Havana, Washington, Pretoria and the Struggle for Southern Africa, 1976–1991* (Chapel Hill: University of North Carolina Press, 2013).

3. Noam Chomsky, *Pirates and Emperors, Old and New: International Terrorism in the Real World* (Chicago: Haymarket Books, 2015), p. viii.

4. Kenneth B. Nobel, "Savimbi, Trailing, Hints at New War," *New York Times*, 4 October 1992.

5. Isaac Risco, "Mandela, a Loyal Friend of Cuba's Fidel," *Havana Times*, 7 December 2013.

6. William M. LeoGrande and Peter Kornbluh, *Back Channel to Cuba: The Hidden History of Negotiations Between Washington and Havana* (Chapel Hill: University of North Carolina Press, 2014), 145.

7. Summary of International Court of Justice ruling, "The Military and Paramilitary Activities In and Against Nicaragua," *Nicaragua v. United States of America*, 27 June 1986, http://www.icj-cij.org/docket/?sum=367&p1=3&p2=3&case=70&p3=5.

8. Keith Bolender, *Voices From the Other Side: An Oral History of Terrorism Against Cuba* (London: Pluto Press, 2010).

9. WIN/Gallup International, "End of Year Survey 2013," http://www.wingia.com/en/services/end_of_year_survey_2013/7/.

18. OBAMA'S HISTORIC MOVE

1. Jon Lee Anderson, "Obama and Castro Seize History," *New Yorker*, 18 December 2014.

2. Papers of John F. Kennedy, Presidential Papers, National Security Files, Meetings and Memoranda Series, National Security Action Memoranda, National Security Action Memorandum Number 263, John F. Kennedy Presidential Library and Museum, Boston, Massachusetts.

3. Michael Glennon, "Terrorism and 'Intentional Ignorance,'" *Christian Science Monitor*, 20 March 1986.

4. U.S. State Department Office of the Historian, Foreign Relations of the United

States, 1961–1963, Document 158, "Notes on Cabinet Meeting," 20 April 1961, https://history.state.gov/historicaldocuments/frus1961-63v10/d158.

5. Ernest R. May and Philip D. Zelikow, eds., *The Kennedy Tapes: Inside the White House During the Cuban Missile Crisis* (Cambridge, MA: Harvard University Press, 1998), 84.

6. Tacitus, *Annals of Tacitus, Book XI* (New York: Macmillan, 1888), 194.

7. Michael R. Beschloss, *Taking Charge: The Johnson White House Tapes 1963–1964* (New York: Simon & Schuster, 1998), 87.

8. Lars Schoultz, *That Infernal Little Cuban Republic: The United States and the Cuban Revolution* (Chapel Hill: University of North Carolina Press, 2011), 5.

9. Nancy Reagan, *My Turn: The Memoirs of Nancy Reagan* (New York: Random House, 2011), 77.

10. Theodore Roosevelt to Henry L. White, 13 September 1906, Roosevelt Papers, Library of Congress.

11. Noam Chomsky, *Hopes and Prospects* (Chicago: Haymarket Books, 2010), 50.

12. William M. LeoGrande and Peter Kornbluh, *Back Channel to Cuba: The Hidden History of Negotiations Between Washington and Havana* (Chapel Hill: University of North Carolina, 2014).

13. White House, Office of the Press Secretary, "Statement by the President on Cuba Policy Changes," press release, 17 December 2014, https://www.whitehouse.gov /the-press-office/2014/12/17/statement-president-cuba-policy-changes.

14. CNN/ORC Poll, 18–21 December 2014, http://i2.cdn.turner.com/cnn/2014 /images/12/23/cuba.poll.pdf.

15. Chomsky, *Hopes and Prospects*, 116; Dennis Merrill and Thomas Paterson, *Major Problems in American Foreign Relations, Volume II: Since 1914* (Boston: Cengage Learning, 2009), 394.

16. Noam Chomsky, *Deterring Democracy* (New York: Hill and Wang, 1991), 228.

19. "TWO WAYS ABOUT IT"

1. Dan Bilefsky and Maïa de la Baume, "French Premier Declares 'War' on Radical Islam as Paris Girds for Rally," *New York Times*, 10 January 2015.

2. Jodi Rudoren, "Israelis Link Attacks to Their Own Struggles," *New York Times*, 9 January 2015.

3. Liz Alderman, "Recounting a Bustling Office at Charlie Hebdo, Then a 'Vision of Horror,'" *New York Times*, 8 January 2015; Anand Giridharadas, https:// twitter.com/anandwrites/status/552825021878771713.

4. Steven Erlanger, "Days of Sirens, Fear and Blood: 'France Is Turned Upside Down,'" *New York Times*, 9 January 2015.

5. Unless otherwise cited, the preceding material is quoted from Steven Erlanger, "Crisis in the Balkans: Belgrade; Survivors of NATO Attack on Serb TV Headquarters: Luck, Pluck and Resolve," *New York Times*, 24 April 1999.

6. Amy Goodman, "Pacifica Rejects Overseas Press Club Award," *Democracy Now!*, Pacifica Radio, 23 April 1999.

7. Roy Gutman and Mousab Alhamadee, "U.S. Airstrike in Syria May Have Killed 50 Civilians," McClatchyDC, 11 January 2015.

8. David Holley and Zoran Cirjakovic, "Ex-Chief of Serb State TV Gets Prison," *Los Angeles Times*, 22 June 2002; United Nations International Criminal Tribunal for the former Yugoslavia, "Final Report to the Prosecutor by the Committee Established to Review the NATO Bombing Campaign Against the Federal Republic of Yugoslavia," http://www.icty.org/x/file/Press/nato061300.pdf.

9. Floyd Abrams, "After the Terrorist Attack in Paris," letter to the editor, *New York Times*, 8 January 2015.

10. Richard A. Oppel Jr., "Early Target of Offensive Is a Hospital," *New York Times*, 8 November 2004.

20. ONE DAY IN THE LIFE OF A READER OF THE *NEW YORK TIMES*

1. Jonathan Mahler, "In Report on Rolling Stone, a Case Study in Failed Journalism," *New York Times*, 5 April 2015.

2. Thomas Fuller, "One Woman's Mission to Free Laos from Millions of Unexploded Bombs," *New York Times*, 5 April 2015.

3. Ibid.

4. Fred Branfman, *Voices from the Plain of Jars: Life Under an Air War* (Madison: University of Wisconsin Press, 2013).

5. Ibid., 36.

6. Fuller, "One Woman's Mission to Free Laos from Millions of Unexploded Bombs."

7. Thomas Friedman, "Iran and the Obama Doctrine," *New York Times*, 5 April 2015.

8. Ibid.

9. Enrique Krauze, "Cuba: The New Opening," *New York Review of Books*, 2 April 2015.

10. David Martosko and Associated Press, "Obama Tries 'New Approach' on Cuba with Normalized Trade Relations and Diplomacy Between Washington and Havana for the First Time in a Half-Century," *Daily Mail* (London), 17 December 2014.

11. Peter Baker, "A Foreign Policy Gamble by Obama at a Moment of Truth," *New York Times*, 2 April 2015.

12. Jessica Matthews, "The Road from Westphalia," *New York Review of Books*, 19 March 2015.

21. "THE IRANIAN THREAT": WHO IS THE GRAVEST DANGER TO WORLD PEACE?

1. Kelsey Davenport, "The P5+1 and Iran Nuclear Deal Alert, August 11," Arms Control Association, 11 August 2015, http://www.armscontrol.org/blog/ArmsControlNow/08-11-2015/The-P5-plus-1-and-Iran-Nuclear-Deal-Alert-August-11.

2. Scott Clement and Peyton M. Craighill, "Poll: Clear Majority Supports Nuclear Deal with Iran," *Washington Post*, 30 March 2015; Laura Meckler and Kristina Peterson, "U.S. Public Split on Iran Nuclear Deal—WSJ/NBC Poll," Washington Wire, 3 August 2015, http://blogs.wsj.com/washwire/2015/08/03/american-public-split-on-iran-nuclear-deal-wsjnbc-poll/.

3. Philip Weiss, "Cruz Says Iran Could Set Off Electro Magnetic Pulse over East Coast, Killing 10s of Millions," *Mondoweiss*, 29 July 2015.

4. Simon Maloy, "Scott Walker's Deranged Hawkishness: He's Ready to Bomb Iran During His Inauguration Speech," *Salon*, 20 July 2015.

5. Amy Davidson, "Broken," *New Yorker*, 3 August 2015; "Former Top Brass to Netanyahu: Accept Iran Accord as 'Done Deal,'" *Ha'aretz*, 3 August 2015.

6. Thomas E. Mann and Norman J. Ornstein, "Finding the Common Good in an Era of Dysfunctional Governance," *Daedalus* 142, no. 2 (Spring 2013).

7. Helene Cooper and Gardiner Harris, "Top General Gives 'Pragmatic' View of Iran Nuclear Deal," *New York Times*, 29 July 2015.

8. Dennis Ross, "How to Make Iran Keep Its Word," *Politico*, 29 July 2015.

9. Dennis Ross, "Iran Will Cheat. Then What?" *Time*, 15 July 2015; "Former Obama Adviser: Send B-52 Bombers to Israel," *Ha'aretz*, 17 July 2015.

10. Javad Zarif, "Iran Has Signed a Historic Nuclear Deal—Now It's Israel's Turn," op-ed, *Guardian* (London), 31 July 2015.

11. Jayantha Dhanapala and Sergio Duarte, "Is There a Future for the NPT?" *Arms Control Today*, July/August 2015.

12. WIN/Gallup, "Optimism Is Back in the World," 30 December 2013, http://www.wingia.com/web/files/services/33/file/33.pdf?1439575556.

13. Anthony H. Cordesman, "Military Spending and Arms Sales in the Gulf," Center for Strategic and International Studies, 28 April 2015, http://csis.org/files/publication/150428_military_spending.pdf.

14. Department of Defense, Unclassified Report on Military Power of Iran, April 2010, http://www.politico.com/static/PPM145_link_042010.html.

15. SIPRI Military Expenditure Database, http://www.sipri.org/research/armaments/milex/milex_database; Trita Parsi and Tyler Cullis, "The Myth of the Iranian Military Giant," *Foreign Policy*, 10 July 2015.

16. Parsi and Cullis, "The Myth of the Iranian Military Giant."

17. Cordesman, "Military Spending and Arms Sales in the Gulf," 4.

18. Seyed Hossein Mousavian and Shahir Shahidsaless, *Iran and the United States: An Insider's View on the Failed Past and the Road to Peace* (New York: Bloomsbury, 2014), 214–19.

19. William A. Dorman and Mansour Farhang, *The U.S. Press and Iran: Foreign Policy and the Journalism of Deference* (Berkeley: University of California Press, 1988).

20. Pervez Hoodbhoy and Zia Mian, "Changing Nuclear Thinking in Pakistan," Asia Pacfic Leadership Network for Nuclear Non-Proliferation and Disarmament and Centre for Nuclear Non-Proliferation and Disarmament, Policy Brief No. 9, February 2014, http://www.princeton.edu/sgs/faculty-staff/zia-mian/Hoodbhoy-Mian-Changing-Nuclear-Thinking.pdf.

21. Haroon Siddique, "Bush: Iran 'the World's Leading Supporter of Terrorism,'" *Guardian* (London), 28 August 2007.
22. Peter Bergen and Paul Cruickshank, "The Iraq Effect: War Has Increased Terrorism Sevenfold Worldwide," *Mother Jones*, 1 March 2007.
23. Somini Sengupta, "U.N. Moves to Lift Iran Sanctions After Nuclear Deal, Setting Up a Clash in Congress," *New York Times*, 20 July 2015.
24. Helene Cooper, "U.S. Defense Secretary Visits Israel to Soothe Ally After Iran Nuclear Deal," *New York Times*, 20 July 2015.
25. Anne Barnard, "120 Degrees and No Relief? ISIS Takes Back Seat for Iraqis," *New York Times*, 1 August 2015.
26. WIN/Gallup, "Happiness Is on the Rise," 30 December 2014, http://www.wingia.com/web/files/richeditor/filemanager/EOY_release_2014_-_FINAL.pdf.
27. James Chace, "How 'Moral' Can We Get?" *New York Times Magazine*, 22 May 1977.
28. Leon Wieseltier, "The Iran Deal and the Rut of History," *Atlantic*, 27 July 2015.
29. Shane Harris and Matthew M. Aid, "Exclusive: CIA Files Prove America Helped Saddam as He Gassed Iran," *Foreign Policy*, 26 August 2013.
30. See Alex Boraine, "Justice in Iraq: Let the UN Put Saddam on Trial," *New York Times*, 21 April 2003.
31. Gary Milhollin, "Building Saddam Hussein's Bomb," *New York Times Magazine*, 8 March 1992.
32. Robert Litwak, "Iran's Nuclear Chess: Calculating America's Moves," Wilson Center report, 18 July 2014, 29, https://www.wilsoncenter.org/publication/irans-nuclear-chess-calculating-americas-moves.
33. For example, David E. Sanger, "Obama Order Sped Up Wave of Cyberattacks Against Iran," *New York Times*, 1 June 2012; Farnaz Fassihi and Jay Solomon, "Scientist Killing Stokes U.S.-Iran Tensions," *Wall Street Journal*, 12 January 2012; Dan Raviv, "US Pushing Israel to Stop Assassinating Iranian Nuclear Scientists," *CBSNews.com*, 1 March 2014.
34. "Contemporary Practices of the United States," *American Journal of International Law* 109, no. 1 (January 2015).
35. Charlie Savage, "Bush Asserts Authority to Bypass Defense Act," *Boston Globe*, 30 January 2008.
36. Elaine Sciolino, "Iran's Nuclear Goals Lie in Half-Built Plant," *New York Times*, 19 May 1995.
37. Mousavian and Shahidsaless, *Iran and the United States*, 178.
38. CIA report (declassified by NSA and published on NSA archive), "Special National Intelligence Estimate 4-1-74: Prospects for Further Proliferation of Nuclear Weapons," 23 August 1974, http://nsarchive.gwu.edu/NSAEBB/NSAEBB240/snie.pdf.
39. Roham Alvandi, *Nixon, Kissinger, and the Shah: The United States and Iran in the Cold War* (Oxford: Oxford University Press, 2014); Mousavian and Shahidsaless, *Iran and the United States*, 178.
40. Farah Stockman, "Iran's Nuclear Vision Initially Glimpsed at Institute," *Boston Globe*, 13 March 2007.

41. Dafna Linzer, "Past Arguments Don't Square with Current Iran Policy," *Washington Post*, 27 March 2005.
42. Samuel P. Huntington, "The Lonely Superpower," *Foreign Affairs* 78, no. 2 (March/April 1999).
43. Robert Jervis, "Weapons Without Purpose? Nuclear Strategy in the Post–Cold War Era," review of *The Price of Dominance: The New Weapons of Mass Destruction and Their Challenge to American Leadership*, by Jan Lodal, *Foreign Affairs* 80, no. 4 (July/August 2001).
44. Bill Clinton, "A National Security for a New Century," National Security Strategy Archive, 1 December 1999, http://nssarchive.us/national-security-strategy -2000-2/.

22. THE DOOMSDAY CLOCK

1. "2015: It Is Three Minutes to Midnight," *Bulletin of the Atomic Scientists*, http:// thebulletin.org/clock/2015.
2. "In Greenland, Another Major Glacier Comes Undone," Jet Propulsion Lab, California Institute of Technology, 12 November 2015, http://www.jpl.nasa.gov /news/news.php?feature=4771.
3. Hannah Osborne, "COP21 Paris Climate Deal: Laurent Fabius Announces Draft Agreement to Limit Global Warming to 2C," *International Business Times*, 12 December 2015. http://www.ibtimes.co.uk/cop21-paris-climate-deal-laurent -fabius-announces-draft-agreement-limit-global-warming-2c-1533045.
4. Coral Davenport, "Paris Deal Would Herald an Important First Step on Climate Change," *New York Times*, 29 November 2015.
5. Coral Davenport, "Nations Approve Landmark Climate Accord in Paris," *New York Times*, 12 December 2015.
6. Evangelicals heavily dominate the first Republican primary, in Iowa. Polls there show that of likely Republican voters, "nearly six in 10 say climate change is a hoax. More than half want mass deportations of illegal immigrants. Six in 10 would abolish the Internal Revenue Service" (thereby providing a huge gift to the superrich and corporate sector). Trip Gabriel, "Ted Cruz Surges Past Donald Trump to Lead in Iowa Poll," *New York Times*, 12 December 2015.
7. Sociologists Rory McVeigh and David Cunningham found that a significant predictor of current Republican voting patterns in the South is the prior existence of a strong chapter of the Ku Klux Klan in the 1960s. Bill Schaller, "Ku Klux Klan's Lasting Legacy on the U.S. Political System," *Brandeis Now*, 4 December 2014. https://www.brandeis.edu/now/2014/december/cunningham -kkk-impact.html.
8. Shawn Donnan and Sam Fleming, "America's Middle-Class Meltdown: Fifth of US Adults Live in or near to Poverty," *Financial Times* (London), 11 December 2015.
9. Sewell Chan and Melissa Eddy, "Republicans Make Presence Felt at Climate Talks by Ignoring Them," *New York Times*, 10 December 2015; David M. Herszenhorn, "Votes in Congress Move to Undercut Climate Pledge," *New York*

Times, 1 December 2015; Samantha Page, "America's Scientists to House Science Committee: Go Away," *ClimateProgress*, 25 November 2015.

10. Giovanni Russonello, "Two-Thirds of Americans Want U.S. to Join Climate Change Pact," *New York Times*, 30 November 2015.

11. Melvin Goodman, "The 'War Scare' in the Kremlin, Revisited: Is History Repeating Itself?" *Counterpunch*, 27 October 2015.

12. Aaron Tovish, "The Okinawa Missiles of October," op-ed, *Bulletin of the Atomic Scientists*, 25 October 2015.

13. David Hoffman, "Shattered Shield: Cold-War Doctrines Refuse to Die," *Washington Post*, 15 March 1998.

14. Seth Baum, "Nuclear War, the Black Swan We Can Never See," *Bulletin of the Atomic Scientists*, 21 November 2014.

15. Eric Schlosser, *Command and Control: Nuclear Weapons, the Damascus Accident, and the Illusion of Safety* (New York: Penguin, 2013).

16. Fiona S. Cunningham and M. Taylor Fravel, "Assuring Assured Retaliation: China's Nuclear Posture and U.S.-China Strategic Stability," *International Security*, Fall 2015.

17. After the uprising that established the pro-Western Ukrainian government, its parliament voted "303 to 8, to rescind a policy of 'nonalignment' and to instead pursue closer military and strategic ties with the West . . . tak[ing] steps toward joining NATO." David M. Herszenhorn, "Ukraine Vote Takes Nation a Step Closer to NATO," *New York Times*, 23 December 2014.

18. Jonathan Steele, review of *Frontline Ukraine: Crisis in the Borderlands*, by Richard Sakwa, *Guardian* (London), 19 February 2015.

19. Lauren McCauley, "In Wake of Turkey Provocation, Putin Orders Anti-aircraft Missiles to Syria," Common Dreams, 25 November 2015.

20. Michael Birnbaum, "U.S. Military Vehicles Paraded 300 Yards from the Russian Border," WorldViews, 24 February 2015, http://www.washingtonpost.com /blogs/worldviews/wp/2015/02/24/u-s-military-vehicles-paraded-300-yards -from-the-russian-border/.

21. Ian Kearns, "Avoiding War in Europe: The Risks From NATO-Russian Close Military Encounters," *Arms Control Today*, November 2015.

23. MASTERS OF MANKIND

1. See among others Marc Weisbrot, *Failed* (New York: Oxford University Press, 2015); David Kotz, *The Rise and Fall of Neoliberal Capitalism* (Cambridge, MA: Harvard University Press, 2015); Mark Blyth, *Austerity: History of a Dangerous Idea* (New York: Oxford University Press, 2013).

2. Alison Smale and Andrew Higgins, "Election Results in Spain Cap a Bitter Year for Leaders in Europe," *New York Times*, 23 December 2015, paraphrasing François Lafond, head of EuropaNova. On the Spanish elections, and their background in the disaster of neoliberal austerity policies, see Marc Weisbrot, Al Jazeera America, 23 December 2015, http://america.aljazeera.com/opinions /2015/12/spain-votes-no-to-failed-economic-policies.html.

3. This is a prominent theme of Walter Lippmann's progressive essays on democracy.

4. John Shy, *A People Numerous and Armed* (New York: Oxford University Press, 1976), 146.

5. William Polk, *Violent Politics: A History of Insurgency, Terrorism and Guerrilla War from the American Revolution to Iraq* (New York: HarperCollins, 2007). An outstanding Middle East scholar and general historian, Polk also draws from direct experience on the ground and at the highest level of U.S. government policy planning.

6. Patrick Tyler, "A New Power in the Streets," *New York Times*, 17 February 2003.

7. Bernard B. Fall, *Last Reflections on a War* (New York: Doubleday, 1967).

8. Gideon Rachman, "Preserving American Power After Obama," *National Interest*, January/February 2016.

9. Jeremy Page and Gordon Lubold, "U.S. Bomber Flies over Waters Claimed by China," *Wall Street Journal*, 18 December 2015.

10. Tim Craig and Simon Denver, "From the Mountains to the Sea: A Chinese Vision, a Pakistani Corridor," *Washington Post*, 23 October 2015; "China Adds Pakistan's Gwadar to 'String of Pearls,'" http://store.businessmonitor.com/article/475258. More generally, Alfred McCoy, "Washington's Great Game and Why It's Failing," *Tomdispatch*, 7 June 2015, http://www.tomdispatch.com/blog/176007/tomgram%3A_alfred_mccoy%2C_washington%27s_great_game_and_why_it%27s_failing.

11. Jane Perlez, "Xi Hosts 56 Nations at Founding of Asian Infrastructure Bank," *New York Times*, June 19, 2015.

12. Richard Sakwa, *Frontline Ukraine: Crisis in the Borderlands* (New York: I. B. Tauris, 2015), 55.

13. Ibid., 46.

14. Ibid., 26.

15. On these matters, the definitive scholarly study today is Mary Elise Sarotte, *1989: The Struggle to Create Post–Cold War Europe* (Princeton, NJ: Princeton University Press, 2011).

16. See Noam Chomsky, *Hopes and Prospects* (Chicago: Haymarket, 2010), 185–86.

17. Sakwa, *Frontline Ukraine*, 4, 52.

18. John J. Mearsheimer, "Why the Ukraine Crisis Is the West's Fault: The Liberal Delusions That Provoked Putin," *Foreign Affairs* 93, no. 5 (September/October 2014); Sakwa, *Frontline Ukraine*, 234–35.

19. Polk, *Violent Politics*, 191.

20. Richard A. Clarke, *Against All Enemies: Inside America's War on Terror* (New York: Free Press, 2004). For discussion, see international law scholar Francis A. Boyle, "From 2001 Until Today: The Afghanistan War Was and Is Illegal," 9 January 2016, http://www.larsschall.com/2016/01/09/from-2001-until-today-the-afghanistan-war-was-and-is-illegal/. For further review and sources, see Noam Chomsky, *Hegemony or Survival: America's Quest for Global Dominance* (New York: Henry Holt, 2003), chap. 8.

21. See H. C. van Sponeck, *A Different Kind of War: The UN Sanctions Regime in Iraq*

(New York: Berghahn, 2006). A crucially important study, barely mentioned in the United States and UK. Technically, the sanctions were administered by the UN, but they are correctly described as U.S.-UK sanctions, primarily Clinton's crime.

22. Brian Katulis, Siwar al-Assad, and William Morris, "One Year Later: Assessing the Coalition Campaign against ISIS," *Middle East Policy* 22, no. 4 (Winter 2015).

23. Timo Kivimäki, "First Do No Harm: Do Air Raids Protect Civilians?," *Middle East Journal* 22, no. 4 (Winter 2015). See also Chomsky, *Hopes and Prospects*, 241.

24. Alan Kuperman, "Obama's Libya Debacle," *Foreign Affairs* 94, no. 2 (March/April 2015); Alex de Waal, "African Roles in the Libyan Conflict of 2011," *International Affairs* 89, no. 2 (2013): 365–79.

25. Peter Bergen and Paul Cruickshank, "The Iraq Effect: War Has Increased Terrorism Sevenfold Worldwide," *Mother Jones*, 1 March 2007.

26. Physicians for Social Responsibility, "Body Count: Casualty Figures After 10 Years of the 'War on Terror,' Iraq, Afghanistan, Pakistan," March 2015, http://www.psr.org/assets/pdfs/body-count.pdf.

27. Kivimäki, "First Do No Harm."

28. Andrew Cockburn, *Kill Chain: The Rise of the High-Tech Assassins* (New York: Henry Holt, 2015); Bruce Hoffman, "ISIS Is Here: Return of the Jihadi," *National Interest*, January/February 2016.

29. Polk, *Violent Politics*, 33–34.

30. Scott Atran, "ISIS Is a Revolution," *Aeon*, 15 December 2015, https://aeon.co/essays/why-isis-has-the-potential-to-be-a-world-altering-revolution; Hoffman, "ISIS Is Here."

31. Thomas Friedman speaking on *Charlie Rose*, PBS, 29 May 2003, https://www.youtube.com/watch?v=ZwFaSpca_3Q; Dan Murphy, "Thomas Friedman, Iraq War Booster," *Christian Science Monitor*, 18 March 2013.

32. Atran, "ISIS Is a Revolution."

33. William R. Polk, "Falling into the ISIS Trap," *Consortiumnews*, 17 November 2015, https://consortiumnews.com/2015/11/17/falling-into-the-isis-trap/.

34. Ayse Tekdal Fildis, "The Troubles in Syria: Spawned by French Divide and Rule," *Middle East Policy* 18, no. 4 (Winter 2011), cited by Anne Joyce, editorial, *Middle East Policy* 22, no. 4 (Winter 2015).

35. On the sordid history of U.S. immigration policy, see Aviva Chomsky, *Undocumented: How Immigration Became Illegal* (Boston: Beacon Press, 2014).

INDEX

THE AMERICAN EMPIRE PROJECT

In an era of unprecedented military strength, leaders of the United States, the global hyperpower, have increasingly embraced imperial ambitions. How did this significant shift in purpose and policy come about? And what lies down the road?

The American Empire Project is a response to the changes that have occurred in America's strategic thinking as well as in its military and economic posture. Empire, long considered an offense against America's democratic heritage, now threatens to define the relationship between our country and the rest of the world. The American Empire Project publishes books that question this development, examine the origins of U.S. imperial aspirations, analyze their ramifications at home and abroad, and discuss alternatives to this dangerous trend.

The project was conceived by Tom Engelhardt and Steve Fraser, editors who are themselves historians and writers. Published by Metropolitan Books, an imprint of Henry Holt and Company, its titles include *Hegemony or Survival* and *Failed States* by Noam Chomsky, *The Limits of Power* and *Washington Rules* by Andrew J. Bacevich, *Blood and Oil* by Michael T. Klare, *Kill Anything That Moves* by Nick Turse, *A People's History of American Empire* by Howard Zinn, and *Empire's Workshop* by Greg Grandin.

For more information about the American Empire Project and for a list of forthcoming titles, please visit americanempireproject.com.